# Small Stakes Hold 'em

## Winning Big with Expert Play

*By*

ED MILLER,
DAVID SKLANSKY, and MASON MALMUTH

**A product of Two Plus Two Publishing**

FIRST EDITION

SECOND PRINTING
JANUARY 2005

*Printing and Binding*
Creel Printers, Inc.
Las Vegas, Nevada

*Printed in the United States of America*

# Small Stakes Hold 'em:
# Winning Big with Expert Play
# COPYRIGHT © 2004 Two Plus Two Publishing LLC

For information contact: **Two Plus Two Publishing LLC**
**600 West Sunset**
**Suite 103**
**Henderson, NV 89015**

ISBN: 1-880685-32-9

*For Raymond and Mimi Miller*

# Table of Contents

i

# About Ed Miller

Ed Miller grew up in New Orleans, Louisiana. He received an S.B. in Physics and another in Computer Science and Electrical Engineering from MIT in 2000. After a year teaching, he moved to Redmond, Washington to work as a software developer for Microsoft.

Looking for a new hobby, he deposited a couple hundred dollars in November 2001 to play $1-$2 and $2-$4 hold 'em online. After losing his initial stake, he sought to improve his game, and he found the books and website of Two Plus Two Publishing LLC. He participated in discussions on the forums at www.twoplustwo.com, and after a few months he turned his losses into wins in a $4-$8 game at a local card room.

By January 2003, he had moved up to $10-$20 and $20-$40, and in March he left his job to play poker full-time. By then he had swapped roles on the online discussion forums from beginning player seeking advice to expert player giving it. After six more successful months playing in the Seattle area, he moved to Las Vegas, where he currently resides. Also in 2003, Dr. Alan Schoonmaker, the author of *The Psychology of Poker,* introduced Ed to David Sklansky and Mason Malmuth, and a partnership soon was born with this book being its first result.

Today Ed usually plays between $10-$20 and $30-$60, but he can occasionally still be found in the $2-$4 to $6-$12 games around Las Vegas.

# About David Sklansky

David Sklansky is generally considered the number one authority on gambling in the world today. Besides his nine books on the subject, David also has produced two videos and numerous writings for various gaming publications. His occasional poker seminars always receive an enthusiastic reception including those given at the Taj Mahal in Atlantic City and the World Series of Poker in Las Vegas.

More recently David has been doing consulting work for casinos, Internet gaming sites, and gaming device companies. He has recently invented a new game called *Poker Challenge,* soon to appear in casinos.

David attributes his standing in the gambling community to three things:

1.   The fact that he presents his ideas as simply as possible (sometimes with Mason Malmuth) even though these ideas frequently involve concepts that are deep, subtle, and not to be found elsewhere.

2.   The fact that the things he says and writes can be counted on to be accurate.

3.   The fact that to this day a large portion of his income is still derived from gambling (usually poker but occasionally blackjack, sports betting, horses, video games, casino promotions, or casino tournaments).

Thus, those who depend on David's advice know that he still depends on it himself.

## Other Books by David Sklansky

*Hold 'em Poker*
*The Theory of Poker*
*Getting The Best of It*
*Sklansky on Poker*
*Poker, Gaming, and Life*
*Sklansky Talks Blackjack*
*Tournament Poker for Advanced Players*

*Gambling for a Living* by David Sklansky and Mason Malmuth
*Hold 'em Poker for Advanced Players* by David Sklansky and
Mason Malmuth
*Seven-Card Stud for Advanced Players* by David Sklansky,
Mason Malmuth, and Ray Zee

# About Mason Malmuth

Mason Malmuth was born and raised in Coral Gables, Florida. In 1973 he received his BS in Mathematics from Virginia Tech, and completed their Masters' program in 1975. While working for the United States Census Bureau in 1979, Mason stopped overnight in Las Vegas while driving to his new assignment in California. He was immediately fascinated by the games, and gambling became his major interest.

After arriving in California he discovered that poker was legal and began playing in some of the public cardrooms as well as taking periodic trips to Las Vegas where he would play both poker and blackjack. In 1981 he went to work for the Northrop Corporation as a mathematician and moved to Los Angeles where he could conviently pursue his interest in poker in the large public cardrooms in Gardena, Bell Gardens, and Commerce.

In 1983 his first article "Card Domination — The Ultimate Blackjack Weapon" was published in *Gambling Times* magazine. In 1987 he left his job with the Northrop Corporation to begin a career as both a full-time gambler and a gambling writer. He has had over 500 articles published in various magazines and is the author or co-author of 14 books. These include *Gambling Theory and Other Topics,* where he tries to demonstrate why only a small number of people are highly successful at gambling. In this book he introduces the reader to the concept of "non-self weighting strategies" and explains why successful gambling is actually a balance of luck and skill. Other books he has co-authored are *Hold 'em Poker For Advanced Players,* written with David Sklansky, and *Seven-Card Stud For Advanced Players* written with David Sklansky and Ray Zee. All the "advanced" books are considered the definitive works on these games.

His company Two Plus Two Publishing has sold over 800,000 books and currently has 28 titles to its credit. These books are recognized as the best in their field and are thoroughly studied by those individuals who take gambling seriously.

## Other Books by Mason Malmth

*Gambling Theory and Other Topics*
*Poker Essays*
*Poker Essays, Volume II*
*Poker Essays, Volume III*
*Blackjack Essays*
*Winning Concepts in Draw and Lowball*

*Gambling for a Living* by David Sklansky and Mason Malmuth
*Hold'em Poker for Advanced Players* by David Sklansky and Mason Malmuth
*Seven-Card Stud for Advanced Players* by David Sklansky, Mason Malmuth, and Ray Zee

## Booklets with Mason Malmuth

*Fundamentals of Craps* by Mason Malmuth and Lynne Loomis
*Fundamentals of Poker* by Mason Malmuth and Lynne Loomis
*Fundamentals of "21"* by Mason Malmuth and Lynne Loomis
*Fundamentals of Video Poker* by Mason Malmuth and Lynne Loomis

# Why This Book ...
## by David Sklansky

Writing a good book about small stakes hold 'em is not as easy as you might think. Just because the opponents you encounter in these games have poor to mediocre skill levels does not mean that the explanation of how to beat them can be mediocre as well.

On the contrary, the underlying concepts needed to extract the most from these players are just as deep, though different, from those needed to beat better players in bigger games. The problem is that most great players have little experience in these smaller games. Even those who look at poker theoretically would have trouble writing a great small stakes hold 'em book without significant experience playing in them. They know the concepts, but aren't sure exactly which ones to apply.

It is the reason that no one (until now) has written an excellent book about small stakes hold 'em. To do it properly you must be a good explainer, have experience in these games, *and* be an excellent poker player. It is not enough that you can beat these games. Anyone who beats smaller games, but fails to beat larger games, is almost certainly confused about poker concepts in general. Inevitably, some of that confusion will spill over into anything he writes about small games. The bottom line is that any book written about small limit poker will contain errors if it is written by somebody who doesn't win when he plays higher.

As I noted earlier, most of the best poker players have little or no experience with small games. For various reasons many did not start out on the lower rungs of the totem pole. (Mason Malmuth and I are two examples.) Most great poker players have trouble explaining exactly how they beat the games they play in. Thus, they would fail abysmally if they tried to explain how to beat the smaller games they never played.

1

## 2 Why this Book ...

Mason and I do know how to explain how and why we win. That includes games with loose players that we sometimes encountered in the bigger games. There is a whole section on the subject in our book *Hold 'em Poker for Advanced Players*. But "loose" is different from just plain "bad."[1] Games with most of your opponents playing badly used to be almost unheard of above the $5-$10 level, and we have rarely addressed them. In fact, we had made it a point *not* to do so since we always believed that it was important to set our readers on the path of beating bigger games as soon as possible. We wanted them to skip smaller games altogether or perhaps beat them less than optimally (with simple common sense), and then move higher.

There were two main reasons we shunned teaching how to beat smaller games. First was that the rake and the expected tip made the games tougher to beat than might be expected, in spite of the opponents' weakness. Second was the fact that we didn't want to teach "bad habits."

Techniques that extract the greatest profit in small games won't work in bigger games. (The converse is even more true.) So we didn't even want to mention them much. We wanted our readers to play and beat $10-$20 or higher. Which is of course what they do. It is the reason our books are so popular.

So what has happened to make us reconsider? Simply put it is poker on TV and poker on the Internet. Since anyone reading this book should know what I'm referring to, I won't expound on it here. All that needs to be said is that this poker explosion has made smaller games become a more viable way to win good money. On the Internet you get to play more hands per hour. In fact, because you can play two or three games at once, you may get to play five times as many hands per hour as in a live game. Plus you don't have to tip. Making well over $50,000 per year playing $3-$6 hold 'em is now no big deal. As for "brick and

---

[1] Loose players in bigger games often play surprisingly well on later betting rounds.

mortar" cardrooms, there are now a lot more bad players in them than ever before. And they are playing higher. So it is no longer unusual to see a $6-$12 or even a $10-$20 game filled with them. This is another reason we can no longer ignore writing about how to beat such games.

The only problem is that Mason and I have little experience playing against a table full of bad players. It's not a big problem. On pure theoretical understanding alone, we could explain proper plays and techniques to beat these games far better than the authors who have thus far attempted this task. But not being fully aware of the how people play at these limits, we would fall short of perfection.

That's where Ed Miller comes in. In Ed we have a man who not only plays poker expertly, presently at the $15-$30 or $30-$60 level, but who has recently moved up the ranks, building his bankroll by playing as low as $2-$4 and $3-$6. He is also a great writer, a brilliant guy, a graduate of MIT, and a major contributor to our website www.twoplustwo.com. With him as our co-author there can be no doubt that, if you want to learn how best to beat the bad players you will find in smaller limit hold 'em games, this book is the place to turn.

# Introduction

This is not a beginners' book. We will not explain the rules of Texas hold 'em, show how to read the board, or teach you to identify the nuts.[2] We do not discuss how to select a table, tell you how large a buy-in to make, or teach you proper table etiquette.

This is also not a beginners' strategy book. We do not repeatedly emphasize the importance of playing tightly before the flop. We do not constantly advise you to avoid trouble or warn against the perils of calling down aimlessly with weak hands.

We do not talk about these things, not because they aren't important, but because *we assume that you already know them*. Many books have already been written to teach the fundamentals of winning strategy at small stakes hold 'em. They emphasize starting with only the best hands and continuing after the flop with only a strong holding. They aim to fix the most expensive mistakes that new players make: ones that stem from the natural tendency to play too many hands and to go too far with them.

These beginners' books generally do a good job of starting students on a winning track. They fix the big errors, and most players who study one of these books will improve from a losing player to a break-even or modestly winning player if they stick to very easy games.

*This book picks up where the beginners' books leave off.* We aim to teach you how to transform yourself from a good player to an expert and from a modest winner to a big winner. We want to teach you to squeeze every last penny of value out of your games. To help you do this, we introduce some advanced concepts that you have likely never before considered. In fact, some of them have never before appeared in print.

---

[2] For that see *Hold 'em Poker* by David Sklansky.

Beginners' books usually advocate a style that we would characterize as tight, cautious, and defensive. They discuss the importance of anticipating and avoiding expensive traps. They urge you to forgo potentially profitable situations if attempting to exploit them might leave you in a precarious spot. Teaching you to protect yourself is their top priority.

We advocate a tight, but aggressive and attacking style. We focus on attacking opponents who have weak hands more than defending ourselves when we have a weak hand. Of course, any attacking plan must be tempered by a solid defense, and the lessons taught by the beginners' books are still valuable. But, while you can be a winner by playing defensively, *if you want to be the best, you must attack!*

Even though this is not a beginners' book, a beginning player can start with this book. We present the important fundamental ideas (tight preflop play, calculating drawing odds and pot odds, discussion of when to fold a hopeless hand, etc.), we just do not emphasize and repeat them as a beginners' book would. A beginner will simply have to study this book more thoroughly than someone who already plays fairly well to achieve the same results.

Furthermore, though the title is *Small Stakes Hold 'em*, the ideas in this book are valuable at all limits. We teach you how to win the maximum in any games with players who play too many hands and go too far with them. These games are ubiquitous at small stakes, but are also quite common at medium stakes and sometimes even higher. We do occasionally discuss concepts specific to small stakes games, such as the influence of the rake, but otherwise the advice is not limit-specific. Few players, even professional medium stakes players, could read this book without learning many valuable lessons.

Hold 'em is more popular now than it ever has been, introducing waves of new players, and most of them play poorly. These new players have made most games much looser and more profitable than ever before. While a winning strategy designed for the tighter, tougher games of the past will also win in these new conditions, it will not win the *maximum*. To do that, you must tailor your strategy to the new conditions and specifically exploit your loose opponents' mistakes. We wrote this book to teach you how to do just that.

The authors also want to thank Dr. Alan Schoonmaker for his help in editing this manuscript. Thanks to Dr. Al our words and ideas are expressed clearly and concisely, and the concepts in this book should be understood by all.

In addition we need to thank Dave Clark, Jeff Galian, and Dr. Mimi Miller for their contributions and insights. We do thank Chris Evans and Gary Alstatt of Creel Printing for their cover design and other artwork throughout this book, as well as all the other personnel at Creel Printing that assisted in this project. We thank Portraits Today by Catherine for photography. We also want to thank all the posters on www.twoplustwo.com for their debate, comments, and encouragement.

# Using This Book

While many of the concepts in this book may be difficult to understand the first time you encounter them, we recommend that you read the entire book once before revisiting any sections. You may find that a topic covered later on helps you understand a troublesome concept. Reading the whole book first will also help you get the "big picture" view and will allow you to see how our whole strategy fits together.

Once you feel that you have a solid grasp of the material presented in the conceptual sections, move on to the "Hand Quizzes." Understanding a number of abstract concepts and knowing when to apply each one are quite different. We have designed the quizzes to test your ability to apply the appropriate concepts in common and important situations. You may find the quizzes to be the most valuable chapter.

The game we address (unless otherwise noted) has a structured-limit. It has two blinds, both to the dealer's left, with the first (small) blind being either one-half or one-third the size of the second (big) blind. All bets and raises before the flop and on the flop are equal to the size of the big blind (we sometimes call them small bets), and all bets and raises on fourth street (known as "the turn") and fifth street (known as "the river") are double the size of the big blind (big bets). For example, a $4-$8 game would have a small blind of $2, a big blind of $4, bets and raises preflop and on the flop in increments of $4, and bets and raises on the turn and river in increments of $8. If you play in a game with a different structure, some of the ideas and concepts that this text discusses will not be totally accurate, and you must make adjustments.

Throughout the book, at important points in every hand example, we report the pot size in parentheses. Preflop and on the flop, we report it in terms of small bets. On the turn and river, we

9

report it in terms of big bets. Since the rake structure varies considerably for many games, we report the pot size before the rake or collection is taken. However, when we move from small to big bets, we round down to the nearest half bet. So if the pot is 9.5 small bets after the flop action, we report the size on fourth street as 4.5 big bets, not 4.75. If you would like, you can interpret this rounding down as an effect of the rake.

Occasionally, particularly in the preflop chapter, we refer to starting hands using the following system:

1.  KK represents any pocket pair of kings, such as K♥K♦ or K♠K♣.

2.  A8s (with an "s") represents any combination of an ace and an eight *of the same suit*, such as A♠8♠ or A♦8♦.

3.  KJ represents any combination of a king and a jack *of different suits*, such as K♣J♦ or K♥J♠

4.  The letter "T" refers to a ten.

We also sometimes use the term "ace-rag." That denotes any hand that contains an ace and a small, unspecified side card, such as a trey or a six.

We anticipate that some people will compare the advice in this book to that given in *Hold 'em Poker for Advanced Players* by David Sklansky and Mason Malmuth. For some situations, we may advise you to do one thing here but another there. *This represents neither a retraction of previous advice nor a contradiction.* In *Hold 'em Poker for Advanced Players*, we assume that your opponents play reasonably well. In this book, we assume that many of your opponents play poorly: specifically, that they play too many hands and go too far with them. The different assumptions can cause you to draw two totally different conclusions in situations that seem almost identical! So if you find two pieces of advice that seem to contradict one another, think about how your opponents' tendencies might cause the correct play to change.

Finally, we anticipate that some readers will concentrate most heavily on the preflop chapter, particularly the two preflop charts that we provide. No doubt, some people will compare our recommendations to those made in other books, and they will try to decide which recommendations are better. *We do not recommend that you do this. It is basically a waste of time.* As long as the strategies are essentially tight and eschew calling raises with offsuit hands, there is simply not that much to choose between one particular set of guidelines and another. *Understanding postflop concepts and play is far more essential to maximizing your win rate.* Move quickly through the preflop material, and concentrate on what is important.

# Part One
# Gambling Concepts

# Gambling Concepts

# Introduction

Small stakes hold 'em games are notoriously loose. Some people seem to think they are too loose: "Nobody folds. It turns the game into a crapshoot. It's like playing bingo." The implication is that your opponents' ultra-loose play can somehow prevent you from winning in the long run, just as if you were playing craps or bingo.

This notion, of course, is absurd. Loose small stakes games are potentially the most profitable limit hold 'em games available (in terms of bets won per hour). Skill is as important a factor in small stakes poker as it is at higher limits. People who equate poker to craps lose, not because the game is unbeatable, but because they make numerous mistakes.

Part of their problem is that they often do not view poker as a gambling game. They view success in terms of pots won, not money won. Losing with pocket aces is a failure to them, even if they played theoretically correctly. If you want to become a successful at hold 'em, avoid taking this perspective.[3]

Instead, see poker for what it is — a gambling game. Casino owners do not get upset when a patron wins a blackjack hand, hits his point at the craps table, or wins a jackpot from a slot machine. They know that, as long as they continue to get action, winning is inevitable. They have set the rules of every game to give themselves an edge. As long as people keep playing the games, the casino owners will eventually win at a rate commensurate with that edge.

---

[3] For more on this important topic, see p. 171 of *The Psychology of Poker* by Alan Schoonmaker.

Small stakes hold 'em is the same way. It is a gambling game. If you are a good player, it does not matter if you lose a big pot today, or if you lose five big pots tomorrow. We understand that it can be frustrating to watch big pot after big pot go to players who hit longshot draws against you. But, difficult as it may sometimes be, don't lose your cool. As long as you understand fundamental gambling concepts and make correct decisions, winning will be inevitable. This chapter explains all of the important gambling concepts you must know to be successful at small stakes hold 'em.

# Where the Money Comes From

If your opponents all played "perfect" poker, you could not possibly win in the long run. On nights when your cards ran much better than average, you would win. When your cards ran worse than average, you would lose. Overall, though, no matter how well you played, you could not beat the game long-term. In fact, if you played in a casino or any place that takes a collection or rake, you would be doomed to lose as surely as if you played craps, roulette, or keno.

*Every cent of your long-term profit playing poker comes from exploiting your opponents' errors and predictable tendencies.* The more numerous and egregious their errors, the more money you can make. Some small stakes players who struggle to beat their game think that they would do better if they moved to a higher limit. "If only I played in a game where people respected my raises, I could be a big winner." This notion, appealing to many harried players, is absurd.

Money comes from exploiting mistakes. When your opponents make mistakes, you can make money. When they don't, you don't make money. There is *always* more potential for profit in games where your opponents make frequent and costly errors.

People learn best through practice and feedback. If you wanted to improve your tennis game, you would go to a tennis court and start swinging at balls. At first you might miss completely. If you did, you would make a small adjustment: You might stand in a different place, swing slightly earlier or later, or move your arm in a different motion. After you did this, you might hit the ball, but send it careening into the net. You would then make another adjustment. Eventually, this iterative process of making an adjustment, observing the result, and choosing the next

16

adjustment based on the previous result improves your game. You start hitting the ball where you want to, consistently.

This is the normal human process for learning. Unfortunately, it does not work *at all* for poker. The immediate results in poker are often divorced from your actions. Sometimes you flop a big hand, bet and raise to build a huge pot, and get drawn out on by a miracle river card. You acted correctly, but your result was terrible. Other times, you may make a loose call and be the recipient of the miracle river card. You acted incorrectly, but your result was terrific. These common "backwards" results fool your brain's natural learning process. The random nature of poker fundamentally frustrates most people; their learning processes get so confused that they just give up. From that point forward, they do not improve; they play their same game, full of terrible mistakes, forever. This is one reason that so many people play so poorly.

The correct way to learn poker is to understand it *theoretically*, and make sure you made the correct play, regardless of the results. Do not start chasing wild draws because you hit one once. Do not stop protecting your good hands with raises simply because someone just called anyway and hit a long shot. This is a particularly common vice among small stakes players. They get so frustrated by people making poor calls and laying "beats" on them that they stop playing aggressively. "I just call. They always draw out anyway. At least this way it won't cost me as much." *The beats do not cause you to lose in the long run. Playing passively does.* Learn the concepts in this book and apply them, regardless of individual results.

The strange notion that your profits might be bigger against better players comes from the exact same trick that poker plays on your brain. The most horrifying result in poker is the "bad beat," when you lose a big pot that you were heavily favored to win. When you experience a terrible outcome, your brain tells you to avoid the cause, the same way your brain tells you to avoid a hot stove after you get burnt. It is trying to help you, but instead it is misleading you! Bad beats happen most often in the very best games. Avoiding bad beats by playing against only good players is the worst thing you can do.

Another part of the problem is that many players, even some who play well at higher stakes, do not understand how to adjust their strategy for a small stakes game. They struggle to beat the easiest games, and they assume that bad beats are to blame. Your opponents' mistakes create the potential for more profit, but if you play incorrectly, you may not take advantage of it. *If you do not win in the long run, it is not because your opponents are making too many mistakes; it is because you are.* Fortunately, after you read this book, you won't have that problem.

We wrote this book because small stakes hold 'em games allow you to achieve an amazing return on investment. An expert player can win thousands of dollars per month, yet need a bankroll of only a few thousand dollars to do so. This opportunity exists only because your opponents in these games play so horribly. If you switched to a game where opponents "respected your raises," and you could "move someone off a hand," your win rate would plummet. The sizable rake in these games would finish off what little profit you could hope to make. *Be glad your opponents refuse to fold; if they didn't, you just might go broke.*

# Fundamental
# Gambling Concepts

"Poker isn't gambling." You have surely heard someone say it. You may have said it yourself. Whoever says it usually really means, "In the long run, everyone expects to receive the same distribution of good and bad hands. Being lucky does not make you a long-term winner; playing better than your opponents does. Eventually, the bad players will all lose, and the good players will all win." That is a bit long-winded, though, so most people tend to stick to, "Poker isn't gambling." You are better off not abbreviating, though, because the second statement is true, while the first one is not! *Poker is gambling.*

In fact, while it may seem like a harmless cliché, denying that poker is gambling can cause you to make systematic errors. Expert poker players make their money in fundamentally the same way that casinos, bookmakers, sports handicappers, card counters, and any other long-term winner at gambling make money. With every decision they strive to *maximize their overall expectation.*

## Expectation

*Expectation* is the amount of money that you will win or lose *on average* by making a wager. Say you and a friend agree to bet on the outcome of a coin flip. If the coin lands on heads, he will pay you $1. If it lands on tails, you will pay him $1. Your expectation for this bet is zero. You expect to win $1 half the time and lose $1 the other half. On average, this bet is break-even.

*To calculate expectation mathematically, you must take an average of all the possible results, weighted by the likelihood of each one.* In this case, we have two results: +$1 and -$1. Each result has a likelihood of ½. Thus, your expectation (referred to as "EV" for "expected value") is 0.

$$0 = \left(\frac{1}{2}\right)(1) + \left(\frac{1}{2}\right)(-1)$$

Let's say your friend decides to pay you $2 for heads, but you still pay only $1 for tails. Now your EV is $0.50.

$$0.5 = \left(\frac{1}{2}\right)(2) + \left(\frac{1}{2}\right)(-1)$$

On any given flip, you will either win $2 or lose $1. But *on average*, you expect to win fifty cents per coin flip. Similarly, your friend's EV is -$0.50.

$$-0.50 = \left(\frac{1}{2}\right)(-2) + \left(\frac{1}{2}\right)(1)$$

If you make fifty cents per flip, he must lose fifty cents per flip. Money does not appear from nowhere or disappear into nowhere: *If one person has a positive expectation, another must have a negative one, and the sum of all expectations must be zero.*

Here is a more complicated example that more closely represents how expectations work in a poker hand. You and two friends, Alan and Betty, decide to gamble on the roll of a die. If the die lands on one through five, you will pay Alan $1. If it lands on six, he will pay you $6. If it lands on one or two, Betty will pay you $5. If it lands on three through six, you pay her $2. Alan and Betty never bet between each other. We can represent this arrangement in table form.

| Number Rolled | Win from Alan | Win from Betty | Net Win |
|---|---|---|---|
| 1 | -$1 | +$5 | +$4 |
| 2 | -$1 | +$5 | +$4 |
| 3 | -$1 | -$2 | -$3 |
| 4 | -$1 | -$2 | -$3 |
| 5 | -$1 | -$2 | -$3 |
| 6 | +$6 | -$2 | +$4 |

Each of these rolls will occur one out of six times. Thus, your EV is $0.50.

$$0.50 = \left(\frac{1}{6}\right)(4) + \left(\frac{1}{6}\right)(4) + \left(\frac{1}{6}\right)(-3) + \left(\frac{1}{6}\right)(-3) + \left(\frac{1}{6}\right)(-3) + \left(\frac{1}{6}\right)(4)$$

You expect to win on average fifty cents each time you roll the die. If you make fifty cents per roll, Alan and Betty must, together, lose fifty cents per roll. Let's calculate their expectations:

$$EV_{Alan} = \left(\frac{5}{6}\right)(1) + \left(\frac{1}{6}\right)(-6) = -\frac{1}{6} = -0.17$$

$$EV_{Betty} = \left(\frac{2}{6}\right)(-5) + \left(\frac{4}{6}\right)(2) = -\frac{2}{6} = -0.33$$

On average Alan loses 17 cents per roll, and Betty loses 33 cents. Together they lose what you win.

# Making Gambling Decisions

To win money gambling over the long term, you should make bets and choose options with positive expectation and avoid those with negative expectation. This is how a casino makes its money: It offers a variety of wagers, but almost all of them afford the house a positive expectation and, hence, the player a negative one.[4]

In some gambling games, the only decision you make is how much to bet. For instance, in our coin-flipping and die-rolling games above, you just flip the coin or roll the die and make the appropriate payouts based on the result. Similarly, in roulette you place your wager on one or more numbers and spin the ball. Your expectation is determined solely by the payout structure and the size of your wager. But in other games, such as blackjack or poker, there are additional decisions to make. In all of these games, the correct decision is the one that *maximizes your overall expectation*.

Say you are playing blackjack and are dealt a six and a five (for a total of 11), and the dealer shows a six.[5] You have three choices: stand, hit, or double down. To decide which play is best, you must calculate the expectation of each option.

If you stand, you hope that the dealer busts. He will draw to seventeen or better, and he will either make it or bust. If he makes it, he will beat your eleven. So you win only if he busts. Even with

---

[4] Sometimes intentionally, and more often unintentionally, casinos offer a few bets that offer the player a positive expectation. The nature of these bets is beyond the scope of this book. For more on this topic see *Gambling for a Living* by David Sklansky and Mason Malmuth.

[5] You may wonder what a blackjack example is doing in a book about poker. Blackjack better illustrates this point because it is a much simpler game than poker. You can calculate the expectation for each play exactly. You cannot in poker.

a six up (the dealer will bust more often with a six up than with any other card), he will bust less than half the time. Thus, since the dealer will make his hand (and beat you) more than half the time, standing has a negative expectation.

If you hit (once only), you can win one of two ways. If you catch a bad card (an ace through five), you can stand and again hope he busts. If you catch a good card (six through king), you can stand and win either if he busts or if he makes a hand smaller than yours. This strategy always wins if the dealer busts (as did standing), and it also wins sometimes when you make a hand higher than the dealer's. This combination lets you win more than half the time, so hitting has a positive expectation.

If you double down, you take one more card as you did when you hit, but you also double your bet. Doubling down therefore doubles your expectation from hitting. Standing has a negative expectation. Hitting has a positive one. In this case, doubling down has double the expectation of hitting, so therefore it is the play that *maximizes your expectation.*

# Making Poker Decisions

Likewise, to win at poker you must make as many plays with a positive expectation as possible, while avoiding those with a negative one. You have three choices each time you act during a poker hand: fold, call, or raise.[6] Each of these plays has an expectation associated with it. *Your goal is simply to choose the one with the highest expectation.*

Quantifying your expectation for calling and raising is often difficult, but folding is easy: It is always zero. When you fold, you are guaranteed to win or lose nothing more. If either calling or raising has a positive expectation, you should not fold. Fold only

---

[6] Betting is just raising when the current bet is zero. Likewise, checking is just calling when the current bet is zero.

if both calling and raising have a negative expectation. Otherwise, compare calling to raising and choose the better option.[7]

As we noted before, some people deny that poker is gambling. Thus, they generally do not approach poker decisions from an expectation-maximizing perspective. This causes systematic errors.

In their view, losing players "gamble" while winning players "avoid gambles." To them, gambling means risking money on a long shot with little hope of winning. They bet and raise only when they will usually win, and they fold whenever they are a significant underdog.

For example, many "poker isn't gambling" people do not like to raise before the flop. They hate risking extra money when the flop will ruin their hand so often. For instance, they might choose never to raise with ace-king. "I like to see if I make a pair first before I risk any extra money. Ace-king is just a drawing hand, after all." They view raising as reckless gambling, the choice of foolish "action players."

Experts do not think this way! They evaluate the expectation of calling and raising independently, and they choose the option with the highest overall value. Say you have five opponents, and you estimate that, on average, your ace-king will win the hand about one out of four times. To simplify the math, assume that your raise also leaves you all-in. Therefore, raising risks one bet to win five (since you have five opponents who must call if you raise), and you win one out of four times, so your immediate EV for the raise is 0.5 bets.

---

[7] To be clear, folding does not make your expectation for the *entire hand* zero, it just makes your expectation from that point forward zero. Looked at another way, many poker decisions are correct because they make the expectation for the entire hand less negative than the alternatives.

$$0.5 = \left(\frac{3}{4}\right)(-1) + \left(\frac{1}{4}\right)(5)$$

Even though you are an underdog to win the hand, raising earns more than just calling. It is the play that maximizes your expectation.

We had to assume that the raise left you all-in because future betting affects your expectation. Poker is complicated. But that should just convince you even more that "playing by platitude" is wrong. "Avoiding gambles" is not sound strategy. Simplistic advice like, "Don't draw to inside straights," "Don't raise on the come," or "Fit or fold," is not expert thinking.[8] Skilled players know that poker is a gambling game. There is no way around it: *To maximize your long-term winnings, you must consistently choose the plays that maximize your expectation.*

# Final Thoughts

Some days you will consistently make the plays with the maximum-possible expectation, but your cards will run worse than average, and you will lose. Other days you will make mistakes and sometimes choose plays with an inferior expectation, but still win because your cards will run better than average. In the long run, however, your results will reflect the expectation of your choices. If you consistently choose plays that maximize your expectation, you will make a lot of money playing poker. If you consistently make the wrong plays, you will lose. *Ignore the results and focus on making decisions that maximize your expectation.* This book will teach you to do just that, and the money will take care of itself.

---

[8] As we will show later in the text, "Fit or Fold," while being a catchy expression and appealing to our intuition, fails miserably from an expectation point of view. Thus it is terrible advice.

# Some Poker-Specific Concepts

In poker, as in any gambling game, long-term profits and losses depend on your expectation. Every time you decide to fold, call, or raise, you must consider your expectation. To maximize your winnings, at each point you must consistently choose the decision with the highest overall expectation. This would be easy to do if you could accurately determine each option's expectation.

In many gambling games, it is trivial to determine your exact expectation for every bet you make. For example, there are 38 numbers on an American roulette wheel: 18 red, 18 black, and 2 green zeros. When you bet on a single number, you are paid 35-to-1. Assuming a fair wheel, there is a 1 in 38 chance that the ball will land on your number. If you bet $100 on number 16, you will lose on average 37 out of 38 times, but win $3,500 1 time out of 38. Thus, your EV for this bet is -$5.26.

$$- \$5.26 = \left(\frac{1}{38}\right)(3,500) + \left(\frac{37}{38}\right)(-100)$$

On average, your $100 bet loses $5.26. For a simple game like roulette, you can calculate your expectation for any bet down to the penny.

Unfortunately, poker is not a simple game.[9] Most importantly, you do not have complete information. There are two important pieces of information that you do not have:

---

[9] Actually, it is fortunate that poker is not simple. If it were, everyone would play it well, and you could never gain an edge or win money in the long run.

1.  Your opponents' cards
2.  How your opponents will respond to your action

(You also do not know what board cards will come, but you can exactly calculate their likelihood of appearing, just as you could calculate the likelihood that the roulette ball would land on your number.)

If you have ace-king, your expectation when your lone opponent has pocket queens is radically different from when he has pocket aces. You could ask him to show you his cards to aid your calculations, but he would probably not oblige. Thus, most calculations of expectation in poker must be *estimates*, based on logical guesses at your opponents' hands.[10]

Furthermore, your expectation depends on how your opponents will react to various actions. If you raise, will they fold or call? Your expectation will usually change based on their actions.

Despite all these variables, to make consistently correct poker decisions, it helps to estimate the expectation of your plays. In this section we will introduce several tools to help you derive these estimates.

# Pot Odds

"Pot odds" are the ratio of the current size of the pot to the bet that you must call. For instance, if you must call a $4 bet, and the pot currently contains $40 (including the $4 bet), then your pot odds are 40-to-4 or 10-to-1. Pot odds are the most important factor determining a play's expectation. Just as the expectation in roulette would change significantly if they decided to pay 20-to-1

---

[10] These logical guesses are arrived at using both psychology (knowledge of your opponents' proclivities) and mathematics (knowledge of the probabilistic frequency of the various hands he could have).

or 50-to-1 instead of 35-to-1 on a winning spin, your expectation in poker changes significantly if your pot odds are 4-to-1 or 14-to-1 instead of 8-to-1.

When you are drawing, pot odds can help you decide whether to call or fold. Say you have

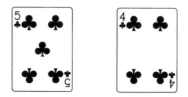

and the board on fourth street is

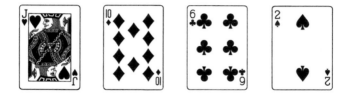

You are heads-up, and your opponent has bet. You are pretty sure he has at least a pair of jacks. Should you call?

It depends on the pot odds. There are four cards (4 treys) that give you the nut straight. No other cards make you a winner. There are 46 unseen cards (you've seen 6 of the 52 total so far), so the river will save you 4 times out of 46. If we ignore the last betting round, you must have pot odds of 42-to-4 or 10.5-to-1 for your call to break even.

$$0 = (4)(10.5) + (42)(-1) = 42 - 42$$

If your pot odds are less than 10.5-to-1, you will not make enough when you get lucky to pay for your single bet investments. If they are more than 10.5-to-1, the call is profitable, and you should draw.[11]

To calculate the break-even point for pot odds on fourth street, follow these quick steps:

1.  Divide 46, the number of total unseen cards, by the number of outs you have.

2.  Subtract one. This converts your results to odds form. For example, ten outs is actually a 3.6-to-1 underdog.

Thus with our four-out gutshot, we take 46/4 = 11.5 and subtract 1 to get 10.5-to-1. For a two-out draw, you would need 46/2 −1 = 23 − 1 or 22-to-1 to break even. Below is a table that relates the break-even point for pot odds on fourth street for draws of one to eighteen outs. You should memorize the numbers you use most to avoid doing repeated arithmetic at the table.[12, 13]

---

[11] The 10.5-to-1 break-even odds are actually still an estimate. As we will explain later, the true break-even point is slightly lower.

[12] These numbers assume that you are certain to win if you catch one of your outs. We discuss how to handle situations where you are not a lock later in the text.

[13] These numbers apply to the next card only. If you want the odds of making your hand with two cards to come, see page 107 of *Hold 'em Poker* by David Sklansky.

| Number of Outs | Break-Even Pot Odds | Number of Outs | Break-Even Pot Odds |
|---|---|---|---|
| 1 | 45-to-1 | 10 | 3.6-to-1 |
| 2 | 22-to-1 | 11 | 3.2-to-1 |
| 3 | 14.3-to-1 | 12 | 2.8-to-1 |
| 4 | 10.5-to-1 | 13 | 2.5-to-1 |
| 5 | 8.2-to-1 | 14 | 2.2-to-1 |
| 6 | 6.7-to-1 | 15 | 2.1-to-1 |
| 7 | 5.6-to-1 | 16 | 1.9-to-1 |
| 8 | 4.75-to-1 | 17 | 1.7-to-1 |
| 9 | 4.1-to-1 | 18 | 1.6-to-1 |

Notice that after about eight outs, the break-even pot odds become so small that virtually any pot on fourth street will offer you profitable drawing odds. Thus, you should almost never fold a draw with eight or more outs for one bet, so do not bother to memorize the numbers for those draws. The most important numbers to know are those for the long shot draws.

Hidden behind this observation is a valuable insight into correct strategy. Small stakes games are known for their many players who will call to the river with very weak hands. These players do not memorize this table; they do not estimate their expectation. They just call. They cannot wait to see what the river will bring, and they certainly would not relinquish their frequently slim winning chances for one or two "measly" bets.

When they have a strong draw, one with eight or more outs, their calling instinct coincides with correct strategy. They will see the river no matter what, and they should. But when your opponents have weak draws, those with fewer than eight outs, whether they can call profitably depends on the size of the bet and pot — that is, on their pot odds.

Say you are playing $2-$4, and the pot is $44 on the turn. You have top pair, and your lone, loose opponent has four outs to beat you. If you bet $4, then the pot will be $48 (the original size plus your bet), and your opponent will have pot odds of 48-to-4 or 12-to-1. Since that is more than the break-even point for his draw (10.5-to-1 for four outs), he can call profitably.

Now assume that you have two opponents, one who has bet, and the other that still has the four out draw. The pot started at $44, so your opponent's bet makes it $48. If you raise, you will make the pot $56 total, but it will be $8 for your opponent with four outs to call. His pot odds will be 56-to-8 or 7-to-1. He can no longer call profitably. If he does call, he will theoretically lose money, and, therefore, you and your other opponent combined will make that money.[14] *Much of your profit in small stakes games comes from players who call when they should fold with weak hands. Small stakes hold 'em is often a game of attacking players with weak draws.*

# Implied Odds

Pot odds alone cannot determine your expectation exactly, however. There is usually more betting (e.g., the river betting round) after you see if you or others have made your draws. This extra betting affects your expectation for the hand. Using our example from before, you have

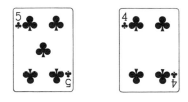

---

[14] In rare cases, only one of you will benefit.

the board is

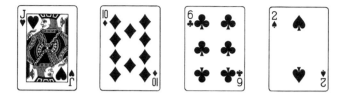

and your opponent has at least a pair of jacks. Using pot odds alone, we concluded that the pot must lay 10.5-to-1 to call profitably.

But we ignored the river betting round. If you miss your draw, you will fold to a bet, so you still lose only one bet (from the turn). But if you make your draw, there will probably be more betting on fifth street. If your opponent has only a pair of jacks, you might win one extra bet. But if he has a strong hand like a set of jacks, he may raise if you bet, losing three or more bets.

So with a draw like this, the river is a freeroll for you: You lose nothing if you miss, but you could make one or more bets if you complete your straight. We did not take that into account when determining the break-even point. "Implied odds" are the pot odds, adjusted for future betting. Calling is profitable if your implied odds are better than the break-even point, even if your pot odds are not.

Say you are trying to decide whether to call with your gutshot. The pot contains $36 before the turn, and your opponent bets $4. Thus, your pot odds are 40-to-4 or 10-to-1, just below the 10.5-to-1 break-even point for a four-out draw. The pot odds say you should fold, but what about the implied odds?

To find your implied odds, you must estimate how much you will win on the river if you make your hand. Sometimes your opponent will have a relatively weak hand and just pay off a single bet. But occasionally he will have a strong hand and raise once or twice, losing a total of two to five bets. So you guess that you will win, on average, about 1.5 bets. Since you will have the nuts if you make your hand (and, therefore, there is no chance that you will actually *lose* those two to five bets to a surprise holding), you should add 1.5 bets to the size of the pot to determine your implied odds. So add $6 (1.5 bets) to the $40 pot, and you have 46-to-4 or 11.5-to-1 implied odds. While your pot odds are only 10-to-1, your implied odds give you a solid overlay. You should call with your gutshot.

# Reverse Implied Odds

So far we have discussed pot and implied odds only in terms of drawing hands on the turn. This situation is simplest for determining your winning chances: If you hit your draw, you win, and if you miss, you lose. But pot and implied odds are important for every hand: made hands, drawing hands, and even when you are not sure whether you are ahead or drawing.

When you are drawing to the nuts, your implied odds are usually better than your pot odds. You often have a "freeroll" situation as you did with the gutshot: You lose nothing extra when you miss, but you make money when you hit your hand.

Just the opposite occurs when you have a weak made hand; the future betting frequently costs you, and you must deal with "reverse implied odds." Sometimes reverse implied odds can turn a hand that looks profitable (according to the pot odds) into a loser. This happens under the following circumstances:

1. The pot is small.

2. You are still on the preflop or flop betting rounds. That is, there are still several big bets to go before the showdown.

3. You have a weak made hand that may be best now, but is easy to draw out on.

For example, say you have

in the big blind. Two players limp, the small blind completes, and you check (4 small bets). The flop is

giving you top pair. The small blind bets (5 small bets). You should fold.

Getting 5-to-1, the pot odds look favorable. These odds suggest that you need to win only 17 percent of the time to call profitably. But your true odds are much worse than 5-to-1.

If you have the best hand, you are unlikely to get a lot of action from weaker hands. You may get one loose player to pay off with a smaller pair, but otherwise you cannot expect to make much on the turn and river.

On the other hand, plenty of cards could make your opponents a bigger pair, straight, or flush. If an opponent does draw out on you, you may not know and end up paying him off.

Finally, you could already be behind to someone with an overpair or a nine and a better kicker. If so, you may again be paying off on the turn and river.

There is a much higher chance that you will be the one paying off the big bets on the later streets than the one getting paid off. You could call profitably if it would leave you all-in (allowing you to see the showdown for free), but since you cannot, we say you are getting reverse implied odds. And in this case, those reverse implied odds are not high enough to allow you to play the hand.

To summarize, implied odds measure your overall expectation for the hand, including all your opponents' future betting. Accounting for future betting can shift your estimate for your hand's expectation in either direction:

1. With a drawing hand, especially one with outs to a strong hand like a flush or the nut straight, implied odds sometimes allow you to call profitably when the pot odds do not seem to justify it. This is particularly true on the flop, when there are two rounds of big bets remaining for the made hands to pay off. *Estimate how much you will make on future betting and add that to the size of the current pot to calculate your implied odds.*

2. With a weak made hand, especially when the pot is small, reverse implied odds sometimes force you to fold when the pot odds seem to support continuing. You will be paying off a better hand for big bets far more often than someone will pay you off. *When the pot is small, if there is a high chance you are either already beaten or will be outdrawn, fold marginal made hands.*

# Pot Equity

Pot and implied odds are useful tools for estimating your expectation when deciding between calling and folding (not so much when you are deciding whether to bet or raise). Thinking in terms of pot equity can help you make both call/fold and call/raise decisions.

Your "pot equity" is the dollar or bet amount equivalent to the percentage of the pot that you expect to win. That is, if the pot contains ten bets, and you have a draw to the nuts that will come in twenty percent of the time, your pot equity is two bets (twenty percent of ten). Thinking in terms of pot equity is most useful when the pot is multiway. It is typically helpful in three situations:

1.  When you are considering folding, your pot equity measures how much you "lose" or give up when you fold. Folding forfeits your claim to a share of the pot, and your pot equity quantifies how much that share is worth. For instance, say you have a draw that will come in ten percent of the time. If the pot is five bets, your pot equity is 0.5 bets. It is not worthwhile to protect that small equity if you must call a bet to do so. Do not spend one bet to protect half a bet of equity.

2.  When you are considering giving a free or cheap card (e.g., slowplaying), your *opponents' combined* pot equity measures how much you are risking if that card beats you. For example, you are heads-up, the pot contains six bets, and your opponent has a draw that will beat you ten percent of the time. His pot equity is 0.6 bets. If you give him a free card (as a slowplay), you grant him his 0.6 bet share of the pot for free. This would be worthwhile if you felt that you could win an average of more than 0.6 bets *extra* from him as a result (perhaps because you think he would now call or bluff on the end even if he misses his draw).

3.  When you have a strong drawing hand (particularly before the flop or on the flop), your pot equity determines whether you can bet or raise for value. For instance, you have flopped the nut flush draw against four opponents. You have a 35 percent chance to make your hand by the river, and therefore, also about a 35 percent pot equity.[15] If all four of your

---

[15] Obviously, you will occasionally make your flush and still lose. But you will also sometimes win when you miss your flush and catch your top card or by backing into another hand like two pair. As an

opponents call to see the turn, you will contribute 20 percent of the money, but your equity is 35 percent. This represents a "pot equity edge," as you will net a profit worth 15 percent of all the flop betting. The more flop raises, the more money you make.[16]

This last application of pot equity is particularly useful for thinking about decisions in small stakes games. When gambling, the best play is the one that maximizes your expectation. In poker, maximizing your expectation usually means raising for value instead of calling when you have a pot equity edge. You need not have the best hand to raise for value, you just need to expect to make the best hand by the river more than your fair share of the time. Hence, you should frequently bet or raise on the flop with a strong draw like a quality open-ended straight draw or flush draw, and you should generally raise a hand like

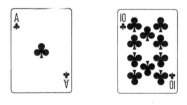

before the flop if no one has yet raised. In both situations you expect to win significantly more than your share by the river.

---

approximation, we assume that these probabilities cancel.

[16] This is not completely true. Many raises may indicate that one of your opponents has a strong hand like a set. If so, you can make your flush, but still lose if the board pairs.

# Counting the Pot

These three concepts — pot odds, implied odds, and pot equity — help you to determine the expectation of your plays. Pot and implied odds help you decide whether calling has a positive or negative expectation (and therefore whether you should prefer it to folding, which always has an expectation of zero). Pot equity can help you determine whether raising or calling has a higher expectation.

To use any of these tools, however, you must first count the pot. The pot size affects your expectation *for every decision you make.* "Should I call or fold? Should I raise or just call?" To answer these questions, you must almost always first ask, "How big is the pot?"

In all of the hand examples in this book, we supply a running count of the size of the pot at important points throughout the hand. We do this for two reasons:

1.  It is a convenience for you as you read the example. You will not have to recount the action to determine the pot size. We do the work for you.

2.  It reminds you that you must use the pot size in every decision you make. We quote the pot size at several points throughout the hand. As you play, you should be able to do the same (it is usually easier to count *bets* rather than actual money), and you should use that information almost every time you act.

*Always know how much is in the pot at all times.*

# Random and
# Independent Events

The human brain is terrific at identifying patterns. We draw squiggles on a page to represent abstract ideas, and every literate person understands them as words. We can instantly identify individuals by looking at their faces alone, even if their appearance has changed, and we haven't seen them for years. Everyone recognizes these incredibly complex patterns effortlessly and reliably.

Sometimes our overzealous brains find patterns where none actually exist. Some of us see faces on the moon or animal shapes in the stars. Of course, no one actually believes that there is a man's face embedded in the moon or that the stars have been specifically arranged to look like a bull or lion, so these false patterns just entertain us.

But sometimes people see false patterns that they believe are real. For example, people take placebo pills, feel better, and conclude that the pills have cured their ailments. In that case, one could argue that this glitch in our pattern-recognition system is helpful.

When it comes to gambling, however, mistaking false patterns as real has led many to ruin. Most gamblers tend to ascribe meaning to purely random, independent events. They are wrong to do so. *The cards dealt on any poker hand are, for practical purposes, completely random and independent of the cards dealt on any previous hand.*[17]

---

[17] "Randomness" actually has a strict mathematical definition, and the process used to shuffle cards does not produce a technically random distribution. For all practical purposes, however, you can treat a well-shuffled deck as random. For more on this topic, see p. 169 of *Gambling*

When most people play poker, they tend to expect that which has recently occurred to recur. For example, if they have drawn to five flushes so far that session and made them all, they tend to expect to complete their flush again if they flop another draw. Likewise, when people miss five flushes in a row, they tend to expect to miss a sixth one.

Of course, each hand is an *independent event*. Cards are pieces of plastic. They have no knowledge, no memory, no cosmic plan. They are scrambled and shuffled thoroughly prior to each hand. Pieces of plastic cannot possibly conspire against you to give you four spades, but not a fifth. Even if you've flopped and missed twenty flush draws in a row, as long as you are not being cheated, your chance to complete your next flush draw by the river is 35 percent, just as it always is.

There is no such thing as "flop lag." If you have been "running good," or "playing a rush," you are no more likely than anyone else to be dealt a good hand in the future. It isn't true that "Someone always makes two pair whenever I have aces," or that "Everyone else always makes their flushes, but I always miss mine." Pocket kings are not actually "ace magnets," and not everyone hits his two-outer against you. Past results do not affect the cards dealt in future hands.

Our brains invented all of this nonsense to explain something it clearly wasn't designed to understand: completely random events with absolutely no pattern or meaning whatsoever. It is natural to begin to think that the cards are out to get you when you are losing, or that you will continue to be lucky when you have been "hot." But being natural does not mean it is helpful. Stop your pattern-recognizer before it goes haywire by telling yourself, "There is no pattern. There is no pattern!"

---

*Theory and Other Topics* by Mason Malmuth.

# Gambling Concepts

# Afterthought

As can be seen, poker is gambling. Anyone who says it's not or states that when he plays he doesn't gamble, does not understand poker as well as he should. Poker is gambling because your outcomes, for the most part, are not certain. This means that sometimes you will do much better than expected and at other times much worse. You may even lose to players who are not nearly as skilled as you.

But what sets poker apart from many other gambling games is that your expectation can be positive. You achieve this mainly by exploiting the errors that your opponents make because the money comes from them. That's why ideas like expectation, pot odds, implied odds, and pot equity are so important. Put another way, these are some of the tools that you need to be successful.

But there is also another tool that's very important. It is a complete understanding of hold 'em and how it should be played at small stakes games. So keep reading.

# Part Two
# Preflop Play

# Preflop Play

# Introduction

Say you are prone to making a particularly bizarre error: Every time you are dealt a royal flush, you check and fold. Well, this error is very expensive, as you forfeit an entire pot you are guaranteed to win. Yet you could make this egregious error *every time* and still be a successful poker player. That is because you get the opportunity to make this mistake only once or twice per year. So even if it costs you $100 on average each time you make it, it still costs you only $100-$200 per year. A good player can easily overcome the effects of such an error with otherwise sound play.

Taken individually, preflop errors tend to be much less expensive. If you call with a hand that you should fold, it can obviously cost you no more than the price of the call. For instance, if you are playing $2-$4 and call a raise with

(a clear error), your mistake cannot possibly cost you more than the $4 you used to call.[18] It does not cost even that much, as you

---

[18] If making the initial error could cause you to make additional errors later in the hand, then it could be said that it has cost more than the price of the call. But really, in that case, you have made several distinct errors, the first of which can cost no more than the price of the call.

will sometimes go on to win the hand. So it theoretically costs a fraction of the $4 call, perhaps more like $1 or $2 in this example. *Yet you cannot call raises with king-ten (and other similar hands) and expect to be a long-term winner.* While each individual mistake is not expensive, you make a preflop decision every time you are dealt a hand. So while you could fold a royal flush only once or twice per year, you can make weak preflop calls *tens of thousands of times per year.* So if each loose call is, on average, a $1 error, over a year making that error could cost you well over $10,000! Thus, a solid, almost mistake-free preflop strategy is critical to long-term success in small stakes hold 'em. This chapter teaches you to avoid bankroll-draining preflop errors and lays a solid foundation for winning hold 'em.

# Preflop Concepts

Good hand selection is the foundation of winning hold 'em. No matter how well you play otherwise, if you often start with the wrong hands, you will be a long-term loser. Fortunately, learning which hands to fold, call, or raise is probably the easiest step toward becoming a big winner.

This chapter is divided into three sections. This first section discusses general concepts for preflop play. It points out several common errors and shows you how to avoid them. The later two sections are more detailed; they recommend exactly when and how to play various hands. After reading the specific advice of the later sections, return to this section. Understand how the general principles guide our recommendations. It is crucially important to understand the underlying concepts. If you just memorize the "rules" for playing hands, you cannot adjust to changing conditions, and while you might win a little, you will still be far away from expert play.

## Tight is Right

The only hand rewarded in poker is the best hand. At the showdown you win nothing if your hand is second- or third- best. Being a little better than average is worthless. Thus, starting hands that are a little better than average tend to lose money in the long run. When selecting starting hands, choose only those few hands that have a positive expectation. If the hand does not figure to show a profit, there is no reason to play it.

The best starting hands make a lot of money. A few more hands are modestly profitable. Most hands lose in the long run. They are the slightly above average, average, and below average hands. Below is a graph of the average profitability of each of the 169 possible starting hands. The hands are ordered from most to least profitable from left to right. Notice how quickly weaker hands lose value.

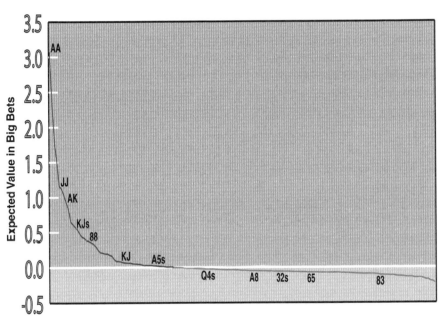

This is real data from an expert player who has a database of 60,000 hands.[19] Of course no two players will be exactly the same, and this graph would probably look fairly different if it were the results of a losing player. But we would still see that the best

---

[19] This sample size is not nearly large enough to determine the win rate of any one particular hand, but it is large enough to show the trend clearly. The downward curve at the right-most edge of the graph is not a real effect. It is an artifact of the limited sample size.

starting hands are highly profitable, and a few more make a small amount of money.

Hand values change a lot based on circumstances. If you are second to act, and the player under the gun has raised, only five or six hands may be profitable. If you are on the button after three limpers, as many as fifty (of the 169 total) hands may be profitable. Even under the best circumstances, though, you should fold most hands. Merely average starting hands do not become the best hand often enough to compensate for the cost of playing them.

# Bad Hands and Dead Money

One characteristic that distinguishes small stakes from medium or high stakes games is that small stakes games tend to feature players who play far too many hands and almost automatically go to the later streets with them.[20] If your opponents limited themselves only to those hands that are profitable, most pots would be contested heads-up or three-handed. The frequency of multiway pots indicates that your opponents play many unprofitable hands.

By definition, an unprofitable hand expects to recover less than its original investment from the pot.[21] The difference between

---

[20] Some medium and high stakes games also fit this description.

[21] A hand's expectation is an average of all the possible outcomes weighted by the likelihood of those outcomes. As a simplified example, assume that your hand has the following possible outcomes: fold on the flop, fold on the turn after calling one bet on the flop, and winning a five bet pot. You will fold on the flop sixty percent of the time, fold on the turn twenty percent of the time, and win the pot the remaining twenty percent. Not counting your original preflop investment (we consider that at the end), folding on the flop costs nothing, folding on the turn costs one bet, and winning the pot gains five bets. Your expected return from

the original investment and the return is "dead" money. That is, it is extra money, contributed by the bad hand's owner, that everyone else in the pot can win. It is as if he were playing a better, break-even, hand, but tossed an extra chip in the pot as a bonus for the winner. If you have trouble seeing how this money is "dead," you can pretend that a generous person walking by the table tossed in the extra chip instead of the player with the hand. All that matters is that the pot is sweetened when someone pays more to see the flop than his hand is worth.

In most small stakes games several of your opponents will frequently play unprofitable hands. Each of these players subsidizes the pot with extra money. These additional chips comprise much of your profit, and they add value to many of your hands. Even a hand as weak as

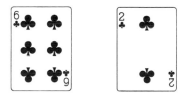

gains value once many loose players are in. However, it may not gain enough value to make it profitable.[22]

---

the pot is exactly 0.8 bets.

$$0.8 = (0.6)(0) + (0.2)(-1) + (0.2)(5)$$

Since it costs one bet before the flop to play the hand, and you expect to get only 0.8 bets back from the pot, the hand is unprofitable. For more discussion of mathematical expectation as it relates to poker and gambling, see *Getting the Best of It* by David Sklansky.

[22] Gaining value and being profitable are distinct. If a hand is worth -$4, it can gain $3 of value and still be unprofitable. The presence of weak

When you raise before the flop, especially when you raise after all your opponents have committed to their hands, you double the total preflop investment for each player. Because some of your opponents are playing unprofitable hands, this increases the number of chips you expect to win on average.[23] With your better hands you should often raise, not to limit the field, but to increase your overall expectation.

# Three Hand Types

There are three types of profitable preflop hands: top pair hands, speculative hands, and powerhouse hands. Not all good hands fit wholly under one type; some hands display characteristics of several types.

# Top Pair Hands

The quintessential top pair hands consist of two big, offsuit cards like

---

opponents adds value to most hands, though, and some of these will go from being unprofitable to being profitable.

[23] It does not double it, though. Money is won and lost after the flop as well as before it. When the pot is larger, more players will stay in longer, and your hand will not win quite as often as if you hadn't raised.

They win many small- to medium-sized pots by making top pair and having it hold up (and occasionally by holding up unimproved). Sometimes, when they make a pair on the flop, you have to "play defense" from that point on. They do not improve often enough, so you hope to survive the turn and river against drawing opponents. If an opponent draws out, he will use the big bets on the turn and river to punish the, now, second-best top pair hand. Thus, these hands make lots of money on the early betting rounds, preflop and flop, when they are favored to win. On later rounds, drawing opponents fold when they miss, but raise when they make their hands. The drawing hands usually have the advantage on the turn and river.[24]

Other things being equal, top pair hands play better against few opponents. Top pair is more likely to be best against two or three hands than it is against six or seven. Other things are not equal, though. As we said before, multiway pots usually indicate opponents playing poor, unprofitable hands (thus, contributing "extra" money to the pot). While multiway action devalues your hand relative to some of the other hands, your overall expectation may still be increased due to the extra money. *The best top pair hands — ace-ten, king-jack, and better — tend to benefit more from the extra money than they lose from multiway action.* They actually make *more* money against many bad hands. Weaker top pair hands — king-nine and ace-six, for instance — lose more in most multiway pots than they gain from the additional chips. So, against many opponents these weaker hands should quickly be discarded.

---

[24] But this is not always the case. See "Two Overpair Hands."

   With a good top pair hand you should usually raise. A hand like

wins far more often than most hands. Many of its wins happen when nobody else makes a good hand (better than a pair of aces or kings). If many of your opponents are playing poorly, get that extra money in the pot preflop, before they know the flop will miss them.

# Speculative Hands

   Speculative hands consist of small, coordinated cards — small pocket pairs, like

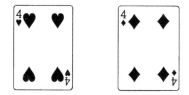

and suited, connected hands, like

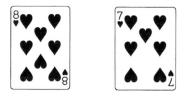

Speculative hands do not prevail frequently, but they make big hands and win big pots when they do. Small pairs make big hands when they flop sets. Suited connectors make big hands when they flop flushes, straights, and strong draws that come in. After the flop, speculative hands often "play offense" when they flop a very strong hand or draw. By the turn many opponents may be drawing dead against a speculative hand (opponents will rarely be drawing dead against top pair). Speculative hands can make a lot of money on the big turn and river bets.

Speculative hands play better against many opponents. They make powerful hands that can beat large fields. Playing in multiway pots leverages this power; many opponents create bigger pots. Against few opponents weak speculative hands like 6♥5♥ and J♦8♦ may not make enough when they get lucky to make up for all the preflop and flop bets lost when they miss.

These hands, especially the weak ones, need to see the flop cheaply. Since they often miss, they lose money with every extra bet that goes in before the flop. Stronger speculative hands, small pocket pairs and big suited connectors like T♥9♥ and up, can afford to pay two bets to see the flop (though they are often more profitable for one bet). Weaker hands like 7♦5♦ usually cannot make up two bets. In almost all situations, none of these hands can afford to pay three or more bets to see the flop.

# Powerhouse Hands

Some very strong hands, powerhouse hands, take the best attributes from each type and the worst attributes from neither. Big pocket pairs, like

and big suited cards, like

often make top pair, but they also make powerful hands like sets and flushes respectively. While offsuit top pair hands frequently "play defense" on fourth and fifth street, these strong hands have the potential to make money on all betting rounds. They play well against many or few opponents. You should raise with them to exploit this advantage.

# The Power of Domination

The community board cards in hold 'em can create a unique preflop relationship sometimes called "domination." It occurs when two hands hold cards of the same rank, but one hand has a higher second card. For instance, if one player holds

and another holds

the player with ace-queen is dominated. If an ace comes, ace-queen will make an expensive second-best hand. So while A♥Q♣ is normally a fairly good hand, it becomes a bad hand if an ace-king is also out.

An even more disastrous form of domination occurs when one player holds a pocket pair of the same rank or higher than an opponent's high card. Take K♥K♠ and K♣J♦. The player with king-jack is at a huge disadvantage. To win, he must catch two jacks, make a straight, or catch an unlikely flush.

Playing a dominated hand before the flop is costly, especially if the pot is short-handed. Against two or three opponents the player with the best pair often wins. When you play a dominated hand, your chance to make the best pair is crippled.

Domination is not as dangerous in multiway pots. When the pot is six- or seven-handed, top pair wins less often, and the ability to make straights and flushes becomes more valuable. Against many players, Q♠J♠ is usually profitable, even if one of your opponents has raised, indicating a strong hand.

Even in a multiway pot, though, domination is trouble for some offsuit hands like K♦J♠. Without strong straight or flush prospects, they have little to compensate for the disadvantage of being dominated.

# The Value of Position

Position is the second most important component of hand value (your own and your opponents' cards are the most important). In late position you have two advantages on all betting rounds:

1.  You can see what your opponents do before you must act. If they bet and raise, you may decide to fold what might normally be a good hand. If they all check, you may decide to bet what might normally be a weak hand.

2.   Your opponents do not know what you will do before they must act. If they check, will you bet or take a free card? If they bet, will you raise? They must play a constant guessing game. Sometimes they will guess wrong; when they do, you profit.

Before the flop, getting to see what your opponents will do is very valuable. With a speculative hand you would usually like to play in an unraised pot. From late position you will know if the pot is raised before you act. From early position you must guess what those behind you will do, and sometimes you will guess wrong and lose money. Furthermore, a raise alerts you that someone has a strong hand that may have you dominated. A hand like K♥J♣ may be profitable against weak hands, but it loses money against strong ones. If you have position, you can play when your opponents are weakest.

After the flop, both seeing what your opponents will do and having your opponents guess at what you will do are valuable. A starting hand's worth is based largely on how much money it expects to earn; much of this earn comes from betting after the flop. With position you make more money after the flop with almost all hands.[25] Thus, many more hands are profitable, and consequently playable, from the button than from under the gun.

# Non-Pair Hand Attributes

In a multiway pot, the best hand will generally be something between a pair and a full house. All non-paired hands have the same chance to make two pair, trips, and a full house. They mainly differ in strength based on their ability to make top pair,

---

[25] An exception sometimes occurs with hands that you might bluff with. Being able to put your money in first is often important when bluffing.

straights, and flushes. There are three valuable attributes to look for (in order of importance):
1. High card strength (top pair likelihood)
2. Suitedness (flush likelihood)
3. Connectedness (straight likelihood)

All non-pair hands can be evaluated along these three dimensions.[26] For example, A♥Q♥ has a lot of high card strength, is suited, but has little connectedness. (It can make only one straight with both cards.) 8♣7♥ is connected, but it has no high card strength, and it is not suited. A♠7♣ has some high card strength, but it is not suited and has no connectedness.

To be worth playing, a non-pair hand usually must be strong in at least two of the three categories. Specifically, hands like T♥4♥ and 7♠6♣ are not worth much. T♥4♥ is suited, but has little high card strength and no connectedness. 7♠6♣ is connected, but has no high card strength and is not suited. Being suited or connected is valuable, but alone these qualities do not make a hand any better than average.[27]

High card strength is generally the most important attribute. Hands like A♠K♥ and A♦Q♣ are very strong despite being offsuit and able to make only one straight. These hands are some of the few exceptions to the "two category" rule from above. Weaker high-card hands like K♥9♠ do not qualify for this exemption.

Hands with two big cards are much stronger than those with only one. There are two reasons:
1. They can make top pair with either card.
2. When they make top pair, they always do so with a good kicker.

---

[26] Gary Carson outlines a similar system of attributes on p. 145 of his book, *The Complete Book of Hold 'em Poker*.

[27] Hands like 8♥7♥ that are suited *and* connected are considerably better than average.

Compare K♥Q♠ to A♣7♦. King-queen can pair either the king or the queen to make top pair. Ace-seven will usually make top pair only by pairing the ace; a pair of sevens will rarely be top pair. Furthermore, when ace-seven makes a pair of aces, it is vulnerable to an opponent who holds an ace with a better kicker (like ace-ten). King-queen will rarely lose to someone with the same pair, but a better kicker.[28, 29]

Hands like A♠J♠ that have strong high card value and are suited are among the very best.

# The Importance of Being Suited

In a multiway pot, a suited hand is much better than its offsuit counterpart. If you hold two suited cards, exactly three more cards of your suit will appear by the river a little less than six percent of the time. This leads some people to conclude that suited and offsuit hands run closely in value.

These people are mistaken. While you usually do not make a flush, when you do, the reward is enormous. In most of those hands being suited will turn a loss into a win. A flush is usually strong enough to beat all of your opponents, even if you started six- or seven-handed. Such multiway pots are often very large. Winning a few extra large pots makes a big difference.[30]

Being suited also affords other advantages. Suited hands have more value on the flop than offsuit hands. One pair is often a

---

[28] This becomes much less true when an opponent raises. Raisers often have ace-king or ace-queen.

[29] For more on this topic, see p. 138 of *The Complete Book of Hold 'em Poker* by Gary Carson.

[30] Put another way, if your suitedness increases your chances of winning from, say, 16 percent to 20 percent, this is not a 4 percent increase, but rather a 25 percent increase!

vulnerable holding, but a pair plus a flush draw is always strong. Or you can flop a backdoor flush draw, adding value to weak holdings like middle pair or a gutshot.

The stronger your hand, the more latitude you have to play aggressively after the flop. If your hand includes a flush draw, you may bet and raise instead of check and call (or fold). You will win some hands where you began drawing to a flush, but backed into something else. You will pick up pots with a bet when no one has a good hand, even though you have not made your hand yet. When your hand is offsuit (with no flush potential), you miss these opportunities.

Since being suited affords a major advantage in a multiway pot, having an offsuit hand sometimes puts you at a disadvantage. If you have six opponents, expect several of them to have suited hands. When you play offsuit hands like Q♥9♣ and A♠4♦ you grant your opponents a big head start. Even expert players cannot usually overcome this starting gap; weak offsuit hands do not get lucky often enough. An offsuit hand must be very powerful, like

to overcome its intrinsic liability. So if you are in doubt about whether to play a hand, be inclined to play it if it is suited, but fold it otherwise.[31]

---

[31] Having said this, you should still fold most of your suited hands. Remember that average suited hands like J♥6♥ and 8♣4♣ are not worth much.

# Avoiding Costly Errors

Most players make two major preflop mistakes. They are so costly, and the opportunity to make them so frequent, that no one prone to making them has a long term win in this game. They are

1.    Playing weak hands out of position, particularly weak offsuit hands

2.    Cold-calling raises with mediocre and potentially dominated hands

# Playing Weak Hands Out Of Position

Many hands require specific playing conditions to be profitable. For instance, some need the pot to be unraised or multiway. Others are better with few opponents. In early position you must act before you know which conditions will be present. For instance, if you limp in up front with a hand like J♠9♠ or Q♥J♣ you are counting on the pot not being raised behind you. If it is raised, your call will have been unprofitable. You should call the raise (the pot will be too big to fold), but you will wish that you had folded for the first bet. By wading in up front with a marginal hand, you have unwittingly wandered into a costly situation.

You should also avoid playing weak hands up front because they tend to make marginal hands on the flop (which is one reason they are weak). Much of the value that marginal hands have is lost when you play out of position. J♠9♠ will often flop middle pair, a gutshot straight draw, or a backdoor flush draw. You would generally like to see fourth street with these weak draws; if you flop a gutshot, it will often be profitable to call for one bet. But when you are out of position, you might call an early bet and then have it raised and reraised behind you. Once again, you will wish that you had not called the first bet and will now probably be forced to fold for the two additional bets.[32]

Weak offsuit hands are significant losers out of position. Hands like K♠T♥ are extremely vulnerable to domination. Since it makes few straights and flushes, king-ten relies heavily on its ability to make top pair. King-ten's top pair potential is crippled when it faces hands like K♣Q♥, A♦T♦, or J♠J♣. Against each of these hands king-ten can pair one of its cards and still be behind. In late position you can reduce your exposure to strong hands by playing only in unraised pots. In early position, without the extra information, it is too likely that a dominating hand is behind you to play. *Avoid marginal hands, particularly offsuit ones, in early position.*

# Cold-Calling Raises with Mediocre Hands

This is the second major error. "Cold-calling" is calling two or more bets when you have not yet invested any money. (Calling a raise from the blind or calling one bet back to you after you have limped in is not cold-calling.)

When someone raises, it typically indicates a strong hand.[33] Unless you are in the big blind, you should usually play only hands that are strong enough to reraise the raiser (against a tight raiser, pocket aces through jacks and ace-king). If the pot is very likely to be multiway, you can flat call with a few other hands,

---

[32] Even if there was only one raise behind you, you would wish that you had not made the first call, though, in that case, you would have to call the raise.

[33] Obviously, you will occasionally run into an opponent who raises with a wide range of hands. We will address later how to handle these players.

specifically smaller pocket pairs and some strong suited hands (e.g., Q♥J♥). Two or three other hands — ace-queen suited, ace-jack suited, and king-queen suited — are also usually marginally profitable. You should fold everything else. This means that you must play *extremely* tightly if someone has raised in front of you.[34]

Many of your opponents will have neither the knowledge nor the discipline to fold so many hands. They will call raises with a wide range of hands, including hands like K♥T♦ and J♠5♠. These calls are *terrible* and cost your opponents lots of money over the long-term. In fact, this mistake is particularly costly, because the opportunity to make it arises time after time. A player prone to make this error will often make it twenty times or more in one session.

For example, you have

in middle position. The player under the gun, a tight, unimaginative player, raises. Everyone folds to you. You should fold. Typically, A♥T♥ is a strong hand. You would probably have raised if no one had raised in front of you. Unfortunately, the raise strongly suggests that your opponent has an even better hand. He is likely to have a big pair, aces through tens, or a big ace like ace-king or ace-queen. If the pot stays two- or three-handed, you can be in major trouble. You will likely be playing against a significantly better hand with only one or two other players' money to pad the pot. If you happen to be against a tough player, he will be in position to win the maximum from you, while you

---

[34] For a more thorough discussion of this concept, see p. 20 of *Hold 'em Poker for Advanced Players* by David Sklansky and Mason Malmuth.

win only the minimum from him. This is particularly true if an ace flops, for you will usually pay off to the river if he has a bigger kicker, but he will usually fold early if he has a smaller pocket pair.

You should still fold even if he might also raise with some slightly worse hands like king-queen. While you would call if he *probably* had king-queen when he raised, he will usually have the other hands that are so detrimental to your holding. Sometimes he will have pocket aces, and calling would put you in a dreadful situation. To play against a raise in this spot, your hand should compare favorably to the *range* of hands that he might raise with, not just the worst of his possible hands.

If your hand were A♥T♣, offsuit, you would be in even worse shape. When your hand is suited, a flush sometimes bails you out. With an offsuit hand, you have no good escape hatch when the raiser has you crushed. In fact, the only offsuit hand you should *usually* play against a raise is ace-king (also ace-queen against a loose raiser). The threat of domination devalues every other offsuit hand too much, even ace-queen (again, as long as the raiser is tight with his raises). Nevertheless, many of your opponents would always call with ace-ten, suited or offsuit, in this spot. It is a major error, one you must assiduously avoid. *Never cold-call preflop raises with easily-dominated, offsuit hands.*

# Final Thoughts

Many of the concepts in this section, particularly dead money and top pair versus speculative hands, are quite difficult. You will probably not understand them fully the first time you read this section; it will take you a while. In the meantime, make sure you avoid the two costly errors: Play very tightly from early position, and do not cold-call raises with offsuit hands (except ace-king and sometimes ace-queen, with which you should reraise). If you follow those rules and learn the postflop material, you will consistently beat small stakes games.

After you gain some winning experience, come back to this section. Reread the parts you did not understand. Abstract concepts are difficult to digest without seeing them applied; your experience will aid your understanding. If you hope to be a big winner, though, you will eventually have to understand all the concepts.

# Preflop Hand Categories

In this section we group hands together that have common playing characteristics. Within a category the hands may range significantly in strength, but they will generally play similarly after the flop and share game texture preferences. For each category we describe its optimal playing conditions and discuss what to expect after the flop. Then we give rough recommendations for when and how to play the hands.

## Pocket Pairs

### Monsters (AA and KK)

These hands are the two best in hold 'em, no matter the situation. They play well in short-handed and multiway pots. They play well in passive games and in aggressive ones. Against few opponents, they will usually win unimproved. Against many opponents, they win unimproved less often (though still frequently), but their big hand potential becomes important. When you make a set, you will sometimes win a very large pot with a big full house or even just three of a kind. You should almost always raise and reraise with these hands, no matter the action.

### Big Pairs (QQ, JJ, and TT)

These are outstanding hands. They too play well in any game conditions. They differ from the monsters chiefly because they win less often unimproved. They still fare well without help and will frequently win even when overcards come. Do not play timidly with these hands before the flop simply because an overcard could beat you.

You should typically raise with these hands from any position if it has not yet been raised. It is also usually right to reraise if it has been raised once.

# Medium Pairs (99, 88, and 77)

These pairs shine in two situations. One is when you are two- or three-handed, and your opponents are likely to have weak hands. In this spot they are strong enough to win a fair number of pots even unimproved. This is particularly true if your opponents' hands might contain cards lower than your pair.

These pairs are also quite profitable against five or more opponents. When you make a set, some of your opponents will likely have one pair. Anyone with only one pair on the flop is drawing almost dead against your set. If these players will pay you off with calls and raises, your medium pair has become very profitable. When you have a set, you prefer that the game be loose and aggressive. Looseness ensures that many players will play against you at a big disadvantage. Aggressiveness increases the likelihood that you will get multiple bets in on each street. Many of the biggest hold 'em pots are won by medium pairs that flop sets in loose, aggressive games.

From early position you should usually limp in. If exactly one loose player has limped in front of you, you may want to raise from late position. You are trying to play short-handed against weak hands. Once two or more players have already limped, you should usually also merely limp to encourage multiway action. If someone has raised, you should typically fold unless you are fairly sure several others will enter the pot. You do not want to play short-handed against a bigger pair. However, when there are already three or more players in the pot, call the raise. You are looking to win a big pot by making a set.

# Small Pairs (66-22)

These pairs do not win often unimproved, even against few opponents. You are hoping to win a big pot with a set or full house. Therefore, they play best when the game is loose and somewhat aggressive. Loose and passive is acceptable as well, but you will not make as much money under those conditions when you flop a set.[35] If the game is tight, usually two to four players to the flop, these hands are not worth much.

You would like to see the flop cheaply, for one, or at most, two bets. You will make a set on the flop only about twelve percent of the time. Since you will fold so frequently after the flop (when you miss your set or occasional straight draw), you need to anticipate collecting a lot of bets those times that you hit your set, and it holds up.

Fortunately, small stakes games are almost always loose. In most games you can play these hands profitably from any position if it has not yet been raised. However, if it is frequently three or more bets before the flop, you should fold from early position. If it has been raised in front of you, to play you need to be almost sure the pot will be five-handed or more. You need a multiway pot to compensate for the extra money you invest before the flop. Against certain players who are almost guaranteed to put many bets into the pot on the flop (and sometimes on the turn as well) you can, on occasion, make do with fewer than five players.

---

[35] On the other hand you will make your set somewhat more often, since you will more likely get a free card.

# Suited Cards

## Big Suited Broadway
## (AKs-ATs, KQs, and KJs)

These are very strong hands. They often make top pair with a strong kicker, usually enough to win. Being suited, they also sometimes make a big flush, capable of winning a massive pot against many opponents. They play well against many or few opponents. They shine in both passive and aggressive games.

If the pot is unraised, you should usually raise with any of these hands. If the game is tight, it may be better to limp from early position to lure opponents with weaker hands into the pot. With a raise in front of you, be careful with AJs, ATs, KQs, and KJs. You may be dominated by the raiser. Call only if the raiser will raise with many hands, or if there are already several others in the pot. With AKs and AQs, you can play against a tight raiser. In fact, you should usually reraise with AKs.

A note about tight raisers: Any tight raiser requires a high-quality hand to raise. Some are aware of position, however. Such a player will loosen his raising requirements as his position improves, especially if he is first to enter the pot. If you have AJs, for instance, and a position-aware, tight raiser raises from under the gun, you should fold unless you expect a multiway pot. But if the same player raises, first to enter the pot, from late position, you should usually reraise with AJs. His range of possible hands is much broader from late position.

Other tight raisers do not adjust their range of hands with position. These players tend to be weak and passive and raise only with the very best hands (perhaps only pocket aces through queens). Against such a player you should fold AJs when he raises, no matter his position. His raise almost always indicates a monster hand, so avoid him.

# Little Suited Broadway
# (QJs, KTs, QTs, and JTs)

These hands are strong against opponents with weak hands. They make top pair with a decent kicker, a good hand if not dominated. Top pair with these hands is not nearly as strong as top pair with the big suited Broadways, though. For instance, if the flop comes ten high, and you hold king-ten suited, three overcards can come to beat your pair. To compensate somewhat for this weakness, they make straights more often than the big suited Broadways. Again, they can also make big flushes and win large pots.

Because their straight potential is strengthened, but their top pair potential weakened, these hands are better multiway. If your opponents are willing to play weak hands, frequently the case in small stakes games, the little suited Broadways are quite profitable even from out of position.

If the pot is unraised, you should limp with these hands from early or middle position. You would like to encourage loose limpers behind you. From late position, you can raise no matter how many limpers there are. Because of its flush potential, your hand plays well in a large pot. To play *against* a raise however, you must be sure the pot will be multiway.

# Suited Aces (A9s-A2s)

Suited aces are good hands in loose games. They have decent high card strength (the ace) and can make the nut flush. They, especially A7s and below, play best in a loose and passive game. In a loose game, they make much more money when they make the nut flush. Notwithstanding their high card strength, the smaller suited aces are fundamentally speculative hands, deriving much of their value from their flush-making ability.

Despite what many players think, the size of the kicker is important. A9s is a much better hand than A2s. First, a pair of nines is far more likely to win a showdown than a pair of deuces. Second, a nine is often enough to win a kicker war, while a deuce obviously never is. Many loose games feature players who play any ace, suited or not, no matter the circumstances. If an ace flops, opponents will often have hands like A6 (offsuit). In that circumstance, a bigger kicker is the difference between winning and "chopping" (or losing).

Some players also mistakenly conclude that A5s-A2s are better than A9s-A6s because they can make a wheel. While the wheel possibility is useful, it generally does not overcome the high card strength of the latter hands. A6s and A5s run closely in strength (the wheel potential is worth slightly more than one pip of high card strength), but otherwise the bigger hands are better.[36]

If the game is passive, you can play any of these hands from any position in an unraised pot. In a somewhat aggressive game, play only A9s and A8s from up front, but fold even these if the pots are frequently going to three bets or more. From middle position or later, limp in with these hands if the pot is still unraised. From late position, consider raising with A9s or A8s after limpers if your opponents are loose. Usually fold all these hands, however, if it is raised in front of you. Cold-calling raises with these hands in short-handed pots is a common and costly mistake.

# Suited Kings (K9s-K2s)

These are weak, speculative hands. They have marginal high card strength: As long as you are not dominated (a common problem with these hands), a pair of kings will win many pots.

---

[36] For more on this topic, see p. 151 of *The Complete Book of Hold 'em Poker* by Gary Carson.

They are significantly weaker than suited aces, though, mainly because a pair of aces is stronger than a pair of kings.[37] They require loose and passive conditions to be profitable. Again, a higher kicker makes these hands more valuable; K9s is a fairly strong hand, while in most circumstances K2s is unprofitable.

In a loose and passive game, you can limp in with K9s from early position (but not with K8s or less). Otherwise, fold all of these hands from up front. From the button, you can limp with most of these hands if two or three weak and loose players have limped in front of you. Never cold-call a raise with any of these hands.

# Suited Connectors (T9s-54s, J9s-64s, Q9s-96s, Q8s, and J7s)

These are all speculative hands with little high card strength. They feature the ability to make flushes and many straights.[38] These hands play best in loose and passive games. Passive play by your opponents after the flop is particularly crucial for the weaker of these hands (87s-54s, T8s-64s, J8s-96s, Q8s, and J7s). You will often flop weak draws: a gutshot straight draw, middle or bottom pair, or a backdoor flush draw. With these hands, aggressive opponents will often bet and raise, knocking you out of the pot.

---

[37] Despite what some players think, they are *not* weaker mainly because an ace-high flush is much stronger than a king-high flush. It isn't. Obviously, an ace-high flush is somewhat better, but the most important difference between A9s and K9s is in highcard strength. This is especially true if you make a pair on the turn or river after flopping a flush draw. There are many spots where kings lose because there is an ace on board, but aces would win.

[38] Keep in mind that the bigger the gap, the fewer straights you can make. For example, 9♠8♠ can make four straights, while J♠8♠ can make only two straights (using both cards).

Against passive opponents, you will get free or cheap cards, giving you more chances to get lucky. You also need to be able to see the flop for one bet. With a few exceptions, you cannot overcome your preflop disadvantage if you must pay two or more bets to see the flop.

Fold all of these hands in early position unless the game is very passive. When that is the case (preflop raises on ten or fewer percent of hands), limp in with only the strongest of these hands (T9s and J9s) from up front. In middle position, limp with the top fifty percent of these hands if the pot will be multiway and a raise unlikely. You can usually play any of these hands for one bet on the button. Fold if the pot has been raised in front of you unless there are many players already in, and you have one of the stronger hands of this category.

# Junk Suited Hands (Any Suited Hand Not Yet Mentioned)

Any suited hand not mentioned so far is too weak, even for one bet on the button, to play profitably. Unless you are in the blinds, fold them every time. Playing junk suited hands is an extremely common error, among the most common in small stakes games. These hands simply do not win enough. Avoid them.[39]

---

[39] Q7s-Q2s on the button is an exception in some games.

# Offsuit Cards

# Big Offsuit Broadway
# (AK, AQ, AJ, and KQ)

These are the best of the offsuit hands. They commonly make a strong top pair. All offsuit hands are at an inherent disadvantage in a multiway pot, but these hands win often enough to play well against many weak limpers. They are strong in either a passive or aggressive game; top pair hands win a large number of pots, so you should welcome preflop action from bad players.

You can open with any of these hands from any position. Raise any of these hands if it has not already been raised.[40] Beware if someone raises in front of you, however; unless you have AK, you are vulnerable to domination. So be prepared to fold all offsuit hands except AK to a raise. Reraise with AK. If the raiser will raise with some weaker hands like AT, KJ, and 77, do not fold AQ; reraise instead. If the raiser is very wild, sometimes raising with hands such as K6s and 33, reraise with AJ and KQ as well.

# Little Offsuit Broadway
# (AT, KJ, QJ, KT, QT, and JT)

These hands are marginal and playable only under favorable circumstances. They tend to make weak top pair hands, the same as the little suited Broadways. Without the advantage of being

---

[40] If the pot is already many-handed, perhaps five or six limpers, consider just limping with AJ and KQ. Your preflop edge is relatively small against so many opponents, and your call should give you strategic advantages which can make up for your small theoretical loss from not raising by allowing you to outplay your opponents after the flop.

suited, though, these hands are not very profitable. They play best in an unraised pot against a few, loose opponents. Tight opponents tend to limp in with hands like AQ, AJ, and KQ, hands that dominate the little offsuits. *So consider who has already limped in before deciding to call.* While weaker in general, the smaller hands, because they make more straights, benefit somewhat from multiway action.

Fold all of these hands in early position with the exception of AT and KJ in loose games. In middle position you can play AT and KJ if loose players have limped.

On the button you can usually play any of these hands in an unraised pot. If the pot is still short-handed, raise (especially with AT and KJ) to try to fold the blinds. Against several limpers, just limp in. Cold-calling raises with these hands is one of the most common, and most costly, preflop mistakes. It is essentially never correct to play these hands against even a loose raiser. So don't do it!

# Junk Offsuit Hands (Any offsuit hand not yet mentioned)

Our recommendation for these hands is even stronger than it is for the suited junk hands: Do not play them. Note that this category contains offsuit aces (A9-A2) and offsuit connectors (T9-54). You will frequently see opponents play them, but they are only rarely profitable. Small stakes games are usually loose, where weak offsuit hands are at their worst. Until you have mastered preflop play, you should avoid these hands altogether.

Possible exceptions might be A9, T9, and 98 on the button for one bet only. But even here, at best, these hands are only marginally profitable.

# Final Thoughts

By knowing to which category a hand belongs, you will know its strengths and weaknesses. In the next section we give specific recommendations for playing your hands. For those recommendations, we assume that your game is a typical small stakes game: loose and either passive or just somewhat aggressive. If your game differs significantly from the assumed texture, you will need to adjust the recommendations. Learning the concepts in this section will help you adjust correctly.

# Preflop Recommendations

In this section we recommend a play for each specific hand in common preflop situations. We list hands that are playable in certain spots and recommend raising with some of them. *These recommendations are not rigid.* View them like training wheels for preflop play: When you feel lost, look to these guidelines for a decent *default* play. An expert player who fully understands preflop and postflop concepts will frequently deviate (correctly) from these suggestions.

Having said that, we have thought seriously about these recommendations, and we feel that they represent the best default play for each hand in a typical situation. So deviate from these recommendations only when you can identify something *specifically atypical* about your game or situation. For example, you might play a hand that we recommend folding because your game is extremely passive. Similarly, you might choose to raise with a "limping" hand because the player in the big blind is particularly tight, or you might fold it if a very tough player has entered the pot.

You should not deviate from these recommendations by applying your own broad preflop concepts. You will usually be wrong. For instance, do not limp with most of the hands we recommend raising because, "I don't like to invest much until I see the flop," or "I just don't think ace-ten suited is a raising hand." We recommend raising for a specific, clearly thought-out reason: After considering all the important principles, we have concluded that it is the best play. Similarly, do not conclude, "These recommendations are way too tight. I can play a whole lot more hands." You will be wrong, and it will cost you money in the long run.

Also, many of these plays are inherently close. The difference in expectation between, say, raising or limping with ace-ten suited

76

from under the gun, is quite small. Game conditions could cause you to favor one play over the other. The most heated debates over preflop play generally occur about decisions with a tiny difference in expectation between one play and another. For instance, there have been myriad arguments about what to do with king-queen offsuit under the gun. Most of the thousands of hours spent debating this point were wasted. Under typical conditions the difference in expectation between raising and calling is quite small. Until you play excellently otherwise, just pick one option and go with it.

In general, do not spend too much time contemplating specific preflop plays. If you have to think about it too long, the options probably run close in value. *Instead, use that time to improve your postflop play.* After you learn to play decently preflop, most of your additional winnings will come from *exploiting your opponents' postflop mistakes.*

Often, you will hear a struggling new player complain, "I don't understand! I play all the right cards, but I still don't win." He may be right. He probably is playing well enough preflop, but he cannot win because his postflop skills are poor. Focus on the important things. Learn a solid, simple preflop system, and then develop your postflop game. Once you learn to play well after the flop, revisit preflop play and fine-tune your skills. This order will maximize your winnings while you learn.

Finally, simplicity was a top priority when we developed these recommendations. Correct play is inherently complex, but we have simplified wherever possible. Specifically, if two choices ran close in value, but one allowed us to simplify the system to make it easier to learn, we used the simpler choice, sometimes at the expense of a small amount of expectation. New players will have enough trouble with this simplified system; we decided not to add complexity.

These recommendations assume a typical ten-handed, small stakes game:[41] It is passive to somewhat aggressive before the flop (about 15 to 35 percent of pots are raised), and most players go too far with their hands. If your game differs from this template, these recommendations will not be accurate. Modify them, promoting hands that play well in your game type and relegating ones that play poorly. For example, if your game is very passive, play more of the weaker suited cards from early and middle positions. The conceptual sections should give you a solid foundation to make these adjustments.

We divide these recommendations into two parts: those for a moderately tight game with 3-5 players on average seeing the flop, and those for a loose game with 6-8 players on average.[42] If your game falls between these two archetypes, play more hands than recommended for the tight game, but fewer than for the loose one.[43] Also, if your game normally falls under one category, but has switched for this particular hand, use the guidelines appropriate for the new conditions. For instance, your game is normally loose with six to eight players on average seeing the flop. In this particular hand, however, you are on the button, and there are only two players, a caller and a raiser. Apply the tight game recommendations.

Again, you need not memorize these specific recommendations. The most important preflop sections are the conceptual ones; this one is designed just to get you started.

---

[41] For a shorter-handed game, assume that your game is ten-handed and that the first few players have folded.

[42] These terms "tight" and "loose" are relative. What we call a tight game is relatively tight for a small stakes game, but would usually be considered somewhat loose for a high stakes game.

[43] Notice that we disagree with the oft-stated saying, "Play tight when they play loose and vice versa." There are a few specific situations where this is true, but not on average, especially against weak players.

Finally, if you remember nothing else about preflop play, remember these four fundamental principles:

1. Play tightly in early position, more loosely in late position.
2. Raise with your better hands.
3. Play only the strongest offsuit holdings.
4. Play *very* tightly if someone has raised in front of you.

# Tight Games
# (3-5 Players on
# Average to the Flop)

| Early Position *The first three seats to the left of the blinds* | Middle Position *The three seats to the left of early position* |
|---|---|
| **If there is no raise** *Play:* AA-77, any two suited cards ten or higher (e.g., AKs, QTs, etc.), AK-AJ, and KQ *Raise:* AA-TT, AKs-AJs, and AK-AQ | **If there is no raise** *Play:* Any pocket pair, AKs-A2s, KQs-K9s, QJs-Q9s, JTs-J9s, T9s-98s, AK-AT, and KQ-KJ *Raise:* AA-99, AKs-ATs, KQs-KJs, AK-AJ, and KQ |
| **Against a Raise** *Play:* AA-TT, AKs-AJs, KQs, and AK *Reraise:* AA-TT, AKs, and AK | **Against a Raise** Same guidelines that you would use from *early position* against a raise |
| **Against a Raise and a Reraise** *Play:* AA-QQ and AKs *Raise:* AA-QQ and AKs | **Against a Raise and a Reraise** *Play:* AA-QQ and AKs *Raise:* AA-QQ and AKs |

## Late Position
### *One off the button and the button*

**If there is no raise**
*Play:* Same hands that you would play from *middle position* plus 87s-54s and any two offsuit cards ten or higher (e.g., KT, JT, etc.)
*Raise:* AA-99, AKs-A8s, KQs-KTs, QJs, AK-AT, and KQ

**Against a Raise**
Same guidelines that you would use from *early and middle position* against a raise, except that if three players have entered the pot so far (the raiser and at least two callers), also call with any pocket pair and QJs-T9s.

**Against a Raise and a Reraise**
*Play:* AA-QQ and AKs
*Raise:* AA-QQ and AKs

## Small Blind

**If there is no raise**
*Play:* Same hands that you would play from *late position,* plus any two suited cards
*Raise:* AA-99, AKs-ATs, KQs-KJs, and AK-AQ

**Against a Raise**
Same guidelines that you would use from *early position* against a raise, except add all pocket pairs (as long as one player besides the raiser has also entered the pot).

## Big Blind

**If there is no raise**
*Raise:* Same hands that you would raise from the *small blind*

**Against a Raise**
*Play:* Same hands that you would play from *late position* for one bet, except remove the weak offsuit hands AT, KJ-KT, QJ-QT, and JT. This leaves any pocket pair, many suited hands, AK-AJ, and KQ.*
*Reraise:* AA-TT, AKs, and AK

* Many of these hands are playable against a possible steal raise in a higher limit game where the impact of the rake is negligible.

# Loose Games (6-8 Players on Average to the Flop)

| Early Position<br>*The first three seats<br>to the left of the blinds* | Middle Position<br>*The three seats to<br>the left of early position* |
|---|---|
| **If there is no raise**<br>*Play:* Any pocket pair. AKs-A2s, KQs-K9s, QJs-Q9s,JTs-J9s, T9s-98s, AK-AT, and KQ-KJ<br>*Raise:* AA-99, AKs-ATs, KQs-KJs, AK-AJ, and KQ<br>(These are the same hands for *middle position* in *tight games.*)<br><br>**Against a Raise**<br>*Play:* Any pocket pair, AKs-ATs, KQs-KTs, QJs, JTs, and AK-AQ<br>*Reraise:* AA-99, AKs-AQs, and AK-AQ<br><br>**Against a Raise and a Reraise**<br>*Play:* AA-TT and AKs-AJs, KQs, and AK<br>*Raise:* AA-QQ and AKs | **If there is no raise**<br>*Play:* Same hands that you would play from *early position*<br>*Raise:* Same hands that you would raise from *early position*<br><br>**Against a Raise**<br>Same guidelines that you would use from *early position* against a raise<br><br>**Against a Raise and a Reraise**<br>*Play:* AA-TT and AKs-AJs, KQs, and AK<br>*Reraise:* AA-QQ and AKs |

## Late Position
### One off the button and the button

**If there is no raise**
*Play:* Same hands that you would play from *middle position* plus K8s-K2s, Q8s, J8s, J7s, 87s-43s, T8s-53s, and any two offsuit cards ten or higher
*Raise:* AA-88, any two suited cards ten or higher, A9s-A8s, K9s, AK-AJ, and KQ

If at least four people have entered the pot in front of you:

**Against a Raise**
*Play:* Any pocket pair, any two suited cards ten or higher, any suited ace (A9s-A2s), and T9s-76s. Also AK and AQ.
*Reraise:* AA-TT, AKs-AJs, KQs, and AK

**Against a Raise and a Reraise**
*Play:* AA-TT, AKs-AJs, KQs, and AK
*Reraise:* AA-QQ and AKs

If fewer than four people have entered, revert to the *tight games* guidelines for *late position.*

## Small Blind

**If there is no raise**
**Play:** Same hands that you would play from *late position* plus any two suited cards
*Raise:* AA-99, AKs-ATs, KQs-KJs, and AK-AQ

**Against a Raise**
*Play:* Same hands that you would play from *early position* against a raise
*Reraise:* AA-TT, AKs-AJs, KQs, and AK

## Big Blind

**If there is no raise**
*Raise:* Same hands that you would raise from the *small blind*

**Against a Raise**
*Play:* Same hands that you would play from *late position* for one bet, except remove the weak offsuit hands AT, KJ-KT, QJ-QT, and JT.*

*Reraise:* Same hands that you would reraise from the *small blind.*

* Many of these hands are playable against a possible steal raise in a higher limit game where the impact of the rake is negligible.

# Some Quick Notes
# About the Recommendations

Many people may be surprised to see that we recommend playing small pocket pairs so often, particularly from early position and against a raise. A typical small stakes game presents ideal conditions for these hands. Pairs thrive when they get lots of action if they flop a set. Since many of your opponents habitually play too many hands and go too far with them, your sets will tend to get plenty of action. When you can be almost sure that at least one, if not several, of your opponents will stay with you to the river, you can play any pair for one or two bets. But if your game is tight, limit yourself to sevens or better from early position. If it is frequently three or more bets before the flop, you might even tighten up to nines or better. But in a typical, loose small stakes game, you should play the vast majority of your pocket pairs.

♣ ♦ ♥ ♠

You should cold-call a raise only rarely, especially if you are the first to do so. For instance, we recommend cold-calling a raise in a tight game with only AQs, AJs, and KQs (also sometimes medium and small pocket pairs and suited connectors when three or more players have already entered the pot). Every other hand you play against a raise you should usually reraise.

To give you an idea about how infrequently you should cold-call, you will be dealt one of these three suited hands once for every 110 hands you play. To cold-call, you cannot be in the blind or under the gun, and someone has to raise in front of you. All those conditions might occur twenty percent of the time. That will leave you in a cold-calling situation once in every 550 hands. If you play live, you might get 35 hands per hour. Thus, one of these cold-calling situations might arise once every 15 hours or so. Even if you add the calls with small pocket pairs and suited connectors and the extra calls you can make when your game is very loose, you still probably should not cold-call a raise more often than once every three hours. *If you find that you cold-call as little as three or four times per session (on average), you are cold-calling too much.* Either you are playing too many hands against a raise (a devastating error), or you are playing too passively with your premium hands (not as devastating, but an error nonetheless).

One of the first things you should watch for when you first sit in a game is the cold-calling frequency. You will find many players who cold-call ten, twenty, or even fifty times per session. No strategy that performs even marginally well includes so much cold-calling. These players are simply hemorrhaging money. Seek them out, but do not emulate them.

♣ ♦ ♥ ♠

If the pot has been raised and reraised in front of you, you must play extremely tightly, even if you do not respect the raisers. Against typical opponents play only AA-QQ and AKs. You may add JJ-TT and AK against loose raisers. If more than about thirty percent of all hands are raised and reraised before the flop (indicating that the raises and reraises are very loose), you may also play 99, AQs-ATs, KQs-KJs, and AQ. If you play very well in large pots, you can loosen up slightly more still, but stick to suited hands with high-card strength. Even if your opponents are extremely loose and crazy, you cannot play speculative hands profitably if you must pay three or more bets to see the flop.

Furthermore, to play hands like ATs and KJs profitably for three bets, you must be very sure of your opponents tendencies. If you are not, it is probably best to give them up.

♣  ♦  ♥  ♠

So far, the guidelines for playing in raised pots apply only when the raise occurs *before* you act. If someone raises *afterwards*, call with any hand if it is one bet back to you. For instance, if you limp with

an opponent limps, and then someone raises, always call the raise as long at it is only one more bet.

If it is two bets back to you (i.e., raised and reraised), tighten up almost as much as you would if cold-calling a raise. The pot will be bigger, so you can play a little looser, but avoid hands that are easily dominated. Say you limp from under the gun, and another player limps behind you. A player in middle position raises, and the button reraises. The big blind calls (10.5 small bets). You should usually call if your hand is

but fold if it is

With pocket eights (or any pocket pair), the extra money in the pot provides enough value to try to flop a set against four opponents. However, despite the large pot, ace-jack is just too likely to be dominated to call.

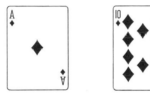

We advocate lots of raising with big suited hands like

and

These hands are strong in any game, but the loose conditions in most small stakes games make them even more valuable. In general, if the pot has not yet been raised, you should almost always raise these hands from any position.[44]

You often make an important trade-off when you raise before the flop. When you have a pot equity edge, your raise has an immediate positive expectation because you will win more than your share. But that raise usually simultaneously *cuts your postflop expectation*. There are several reasons this happens, but an important one is that you tie yourself to the pot.

Say you are playing heads-up against an opponent who will always call to the river no matter what. Depending on the flop, assume for simplicity that either you or he will be a 4-to-1 favorite. Also assume that you can instantly identify who the favorite is by looking at the flop. If you do not raise preflop (so the pot on the flop is two bets), when you are the favorite, if you bet, he will call, and you make money. But when you are the underdog, you can fold when he bets (because your pot odds are not sufficient). Thus, you get the best of it after the flop, since you profit when he calls, but he does not profit when you fold.

Now consider this situation if you raise preflop. The pot is four bets on the flop. When you are the favorite, you will bet, and he will call, again making you money. But now when he bets, you must call for the size of the pot. Now you no longer have a positive expectation after the flop, since you both play the same way.

One reason we zealously suggest raising with big suited cards is because they do not suffer much from this effect. They hit the flop so frequently that you will often want to play on anyway, whether the pot was raised or not. For instance, with a hand like K♠J♠ you will often flop at least two overcards and a backdoor flush draw. For one bet, you should frequently see the turn whether the pot was raised or not. Your preflop raise has an

---

[44] We recommend that you limp with them from early position in a tight game. But even in that case, raising is close and sometimes slightly better.

immediate positive expectation because this strong hand wins more than its share, and it does not sacrifice much expectation after the flop because you often should continue no matter how small the pot.

For loose games we recommend that you play the same hands from middle position that you would from early position. You may be surprised that we do not add hands as your position improves. The gap between your profitability in early and middle position closes when the game is very loose. There are two major reasons:

1.  In a tight, aggressive game, you must play very few hands from early position because someone on your left could raise. This will often limit the pot to only three or four players and leave you paying double to see the flop, out of position. A marginal hand like

only slightly profitable if no one raises behind you, becomes a money-loser in such a scenario. In middle position, because there are fewer players yet to act, it is significantly less likely that someone on your left will raise. Thus, more hands are playable.

However, in a loose game, this "nightmare" scenario is always unlikely because even if someone on your left does raise, five or more players will often call anyway. You are fine playing Q♠9♠ for two bets as long as you have many opponents. You do not have to fear the nightmare scenarios, so you can play more hands up front.

2.    Being in early position actually affords an advantage in loose games that middle position does not offer. After the flop you will frequently want to go for a check-raise to protect your hand or to build the pot when you flop a monster. Check-raising from middle position is both more difficult (fewer potential bettors act behind you) and less effective, since players whom you want to knock out have already checked and will often have an opportunity to call for one bet before the action returns to you. Once they have called one bet, they will usually automatically call your raise as well.

There are probably a few marginal hands that become slightly profitable in middle position. But in the interest of keeping our recommendations simple, we ignored them.

♣   ♦   ♥   ♠

When you are *first* to enter the pot from middle position, you are more likely than usual to play against only one or two others. As a result, some hands that prefer multiway action, particularly small pairs and small suited connectors, that should usually be played are no longer worth playing. For example, normally we recommend playing 2♥2♣ in middle position. But if you are three off the button, and nobody has yet entered the pot, you should fold.

Additionally, you should tend to raise some hands that you might ordinarily just limp with. For example, with medium pairs and suited aces you prefer to play either against many players or against one or two blind defenders. Against many players you hope to make a big hand to beat everyone. Against just the blinds you will often win unimproved. With these hands, once a multiway pot is unlikely, if your raise may cause most of your remaining opponents to fold, tend to open-raise. Besides cutting down the number of opponents, when you raise, you have a chance to win the blinds without a flop.

♣  ♦  ♥  ♠

From late position, if you are the first player to enter the pot, you should almost always raise. The chance to "steal" the blinds without a fight is worth risking an extra bet. However, those of you familiar with preflop strategy for medium stakes games should tighten up substantially on your blind steals when you play in small stakes games. In the bigger games, you should often take a shot at the blinds with many weak hands, such as 7♠5♠ or Q♣9♥, Fold these hands in a small stakes game. There are two important differences that force you to adjust your strategy:

1.  In small stakes games, people usually play more loosely from the blinds. Since you are more likely to be called, marginal stealing hands are no longer profitable.

2.  The rake is proportionally higher in small stakes games. For example, at $15-$30, the rake usually caps at around $4. If you raise from the button, and the big blind calls, the pot is already $70. The $4 rake is generally five percent or less of a heads-up $15-$30 pot. In $3-$6, the same action produces a $13 pot. This is not nearly enough to trigger a cap, so the full ten percent of the pot will be raked (sometimes even more if there is a jackpot rake). Because the pot you win is proportionally smaller, you need a bigger edge to play.

♣  ♦  ♥  ♠

Most games use a small blind that is half the size of the big blind. For instance, in a $4-$8 game, the small blind is typically $2 and the big blind $4. In this structure you can play quite loosely for $2 more. We recommend that you play any pocket pair, any two suited cards, and any two offsuit cards ten or higher. The ratio of the potential size of the final pot to your immediate investment (that is, your implied odds) is roughly double what it is outside the blinds. Doubling your implied odds turns many unprofitable hands into profitable ones (assuming that you play well postflop).

Some games use small blinds of different proportional sizes. For instance, a $3-$6 game usually uses a $1 small blind, one-third of the big blind. A $5-$10 game usually has a $2 small blind, two-fifths of the big blind. You must play more tightly in these structures than we have recommended above. We suggest that you play only those hands from the small blind that you would play on the button.

# Final Thoughts

Use the recommendations in this section as a foundation for your preflop strategy. Adjust them as your game conditions change. But while you may play some hands differently than we suggest, do not stray from the four general principles from the beginning of the section:
1. Play tightly in early position, more loosely in late position.
2. Raise with your better hands.
3. Play only the strongest offsuit holdings.
4. Play *very* tightly if someone has raised in front of you.

Violating these principles at the wrong time is costly. Habitually ignoring them will, in the long run, guarantee that you will lose.

# Preflop Play

# Afterthought

Suppose you sit down in a small stakes game and you're unfamiliar with your opponents. Thus you aren't sure which starting hand strategy to use, the one for tight games or the one for loose games.

Clearly, if you use the tight game approach you will win whether the game is tight or loose. In addition, if the game is tight, playing a hand like a small pair or ace-little suited up front which you normally shouldn't play (in a tight game) should cost you a little money in the long run. So from this logic it appears that the best approach is to be conservative. But we disagree.

Our advice is to follow the loose game guidelines until proven otherwise. That's because at the small stakes there are so many confused and poorly-skilled players that failing to play the extra hands should prove far more costly those times when you should play them than they will save you those times you should throw them away.

So assume the game is loose until proven otherwise. Remember, the purpose of this book is to maximize your profits. We want you to do much better than minimum wage.

# Part Three
# Postflop Concepts

# Postflop Concepts

# Introduction

In small stakes hold 'em, the real money is won and lost after the flop. "Playing better cards" than your opponents only goes so far; experts get most of their edge from their superior postflop play.

Furthermore, while it is relatively easy to judge good preflop play from bad, it is much harder to do so for postflop play. Look at this hand from the perspective of a poor player: One player limps, and the next one raises. Our hero is next to act with

and calls. Everyone folds to the blinds, who both call. The limper calls (10 small bets). The flop is

giving him middle pair and a backdoor flush draw. It is checked to the preflop raiser who bets. Our hero calls.

Our hapless hero has made two plays so far, and he has gotten them both wrong. Most people instantly identify his preflop play

**96**

as an error: It is clearly incorrect to cold-call the raise with queen-seven. But a much smaller percentage of poker players could identify his error on the flop. Yet, of his two mistakes, his flop play is worse by far! *Raising* is the correct play; calling and folding are both major mistakes! So even most players who are "trying to play well" by playing tightly before the flop still make very costly mistakes after the flop because they do not know any better. If you fall into this category, and you could not identify the flop mistake, do not worry. This chapter will teach you all the postflop concepts necessary to become a big winner in small stakes games.

# Counting Outs

Very often you will conclude that you probably do not currently hold the best hand. Sometimes you will have a small flush or straight draw, so virtually any two cards have you beaten. Other times you may have an overpair, but suspect that you are behind to an opponent's two pair. Whenever you are behind, it is crucial to count your outs accurately.

"Counting outs" means determining how many cards will give you the best hand. Sometimes counting outs is very simple. For instance, you hold

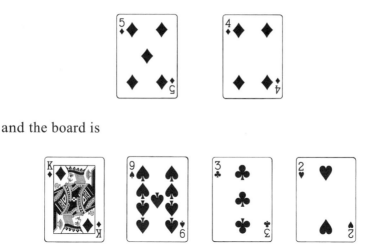

and the board is

You certainly do not have the best hand now; no hand ranks lower than your five-high. However, eight cards (4 sixes and 4 aces) can come on the river that will give you the nuts. No other cards are likely to give you the best hand. Besides the straight cards, only the fours and fives improve your hand, and one small pair will rarely be best, especially against multiple opponents. So your hand has eight outs.

Counting outs is rarely that simple. Many times there will be cards that improve your hand, but do not give you the nuts. Whenever this is the case, your hand could improve, but still be second-best. For example, suppose you hold Q♠J♠, and the board is 9♠8♥4♥2♣ The four tens will give you a straight, but only three of them make the nuts. The T♥ makes your straight, but it puts three hearts on board, which could make someone a flush.

In addition to the tens, any queen or jack will give you top pair. Top pair will win many pots, but lots of hands can beat you. If a queen comes, someone may have jack-ten, completing a straight, or queen-nine, making two pair. If the queen is the Q♥, someone can again make a flush. In fact, someone may already have the pair you hope to make beaten.

So, in this example you have three outs to a cinch (3 tens), one out to a possibly strong hand (the T♥), and six more outs to a possible winner (3 queens and 3 jacks). Your next task is to reconcile these outs of varying value into one number that you can use to estimate your winning chances.

# Partial Outs

Cards that improve your hand but do not give you the nuts are "partial outs." Some percentage of the time, they will give you the best hand. Say you hold

and the board is

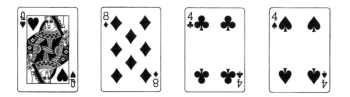

You have one opponent, and given the way he has played his hand, you are almost sure that he holds either pocket kings or queens. You are drawing dead if your opponent has pocket queens, but you have three outs (the remaining aces) if he has kings. Your opponent is equally likely to have either hand.[45] Therefore, each of the aces is worth about half an out. That is, half of the time the ace makes you a winner, and half of the time it does not. You should play your hand as if it had 1.5 outs.[46]

Continuing the example of Q♠J♠ on a 9♠8♥4♥2♣ board, the T♥ does not give you the nuts, but it is frequently a valuable out; often no one will have a flush, and your straight will be the best hand.[47] The outs to top pair are worth significantly less, for it is much easier to beat top pair than a straight. The Q♥ and J♥ are worth even less, since they allow an extra way to beat you.

So you might estimate that the T♥ is almost a full out, but that queens and jacks are somewhat less than half an out each.

---

[45] There are three kings unaccounted for (the K♥, K♦, and K♣). There are also three queens unaccounted for (the Q♠, Q♦, and Q♣). Thus, if you have no other information about your opponent's hand, pocket kings and queens are equally likely.

[46] Therefore, your pot odds should be at least 30-to-1 to call — not really possible here.

[47] Sometimes, based on the number of opponents and how the hand was played, you can be fairly sure that the T♥ does complete a flush for someone else. In that case your straight is not a strong hand.

That would give you three sure outs, a card worth almost a full out, and six cards worth between two and three outs total. Your hand is worth about seven outs.

Even if a card makes you the nuts, you should count it as only a partial out if someone else is likely to have the same hand, splitting the pot. This situation commonly occurs with one card straight draws. If you have A♠6♠, and the board is K♠Q♥J♦4♣, any ten gives you the nuts. But if you have several opponents, one of them may also have an ace. You could make your hand, but win only half (or even one-third) of the pot. If you *knew* someone was drawing to the same hand, you would count each ten as about half an out. You might win the whole pot if a ten comes, though, so the four tens are together probably worth between two and three outs.

You *must* account for partial outs when you are counting. If you count them for full value, you will overvalue your hand and call too often. If you discount them entirely, you will undervalue your hand and fold too much.

# Backdoor Draws

The examples given so far all take place on the turn. When there are two cards to come instead of just one, you will often have one or more backdoor draws. A backdoor draw requires help on both the turn and river. You have a backdoor flush draw, for instance, if you hold two suited cards, and one of your suit appears on the flop. Fourth and fifth street must both be of your suit to make a flush.

Backdoor draws come in only rarely, so by themselves they have little value. For example, if you hold

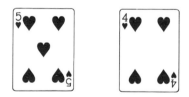

in a multiway pot, and the flop is

your hand is worth very little. Your only reasonable chance to make the best hand is your backdoor heart draw. There are ten hearts out of forty-seven unseen cards on the turn. If a heart comes on the turn, then there will be nine hearts left out of forty-six unseen cards. Therefore, the chance that both the turn and river are hearts is $(10/47)(9/46) \approx 1/24$. You are over a 23-to-1 dog to make your backdoor draw. If it is your only winning chance, the pot must be enormous for you to consider calling a flop bet. (Even 23-to-1 isn't usually enough unless you are all-in because you sometimes have to call a bet on the turn.)

Backdoor draws are more important when they add value to a hand that has other winning chances. For instance A♥4♥ has more value if the flop is K♣8♥4♣ than if it is K♣8♦4♣. The 8♥ gives you a backdoor flush draw, but you have other ways to win. The next step is to quantify the extra value that the backdoor draw adds.

As we calculated before, a backdoor flush draw is a 23-to-1 dog to come in. A hand with one out has a 2/47 chance to improve by the river, so it is a 22.5-to-1 dog. Therefore, a backdoor flush draw is worth about one out. It is usually worth slightly more because when you do not pick up your draw on fourth street, you can fold (saving a bet). Also, if you do complete your flush, your observant opponents will often not suspect it (as they would if a third flush card came to a flopped two-flush), so you can frequently collect extra river bets. A reasonable estimate for the value a backdoor flush draw adds is 1.5 outs.

Backdoor straight draws are a little trickier because their value depends on how many gaps they have. With no gaps (i.e., queen-jack-ten) they are worth about the same as a backdoor flush draw. These draws come in approximately 4.5 percent of the time

$$0.045 \approx \left(\frac{8}{47}\right)\left(\frac{8}{46}\right) + \left(\frac{8}{47}\right)\left(\frac{4}{46}\right)$$

or are about a 21.5-to-1 dog.[48] With one gap (i.e., queen-jack-nine) they are worth about one out. They come in approximately three percent of the time, or are about a 33-to-1 dog. With two gaps (i.e., queen-ten-eight) they are worth half an out. They come in approximately 1.5 percent of the time, or are about a 66-to-1 dog.

Sometimes your hand consists of multiple weak draws. For example, say you have

and the flop is

---

[48] The first term, (8/47)(8/46), represents those times you catch a king or nine on the turn (8 cards) to give you an open-ended river draw (8 outs). The second term, (8/47)(4/46), represents those times you catch an ace or eight on the turn (8 cards) to give you a gutshot river draw (4 outs).

You have two overcards, a backdoor flush draw, and a zero-gap, backdoor straight draw. None of your draws is very strong individually, but there are 22 turn cards that improve your hand significantly (10 hearts and 3 non-heart kings, queens, jacks, and nines). Counting outs, you might estimate that your two overcards are worth a total of three outs (six cards are worth about half an out each; you should not count them as full outs because top pair is often beaten), and your backdoor flush and straight draws are each worth 1.5 outs. Your hand has a value of about six outs.

# Redraws

When there are two cards to come, you will also be exposed to "redraws." If you improve to the best hand on the turn, your opponents will rarely be drawing dead. There is usually some chance that you will be outdrawn on the river. While the possible presence of redraws devalues any draw on the flop, some draws are much more sensitive to redraws than others.

If you hold

and the flop is

your draw is not very sensitive to redraws. Assuming that you are currently behind, you have five outs to improve to the best hand. No matter which of your five cards comes on fourth street, it will be relatively difficult for your opponents to draw out on fifth street.

Contrast that to 8♦7♦ on a flop of 9♥7♣2♥. The same cards improve your hand, but you are now much more vulnerable to redraws. For instance, if you improve by catching the 8♥, anyone holding a ten, six, or heart will have a draw to beat you. Even if you catch a third seven, someone who flopped a straight or flush draw will sometimes draw out on you. With two or three opponents there is a large chance that, even if you improve, you will still lose.

Redraws also strongly affect the value of a straight or flush draw with overcards. Compare K♠Q♠ on a T♥9♣2♦ flop to 9♠8♠ on a 6♥5♣2♠ flop. In both hands you hold a gutshot draw to the nuts and two overcards. Nevertheless, the king-queen hand is significantly stronger. If you spike a pair with the king-queen, only an ace can make someone a bigger pair on the river. With the nine-eight, there are five overcards that can beat you. In addition, a four or three may make someone a straight. You should play hands that are very vulnerable to redraws cautiously.

# Relative Position

Your position relative to the bettor also affects the value of a weak draw. These hands are often profitable for one bet, but unprofitable for two or more bets. When the bettor is on your immediate left, so your call closes the action, you are guaranteed to see the next street for just one bet. If there are players yet to act after you call, there is some chance that they will raise. The higher this chance, the less value your weak draw has. For instance, a certain draw might be profitable if there is only a ten percent chance of a raise behind you, but unprofitable with a fifty percent chance. The better your relative position, the less likely a raise is, and, hence, the more valuable your weak draw is.

Particularly with very weak draws, such as a small pocket pair (two outs) or a lone backdoor flush draw (1.5 outs), you must usually be very sure that it will not be raised behind you to continue. Even if the pot lays 25-to-1, making these draws slightly profitable for one bet, the threat of a raise may be enough to force you to fold. The chance of a raise behind you should not dissuade you as much with a stronger draw (four or more outs).

# Final Thoughts

Many small stakes players misplay their draws constantly. They call with weak ones that they should fold. They play their strong ones too passively. Some even fold ones that they should call or raise with. Many of these players have no idea how to quantify the value of their draws. They just guess wildly and hope for the best.

This section outlines a systematic approach to assessing the value of a draw. When you flop a draw, you should

1.  Identify every card that could give you the best hand. You must be thorough; sometimes they can be easy to miss.

2.  Decide how likely each card is to make you a winner. Some cards give you the nuts and are full outs. Others like overcards that may not be enough to win if hit, or any card that may cause a split pot, should be counted as partial outs.

3.  Look for backdoor draws. If you have a backdoor straight or flush draw, add the appropriate number of outs to the value of your hand.

4.  Decide how likely redraws are if you make your hand on the turn. Potential redraws devalue your hand.

5. Evaluate your position. With many players to act behind you, weak draws lose value because you may have to call a raise.

When you first start out, this process will be cumbersome. In time it will become second nature; you will see the same scenarios again and again and not have to recalculate every time.

A lot of players see drawing hands from an irrational perspective, "Other people hit their crazy draws every time, but I can't buy a diamond when I need one." As a result, they consistently misplay their hands. Using the logical approach to draw evaluation presented in this section will allow you to make reliably sound playing decisions.

# Finding Hidden Outs

When your opponent has a hand that can be counterfeited, you often have more outs than is obvious.[49] You should learn to recognize these hidden outs.

Say you have

on the button. Two loose, passive opponents limp, and you raise. The blinds and the limpers call (10 small bets). The flop is

It is checked to the player on your right, who bets. You raise. The big blind calls two cold, and the bettor calls (8 big bets). The turn

---

[49] A turn or river card counterfeits a strong hand if it "improves" it in a way that causes one or both hole cards no longer to play. For example, if you have K♥4♥, and the board is K♣7♦4♠ (giving you two pair, kings and fours), the 7♥ on the turn counterfeits your hand. You now have "improved" to kings and sevens, but the 4♥ in your hand no longer plays. The relative strength of your hand is reduced, as any king with a kicker higher than a four now beats you (as does any seven).

is the 3♦. It is checked to you, and you bet. The big blind calls, but the flop bettor raises (12 big bets). What should you do?

It appears that you are behind, but the pot lays 12-to-1. Your passive opponent would almost certainly not check-raise the turn with less than two pair. To decide whether you should call or fold, you need to count your outs. There are three obvious cards (the jacks) that might be outs. These are not your only potential outs, however.

Let us assume that your opponent plays so loosely that he might start with any two cards. His possible hands are king-nine, king-five, king-trey, or nine-five for two pair. (Nine-trey and five-trey are unlikely because he bet the flop.) He could also have pocket kings, nines, or fives for a set. (Pocket treys are also unlikely because he bet the flop.)

There are 2 kings, 3 nines, 3 fives, and 3 treys unaccounted for. Thus he can have king-nine, king-five, and king-trey six ways each, nine-five nine ways, a set of nines or fives three ways each, and a set of kings one way.

You have three outs to beat king-nine (3 jacks). Against king-five, you have six outs (3 jacks and 3 nines). A nine counterfeits his two pair. If a nine comes, you will have kings and nines with a jack. Your opponent will have kings and nines with a five. You have nine outs to beat king-trey (3 jacks, 3 nines, and 3 fives). You have eight outs to beat nine-five (2 kings, 3 jacks, and 3 treys). Against a set you have zero outs.

To approximate your effective number of outs, you can calculate a weighted average of all your opponent's possible hands and your outs against each. Thus, you have approximately five outs.

$$5 \approx \frac{\left[(6)(3) + (6)(6) + (6)(9) + (9)(8) + (3)(0) + (1)(0)\right]}{6 + 6 + 6 + 9 + 3 + 3 + 1}$$

Since you are getting 12-to-1, and you have about five outs, you should call.[50]

You cannot expect to calculate this weighted average while you are making your decision at the table. Still, you should be aware of possible hands like king-trey against which you have nine outs. If you had counted just three outs, you would have decided to fold. The presence of the "hidden" outs changed your correct play.

# Hidden Out Exercises

Below are ten common situations in which there are important hidden outs. For each hand determine how many outs you have to win and how many to tie. Solutions are below. Try to answer for each hand on your own before you consult the solutions.

|  | Your Hand | Your Opponent's Hand | The Board on Fourth Street |
|---|---|---|---|
| 1. | A♥2♥ | A♦8♦ | A♣K♣7♠4♥ |
| 2. | A♥2♥ | A♦8♦ | A♣K♣9♠4♥ |
| 3. | A♥K♥ | K♣3♣ | K♦T♥7♣3♠ |
| 4. | K♥9♥ | K♣3♣ | K♦T♥7♣3♠ |
| 5. | A♦Q♣ | 3♠3♥ | J♣J♥8♦4♠ |
| 6. | A♠2♠ | A♦T♣ | A♥A♣Q♥6♦ |
| 7. | A♠2♣ | A♥T♦ | A♠8♦8♥3♣ |
| 8. | A♦2♦ | A♠3♠ | A♣8♦8♥2♥ |
| 9. | Q♠Q♣ | 3♠3♣ | A♦A♥7♥3♦ |
| 10. | A♣K♣ | 3♠3♣ | 8♣2♠2♦2♥ |

---

[50] (6)(3) in the above equation represents the six ways your opponent can hold king-nine multiplied by your three outs against that hand; (6)(6) represents the six ways your opponent can hold king-five multiplied by your six outs against that hand, etc.

1. A♥2♥ vs. A♦8♦ with A♣K♣7♠4♥. You have three outs to win (3 deuces) and six outs to tie (3 sevens and 3 fours). When there is one kicker on the board bigger than your opponent's kicker, pairing either of the bottom two cards will counterfeit his kicker. Notice that pairing the king does not counterfeit his kicker.

2. A♥2♥ vs. A♦8♦ with A♣K♣9♠4♥. You have three outs to win (3 deuces) and 22 outs to tie (1 ace, 3 kings, 4 queens, 4 jacks, 4 tens, 3 nines, and 3 fours). When there are two kickers on the board bigger than your opponent's kicker, pairing any board card will counterfeit his kicker. Also, any card larger than his kicker will put three higher kickers on board.

3. A♥K♥ vs. K♣3♣ with K♦T♥7♣3♠. You have nine outs to win (3 aces, 3 tens, and 3 sevens) and zero outs to tie. Any board pair larger than your opponent's bottom pair counterfeits his hand. Since your ace kicker always plays, you win whenever he is counterfeited.

4. K♥9♥ vs. K♣3♣ with K♦T♥7♣3♠. You have six outs to win (3 tens and 3 nines) and three outs to tie (3 sevens). Your kicker plays when the ten pairs, but it does not play when the seven pairs. If you both have two pair, and your kicker does not play, you tie. Just as with A♦8♦ in Hand No. 1, a board card larger than your kicker weakens your hand.

5. A♦Q♣ vs. 3♠3♥ with J♣J♥8♦4♠. You have twelve outs to win (3 aces, 3 queens, 3 eights, and 3 fours) and zero outs to tie. Two higher pair on board counterfeits your opponent's pair.

6. A♠2♠ vs. A♦T♣ with A♥A♣Q♥6♦. You have three outs to win (3 deuces) and fourteen outs to tie (4 kings, 3 queens, 4 jacks, and 3 sixes). If your opponent has trips, any board pair

will give him a full house and counterfeit any kicker. If there is one card on board higher than his kicker, any river card bigger than his kicker will put two higher cards on board. His kicker will not play.

7. A♣2♣ vs. A♥T♦ with A♠8♦8♥3♣. You have zero outs to win and fifteen outs to tie (1 ace, 4 kings, 4 queens, 4 jacks, 2 eights). A deuce does not help you. You already have two pair, aces and eights. Any ace or eight will give you both the same full house. Any card larger than your opponent's kicker counterfeits his hand. When two players have top pair, and there is a smaller pair on board, it will often be a tie. Just one board card bigger than both kickers forces a split pot.

8. A♦2♦ vs. A♠3♠ with A♣8♦8♥2♥. You have two outs to win (2 deuces) and 42 outs to tie (every other card). The pair of eights counterfeits your bottom pair, so you have aces and eights with a deuce. Your opponent has aces and eights with a trey, so he is currently "ahead." A deuce on the river gives you deuces full of aces, but it does not improve your opponent. Any other card counterfeits your opponent's kicker — he cannot win. Even a trey counterfeits his kicker, since it will leave you both with aces and eights with a trey.

9. Q♠Q♣ vs. 3♠3♣ with A♦A♥7♥3♦. You have four outs to win (2 aces and 2 queens) and zero outs to tie. A third ace counterfeits your opponent's treys full.

10. A♣K♣ vs. 3♠3♣ with 8♣2♠2♦2♥. You have seven outs to win (3 aces, 3 kings, and 1 deuce) and three outs to tie (3 eights). The case deuce counterfeits your opponent's pair, leaving him to play the board. If the eight pairs, it counterfeits his pair, but it also counterfeits your ace kicker, so it is a tie.

# Final Thoughts

One of the first adjustments many players make when they begin to study hold 'em is to start habitually folding top pair or an overpair when they are raised on the turn. They reason that their opponent almost always has two pair or better, so they can save money by folding.

In the long run this adjustment is very expensive. First, their opponents are bluffing them far more often than they suspect. Folding predictably to turn raises will encourage even passive players to take occasional shots at you. Many players who complain about how often loose players draw out on their big pairs are actually just folding far too often.

But even if they could be certain that a turn raise represented two pair or better, the pot is often large enough that they should call anyway. With an overpair you usually have eight outs to beat someone with two pair, and with top pair you can have up to nine. The presence of hidden outs can often swing a fold to a call. When you suspect that you are behind, always count *every* out that you might have. If you miss some, you will lose money by folding too much.

# Evaluating the Flop: Made Hands

Many people compare their hand to the flop and quickly categorize it. They think, "I have top pair," or, "I have a straight draw," playing every top pair and every straight draw the same way. This approach is far too simplistic. There are many variables that affect the value of top pair or a straight draw (or any other hand). This section and the next present several examples of each hand type and examine the important differences. For each example assume that you are in a multiway pot.[51] Examples within the same category are listed in order of descending strength. When two hands are given the same ranking (e.g., "strong" or "marginal"), the example that comes first is the stronger hand. Use these rough interpretations for each ranking:

| | |
|---|---|
| **Monster** | Your hand is strong enough to win the overwhelming majority of the time. Concentrate on building a pot, not eliminating opponents. |
| **Very Strong** | Your hand will win the majority of the time. If the pot is small, it may be better to try to build it instead of eliminating opponents. If the pot is large, it is probably better to protect your hand. |
| **Strong** | You will win first- or second-most often. You should rarely fold, even in a small pot, but you should also try to protect your hand. |

---

[51] Hand values change in heads-up and short-handed pots. Any pair is often a good hand, even when the board is scary.

| | |
|---|---|
| **Marginal** | Your hand has winning chances. If you think you can eliminate opponents, you might bet or raise. If your opponents have stronger hands than usual, you might fold. Playing marginal hands well is a hallmark of expert play. |
| **Poor** | Your hand has dubious chances. You might bet if your opponents appear weak, but you should generally fold to aggression unless the pot is very large. |

# Top Pair or an Overpair

When you flop top pair, you will usually have the highest-ranking hand. Some top pairs are more likely than others to be best. Some are also more vulnerable to being drawn out on than others. Here are a few examples.

# Hands with No Redraws

When you do not have redraws to a straight or flush, you are hoping that your top pair is best and that it will still be best after the turn and river. With little chance to improve, your hand is sensitive to unfavorable conditions.

on a flop of

This is a very strong hand. You have top pair with the best possible kicker. Unless an opponent has pocket aces, a set, or a raggedy two pair, you have the best hand. In addition, there are no straight or flush draws available, making either of those hands unlikely at the river. An opponent with a seven or deuce (not also holding an ace) has five outs. No other hand has a strong chance to overtake you. Even against four or five opponents, you will usually still have the best hand on the river.

A♣T♣ on a flop of A♥6♠2♦. This is a strong hand. You have top pair with a decent kicker. You probably have the best hand, but beware someone who raised before the flop. If he has an ace with a bigger kicker, you have to spike a ten to win. No flush draws are available, and no overcards can come to your pair; if you have the best hand, it is likely to hold up.

A♣T♣ on a flop of T♥6♠2♦. This is a strong hand. You have top pair with the best possible kicker. You probably have the best hand. No flush draws are available, but someone could have overcards to your pair or have flopped a gutshot draw. Several hands could have four or more outs. Again, beware someone who raised before the flop. He is much more likely than average to hold an overpair. You will be outdrawn reasonably often in a multiway pot.

on a flop of

This is a strong hand. You have an overpair. Unless someone has an eight or pocket kings, you have the best hand. There are no straight or flush draws available. Someone with a king or pocket pair has only two outs (spiking his kicker will not improve a king to beat you because you already have aces up). Anyone else is virtually drawing dead. If someone has an eight, however, you are drawing to two outs. In this situation you are either way ahead or way behind: If you are ahead, you will almost always win, even against five or more hands. If you are behind, you will lose unless the miracle ace comes on the turn or river.

A♥6♥ on a flop of 6♣4♦2♠. This is a marginal hand. While you have top pair with the best kicker, any turn card (except for an ace or six) is dangerous. Sevens through kings are overcards. Fours and deuces could help someone who flopped middle or bottom pair. Fives and treys put four to a straight on board. Furthermore, someone will often have an overpair. With a big top pair, overpairs are unlikely, and someone who has one usually alerts you with a preflop raise. But against your top pair of sixes, someone will more often have an overpair. Many players do not raise with pocket sevens through tens. Against four or five opponents, you will often lose.

on a flop of

This is a marginal hand. You have top pair with the best kicker, but you are very vulnerable. A third spade could give someone a flush. Running spades will almost always sink you. A queen, nine, or seven puts four to a straight on board. Also, it is likely that someone flopped two pair; people often play hands like jack-ten and ten-eight. If you have the best hand, someone is likely to draw out. If you are behind, you are drawing slim. If someone flopped a straight, you are drawing nearly dead.

Also, anyone who holds a nine and has made a pair with his other card has many outs to beat you and will frequently play his hand strongly on the flop. This makes it difficult to "read" your opponent's hand, increasing the chance that you will make a playing error on fourth or fifth street. This further diminishes the value of your hand.

A♥4♥ on a flop of A♣T♠9♣. This is a poor hand. You have top pair, but no kicker. Unless you spike a four, you can do no better than tie against another ace. The two high side cards (ten and nine) are dangerous. Even if no one else has an ace, many people are likely to have bottom or middle pair, or a straight or flush draw. In a multiway pot there could be several opponents with good draws. You will win the whole pot only rarely; usually you will be beaten or tied by the river.

However, with redraws, even as little as a backdoor flush draw, top pair becomes more robust. It has two ways to win: being the best hand and holding up, or drawing out on a better hand. The presence of redraws sometimes makes the difference between a profitable and an unprofitable hand. So in this example, if the ten or nine were a heart, your hand would move up at least to the marginal category.

# Hands with Redraws

on a flop of

This is a very strong hand. You have top pair with a very good kicker and a flush draw. You will usually have the best hand; if you do not, you have a redraw to beat someone with a set or two pair.[52] No straight draws are possible. You will win most of the time even in a multiway pot.

Q♠J♠ on a flop of Q♣T♥4♠. This is a strong hand. You have top pair with a good kicker. You also have backdoor straight and flush draws. Two overcards can beat your pair, but any ace or king on fourth street gives you a straight redraw. The A♠ or K♠ gives you both a straight and a flush draw. This is a robust hand that will often win unimproved and will sometimes improve to overtake a better hand.

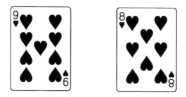

on a flop of

This is a strong hand. You have top pair with open-ended straight and backdoor flush draws. Your top pair is very vulnerable; four of the five overcards can beat you (a ten makes you a straight), and someone could easily have an overpair or have you outkicked. Without the redraws your hand is not nearly as strong. With no redraws and a poor kicker, such as 9♦3♦, it could be very questionable whether you should continue depending on the

---

[52] Two pair is less likely with this disconnected board, but never rule out any holding for a loose player.

action. But here your combined chances to win unimproved and to make a straight or flush make this hand strong.

A♣8♣ on a flop of A♠6♥2♣. This is a strong hand. You have top pair with a marginal kicker and a backdoor flush draw. No overcards can come to give someone a higher pair, and the backdoor flush draw improves this hand significantly. If someone has you outkicked, you can win by spiking an eight *or* by catching running clubs. Also, both board cards are smaller than your kicker, making it likely that your kicker will play on the river.[53] Thus, you will usually beat, not tie, someone with a smaller kicker.

on a flop of

This is a marginal hand. However, it is better than the similar hand in the no redraws section (A♣J♦ on a J♣T♠8♠ flop), because in this hand you have the A♠. Those times that you are beaten by a third spade on the turn, you have a redraw to the nut flush. In the previous hand you had no such redraw.

---

[53] See the section, "Hidden Outs," for more on this idea.

# Pairs Smaller than Top Pair

When you have a pair smaller than top pair, the probability that you have the best hand is obviously reduced. You usually play these hands under one of two circumstances:

1.  No one has shown much strength, so you might have the best hand.

2.  The pot is large, and you are drawing to a probable winner.

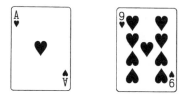

on a flop of

This is a very strong hand. You have middle pair, ace kicker, and the nut flush draw. If no one has a queen, you will usually have the best hand. Even if you are behind to someone with a queen (but not ace-queen), you have fourteen outs (3 aces, 2 nines, and 9 hearts) to overtake him. Even against a large field, you will often win.

You should usually raise and reraise with this hand on the flop, especially against multiple opponents. With so many outs you will usually have a lot of pot equity, even if you do not currently have the best hand.

3♣2♣ on a flop of Q♣8♣2♥. This is a strong hand. You have bottom pair with a small flush draw. Although obviously not as strong as the previous example, this is still a robust holding. Your bottom pair, no kicker is not likely to be the best hand unless you are heads-up, but you still have a fourteen out draw. Any time you flop a pair and a flush draw, you have a strong hand.

on a flop of

This is a strong hand (though it is on the low end of that category). You have a pocket pair much higher than middle pair. If you have the best hand, you are unlikely to be outdrawn. Only one additional overcard can come, and there are no straight or flush draws. If someone has a king, however, you are drawing to two outs.

A♥7♥ on a flop of K♠7♦2♥. This is a marginal hand. You have middle pair, ace kicker. You may have the best hand. If you do not, you have five outs to two pair or trips and a backdoor flush draw. Between this hand and the previous one, if no one has a king, the queens hand is stronger; fewer overcards can outdraw you. But if someone does have a king, this hand is stronger, since you have more outs.

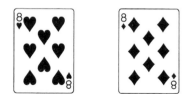

on a flop of

This is a marginal hand. You have a pocket pair higher than middle pair. This hand combines the weakness to overcards of the ace-seven hand with the lack of outs of the queens hand. Despite being a higher-ranking poker hand than ace-seven (a pair of eights versus a pair of sevens), this hand is clearly inferior to both the queens and the ace-seven hands.[54]

Q♥Q♦ on a flop of K♠J♣8♥. This is a poor to marginal hand. You have a pocket pair higher than middle pair. You may have the best hand. If you do, the three big cards and two-flush are dangerous. They make it likely for someone to have flopped a pair or a straight or flush draw (though you do hold two "stopper" cards for many of the possible straights). If behind, you are drawing to two outs and a backdoor straight draw.

---

[54] For a similar example, see p. 88 of *The Theory of Poker* by David Sklansky.

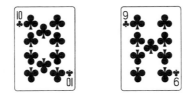

on a flop of

This is a poor hand. You have bottom pair and the bottom end of a one card gutshot. You are unlikely to have the best hand. If you catch a nine, anyone with a bigger two pair or a queen beats you. If you catch a queen, anyone with an ace makes a bigger straight. This hand will make a second-best hand far more often than it makes the best hand, and in most circumstances you should fold it.

6♥6♣ on a flop of Q♦T♦5♣. This is a poor hand. You have a pocket pair higher than bottom pair. You are unlikely to have the best hand. If you do, someone could catch a flush, straight, or one of seven overcards to beat you. If you are behind, you have two outs to improve. One of those outs, the 6♦, puts three to a flush on board. In a multiway pot your hand is terrible (although you should take a card off getting 30-to-1 odds or so which sometimes happens).

# Two Pair

Two pair, even bottom two, is usually a strong hand. You will almost always have the best hand on the flop with two pair (not talking about the times a pair is on board). Its value varies most with the availability of redraws.

on a flop of

This is a very strong hand. You have top two and a backdoor flush draw on an uncoordinated board. The only real threat is a gutshot draw (e.g., jack-ten).

Q♣3♠ on a flop of Q♥9♥3♣. This is a strong hand. With top and bottom pair, you are vulnerable to the middle card pairing, counterfeiting your lower pair. In addition, on this board, straight and flush draws are possible. With two pair, you always have a four out redraw to a full house against those hands.

on a flop of

This is a marginal hand. With any bottom two you are vulnerable to the top card pairing, counterfeiting your lower pair. Plus in this case, the very coordinated nature of the board makes it likely that someone is drawing to a straight or flush. The turn card will drastically affect your hand's value. A straight or flush card will likely leave you behind and drawing to four outs. A blank, on the other hand, puts you in a strong position. (Thus you may want to wait until the turn to play your hand strongly. See the section, "Protecting Your Hand.")

Despite its potential weaknesses, if your opponents did not connect well with the flop, any two pair is quite strong. This hand varies significantly in strength based on the situation.

# Sets

A "set," a pair in your hand and a matching card on the board, is always a very strong hand. If the board is uncoordinated, even bottom set is a monster. On a coordinated board, a set gives you a strong chance to have the best hand combined with a good draw to beat a straight or flush.

on a flop of

This is a monster. There is no need to knock out opponents.[55] You have no real threats; even against a field of five opponents, you will win a very high percentage of the time.

7♥7♠ on a flop of T♥7♣6♣. This is a very strong hand. Unless someone flopped a straight or has pocket tens, you have the best hand. You are vulnerable to straight or flush draws, but you have a good redraw to beat those hands.

# Trips

"Trips," a pair on board and a matching card in your hand, is usually a very strong hand. It is weaker than a set for two reasons:

1.  Someone else can have the same trips, but with a better (or paired) kicker.

2.  The pair on board alerts everyone to the possibility of trips.

You still usually have a strong draw to beat a straight or flush and to tie with someone who has you outkicked.[56]

---

[55] That doesn't necessarily mean you should slowplay on the flop as you will often get action from a king or even an eight. Three kings, on the other hand, usually does call for a slowplay on the flop.

[56] That is, if you have 3♥2♥, your opponent has T♣3♣, and the flop is K♥3♦3♠, you are behind, but have fifteen outs to tie (4 aces, 3 kings, 4

on a flop of

This is a monster. You have trips with the best kicker and a backdoor flush draw. You almost certainly have the best hand; only pocket kings and king-four beat you. There are no straight or flush draws available. Unless the pot is very big, there is no need to knock out opponents.

8♥7♥ on a flop of 9♣7♣7♠. This is a very strong hand. Unless someone has you outkicked or has pocket nines, you have the best hand. The coordinated board means that one or two opponents could have four or more outs.

# Final Thoughts

In this section we spent very little time analyzing big hands like two pair, sets, full houses, and quads. Many players seem preoccupied with learning to "get the maximum" from these hands. *In fact, playing big hands well is an overrated skill.* These

---

queens, and 4 jacks). See the section, "Hidden Outs," for further discussion.

hands occur rarely, and when they do, it is difficult to play them poorly. Two major mistakes in hold 'em are:

1.  Giving too much action with weak hands in small pots (playing loosely preflop or calling postflop with hopeless hands)

2.  Failing to defend big pots (making bad folds or neglecting to protect your hand through aggressive play)

With a powerhouse hand you will not make either of these mistakes. Do not worry about extracting an extra bet occasionally on your rare monsters.

Instead, learn to evaluate the strength of your pair hands accurately. Many loose and overaggressive players make critical errors here. They jam top pair against three or four opponents when the coordinated board strongly devalues their hand. They call and raise in small pots with very dubious pairs, hands that are unlikely to be best now and even more unlikely to be best on the river. In a multiway pot some top pairs are strong enough to raise and reraise for value. Some aren't. Learn to tell the difference.

# Evaluating the Flop: Drawing Hands

In the previous section we examined made hands and discussed how board textures affect their value. In this section we do the same for drawing hands.[57] We use the same assumptions and rating scale in this section as we did previously. Use these rough interpretations for each ranking:

| | |
|---|---|
| **Monster** | Your draw will win over fifty percent of the time, even against a large field. Raise and reraise for value. |
| **Very Strong** | Your hand will win a multiway pot a large percentage of the time. If the pot is small, try to build it by raising without knocking out opponents. In a large pot, protect vulnerable outs such as overcards. Either way, you should be aggressive with these hands. |

---

[57] The distinction between a drawing hand and a made hand is arbitrary. Almost all "made" hands have some potential to improve. Likewise, many "drawing" hands have some value as made hands, even if their value is only king-high. A few hands, such as a pair and a flush or straight draw, have characteristics of both. Some players put far too much emphasis on this difference; for example, they may refuse to play any "drawing" hand aggressively because they are still "on the come." Anyone who advises you to play drawing hands and made hands differently, based solely on that distinction, should be ignored. Strategically, the division is mostly meaningless. What matters is how often your hand will win at the showdown.

| Strong | Your draw will win a significant percentage of the time. Even if the pot is small, you will almost always be correct to see the turn and river. You need to be strongly convinced that you are drawing dead to abandon this draw. |
|---|---|
| Marginal | Your draw will sometimes win, but it either has few outs or is particularly vulnerable to redraws or drawing dead. You may have to fold if the pot is small, and the circumstances appear unfavorable. Generally you should see the turn if the pot is large, though. Consider betting or raising if doing so will improve your winning chances. |
| Poor | Your draw has few outs and will often lose even if you do make your hand. You might bet once to try to pick up the pot. Do not call unless the pot is very large. |

# Flush Draws

Flush draws are strong hands, stronger than most people seem to understand. A flush draw on the flop comes in by the river 35 percent of the time. You should only very rarely fold a flush draw on the flop: Even small preflop pots are generally big enough to rule out folding. (Weak one card flush draws are an exception. A one card flush draw is where you use only one card from your hand and three of the same suit from the board. Even with small cards, you will usually win if you use both cards from your hand. If you use only one card, you must be wary of losing to a larger flush.)

on a flop of

This is a very strong hand. You have the nut flush draw and two big overcards. You will often win even when your flush does not come in if you spike an ace or king. Against a small field, ace-king may even be the best hand and win unimproved.

A♣6♣ on a flop of J♣9♣4♥. This is a strong to very strong hand. An ace-high flush draw is always a good hand; it assures that you cannot lose to a bigger flush. Plus, you have an overcard.

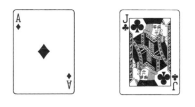

on a flop of

This is a strong hand. You have the one card, nut flush draw and an overcard. When the flop comes all of one suit, even very loose players tighten up. Because of this tendency, you can often pick up the pot without a showdown through aggressive play. One card, nut flush draws are less valuable than their two card cousins, because you rarely get much action on one card flushes as your opponents will fear that you hold the nuts.

J♠9♠ on a flop of K♠7♠5♣. This is a strong hand. You have a flush draw. Also, if no one has a king, you might win the pot by spiking a jack or nine. Consider playing this hand aggressively to encourage hands like ace-jack and pocket queens to fold. Typical players play this hand passively to "avoid losing customers." If the pot is large, knocking players out is better.

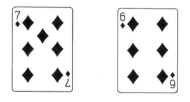

on a flop of

This is a strong hand. Despite your small cards, you will typically win if you make your flush. However, unlike the previous example, you have almost no chance to win by spiking a pair. There is no reason to protect your hand except maybe if the pot is very large. (In that case, you should try to force out single diamonds such as the 9♦ that would beat you if the turn and river both came diamonds.) Your chance to win without a showdown is small, as someone else will almost always like this high-card flop.

Indeed, the chief concern when evaluating the strength of a typical flush draw (two in your hand and two on an unpaired board) is how likely you are to win if you miss your flush, but make a pair. Compare A♥6♥ to Q♥6♥. Few people dispute that the former hand is much stronger, but many argue that it may be primarily attributed to the difference between making an ace-high flush and a queen-high flush. Obviously, making a bigger flush is always better, but a queen-high flush loses to an ace-high far less often than a pair of queens loses to a pair of aces. Ace-six is better than queen-six mostly because you win more often when you miss your flush, but pair your top card. Always consider your chance to win by pairing whenever you have a flush draw.

T♥9♥ on a flop of J♥4♥4♣. This is a strong hand. The pair on board devalues your hand. If you make a flush on the turn, anyone with two pair (a pocket pair, jack, or pair of the turn card) has four outs (2 fours and 2 cards to match their pair). Anyone with trip fours has ten outs (3 jacks, 1 four, 3 pairs of the turn card, and 3 kicker pairs). Furthermore, anyone with a bigger heart than your ten has seven outs (the 7 remaining hearts) to a bigger flush. This plethora of redraws means that you will sometimes make your flush and still lose. Nevertheless, you will also often make your flush and win.

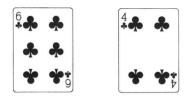

on a flop of

This is a marginal hand. Beware paired boards with three high cards. People love to play hands like jack-ten. You will be drawing dead much more often than usual on flops like this. If a jack or ten comes on the turn, your draw will almost certainly be worthless. This draw suffers all the potential redraws that the previous example does, but the high board cards make it more likely that the hands you fear are actually out against you.

In general, you should continue with a flush draw even if the board is paired. The rare exception is a hand like this if there is a lot of action on the flop.

A♦J♠ on a flop of K♠9♠5♠. This is a marginal hand. You have the third nut, one card flush draw and an overcard. You have two draws, the ace and the flush draw, but neither is sure to win. You are drawing almost dead if one opponent has a king and another has the A♠. With few opponents you are fairly likely to be drawing live. If several opponents have committed to their hands after this flop, you will often be drawing almost dead.

on a flop of

This is a poor hand. You have third pair and a small one card flush draw. Heads-up, it may have a fair amount of value. If your opponent has a bigger pair, you usually have eleven outs (2 nines and 9 diamonds). If he has a bigger diamond, your pair is frequently the best hand. He would have to be lucky to have a bigger pair *and* a bigger diamond or a made flush. As you add opponents, however, this hand loses value quickly. In a multiway pot you will usually have at most two outs and often be drawing virtually dead.

# Straight Draws

Straight draws vary greatly in value. Obviously, open-ended draws arc usually stronger than gutshots. Some gutshots can be fairly strong, though, while some open-ended draws are not worth playing. Poor players commonly misplay their straight draws. Doing so can be costly. (Misplaying flush draws is usually not as bad.)

on a flop of

This is a very strong hand. You have an open-ended straight draw to the nuts, two overcards, and a backdoor flush draw. No four-flush is possible. With eight outs to the nuts and six more to top pair, you will often win.

J♦T♣ on a flop of A♥Q♦8♠. This is a strong hand. You have a double gutshot; any king or nine gives you the nut straight. No flush draw exists. You are unlikely to win if you spike a jack or ten. This draw will win almost as often against six opponents as it will against two.

Double gutshots also tend to be deceptive. Many players who would automatically check if a third flush card came will continue to bet if you make your straight. They do not see the threat (i.e., a nine does not look particularly scary on this board). You will usually get more action on these hands than usual.

on a flop of

This is a strong hand. You have an open-ended straight draw and an overcard on a two-flush board. A non-heart eight gives you the nuts, but ace-queen beats you if a king comes. Furthermore, you can make your straight on the turn, but lose to a flush on the river. Compared with the previous example, your overcard gives you more potential outs, but you have fewer outs to the nuts and are more vulnerable to redraws. Therefore, while the last draw was not, this draw is sensitive to the size of the field.

K♥J♥ on a flop of T♥9♣4♠. This is a strong hand. Your straight draw is only a gutshot, but you also have two overcards and a backdoor flush draw. Most players undervalue hands like this. They think of their hand having only four outs, no stronger than any other gutshot. Actually, the three draws combined give you solid winning chances.

on a flop of

This is a strong hand. You have a one card, open-ended straight draw and an overcard. The board shows three different suits. You will probably win or tie if you catch an eight. Furthermore, a king gives you the nuts, beating anyone who has just a jack (since they make only a king-high straight). You may get a lot of action when a king comes if one or more players have jacks. In general, one card straight draws are worth significantly more if your side card can help make the nuts, as you may get a lot of action when your opponents make a straight but lose to yours. In addition, spiking an ace will often be enough to win.

8♥7♥ on a flop of A♣T♠9♦. This is a marginal hand. You have the bottom end of an open-ended straight draw. A six gives you the nuts, but someone with king-queen or queen-eight beats you if a jack comes. In addition, if a king or queen comes on the turn, your jack outs become even weaker. For example, if the Q♥ comes on the turn, and the J♣ on the river, someone with just an eight ties you. Anyone with a king beats you. With two undercards to the board, you have little hope of winning with a pair. This open-ended draw is weaker than most.

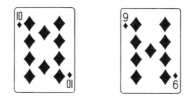

on a flop of

This is a marginal hand. You have a gutshot to the nuts and a backdoor flush draw. In a loose game, this hand is usually strong enough to see the turn. If it is checked to you in a large pot, consider betting. You would like to see many people fold: hands that have you dominated like ace-nine and jack-ten and those like queen-jack that have two overcards to your hand. If these hands fold, you will be much more likely to win if you make a pair.[58]

T♥3♠ on a flop of J♦9♥8♠. This is a marginal hand. You have a one card, open-ended straight draw. With a useless side card, this hand is not very good. Neither a queen nor a seven gives you the nuts. While you will not often lose if you make a straight, you will frequently tie. If several opponents seem committed to the hand, especially in a small pot, you may want to fold. It is too likely that you are drawing to only half the pot.

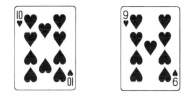

on a flop of

This is a poor hand. You have the bottom end of a gutshot on a paired, two-flush board. If someone holds king-jack, queen-jack,

---

[58] For a similar example with a more complete explanation, see p. 168 of *Hold 'em Poker For Advanced Players* by David Sklansky and Mason Malmuth.

or ace-ten (with the barely notable exception of catching a nine), you are drawing dead. The Q♠ may give someone a flush. Anyone with trip jacks has a redraw if you do make the best hand on the turn. You will often lose even if you do catch a queen.

5♣4♦ on a flop of T♥8♣7♠. This is a poor hand. You have the bottom end of a gutshot. If you catch a six, anyone who holds a nine beats you.

# Big Draws

Big draws combine straight and flush draws. Even in otherwise unfavorable circumstances, these hands are strong. You should usually raise and reraise for value with these draws; many of them come in by the river over fifty percent of the time.

on a flop of

This is a monster. You have an open-ended straight flush draw with two overcards. You have 21 outs to top pair or better! Even against a large field, you will win this hand well over fifty percent of the time.

9♠8♠ on a flop of J♠T♥4♠. This is a very strong hand. You have a flush draw and the bottom end of an open-ended straight draw. Even though a queen gives you the bottom end of the straight, and your flush is not the nut flush, you will win most of the time when you catch one of your fifteen outs.

on a flop of

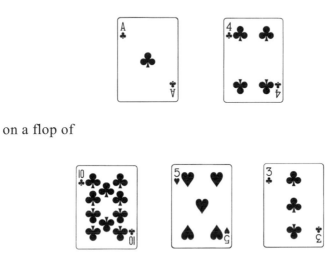

This is a very strong hand. You have the nut flush draw, a gutshot wheel draw, and an overcard. You have twelve outs to a straight or flush and three more to top pair. However, your ace outs are vulnerable to anyone else hanging around with a bigger ace, so if the pot is large you should try to induce any such player to fold (while building the pot that you will often win).

T♥2♥ on a flop of J♥9♥7♠. This is a strong hand. You have a flush draw and a one card gutshot. You will usually win if a heart comes (less often if two hearts come), and you will probably at least tie if an eight comes. Beware opponents playing aggressively (especially if they are normally passive players). If someone already has a set or a made straight, your hand is less valuable.

While all of the above hands are generally quite strong, and you should be willing to put several bets in on the flop, beware a tight, passive player raising with you; he may have a set. These draws are all significantly weakened if one of your opponents has a set. Sets are rare, and under most circumstances you should not fear one. But you should slow down if you suspect one is out.

# Final Thoughts

Flush and straight draws are generally good hands. They become even more valuable in games with very loose and unobservant opponents. These players pad the pot while you are still drawing and pay off frequently after you make your hand. In multiway pots play strong draws aggressively. Eliminating opponents often improves your chance to win by spiking a pair. But you also benefit if all your opponents call; strong draws win far more than their fair share of the time.

While strong draws are very valuable, some flush and many straight draws are not strong. Be careful with your weak and vulnerable draws. In large pots sometimes you should bet or raise with these weaker draws to improve your winning chances or to buy a free card. Usually do not raise for value, though. Weak draws win far less often than strong ones. When you flop a draw, evaluate its strength carefully:
1.	How likely are you to make your hand and still lose?
2.	How likely are you to win if you spike a pair?
3.	How likely are you to split the pot if you hit your straight?
4.	Do you have backdoor draws to go with your main draw?
5.	Will you win much more often in a smaller field, or do you welcome opponents?

Drawing hands can be very profitable in small stakes games. Learn to evaluate them accurately so you make the most out of your strong and weak ones alike.

# Large Pots vs. Small Pots

Pot size is almost always the most important factor to consider when evaluating any poker decision. Poker hands have value that depends directly on the size of the pot. If you flop a royal flush in a $10 pot, bet, and watch everyone fold, hitting your amazing 649,739-to-1 shot turned out to be worth only $10. If you flop a gutshot in a $220 pot, your meager draw is worth about $20, twice as much as your monster hand made you. To make a decision to raise, call, or fold, you should know the value of your hand; you cannot know that without first considering the size of the pot.

## Judging the Size of the Pot

Pot size is determined by the ratio of the value of the pot to the size of current and future bets. A $100 pot is large in a $4-$8 game, but tiny in a $40-$80 game. In this book we describe the size of the pot in terms of the number of bets in it, not the number of chips or dollars. We suggest that you count the pot the same way when you play; thinking in terms of bets allows you to move between limits without doing unnecessary mental arithmetic.

In this book we sometimes give certain playing advice for "large pots," but different advice for "small pots." Unfortunately, there is no bright-line standard that separates the two. The exact pot size where the correct decision changes is different for every situation. It depends on the number of players, the strength of your hand, the playing tendencies of your opponents (e.g., aggressive or passive, tricky or straightforward), and other considerations. In many hands begin to consider the pot to be large if one of the following is true:
1. It is six-handed or more preflop.
2. It is raised preflop and four-handed or more.

145

3.  It is three-bet or more preflop.
4.  At least two of your opponents will usually go to the river.

These rules are *not* rigid or always accurate. They are designed only to give a beginner a general sense of the situations we refer to when we talk about large pots.

# Adjusting to Small Pots

In small pots going too far with weak hands is expensive. You can bet marginal hands on the flop to try to pick up the pot, but if you are raised, usually release your hand immediately or on fourth street if you do not improve. If an opponent is betting or raising, you need to be fairly confident that you have the best hand or a strong draw to call. This principle is especially true after the bet size doubles on the turn. Many loose players repeatedly make the mistake of calling down with weak hands in small pots. *In a small pot if you think you have a close decision between continuing and folding, tend to fold.*

For example, you have

in the big blind. Two players limp, the small blind calls, and you check (4 small bets). The flop is

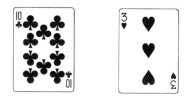

giving you top pair, no kicker. The passive small blind bets. You should usually fold. You have top pair, but, if the small blind or one of the players behind you also has a ten, you are drawing to three outs. The board is somewhat coordinated, and four overcards can come to your pair; even if you do have the best hand now, someone will often draw out on you. Folding the best hand in this tiny pot is not a big mistake, but calling down when you are drawing to only three outs is.

You also need to be more selective with your weak drawing hands when the pot is small. Say you limp from early position with J♦T♦. Two players limp behind you, the small blind calls, and the big blind checks (5 small bets). The flop is Q♥8♣4♦ giving you a gutshot and a backdoor flush draw. The small blind checks, and the big blind bets. You are getting 6-to-1 on a call, but you should probably fold. If you knew that it would not be raised behind you, then you could call. Your hand has just enough strength to take a card off when you are getting 6-to-1 plus implied odds, especially if a couple of opponents might call behind you. Unfortunately, any of the three players yet to act could raise. It is too costly to risk sometimes paying two or three bets to see the turn.

With a weak draw in a small pot, you have little margin for error. If all goes according to plan, your potential reward is small. If someone raises unexpectedly or has you drawing dead, though, the cost is relatively high. *Avoid taking chances with weak draws in small pots.*

# Adjusting to Large Pots

When the pot is large, maximize your chance to win it. Specifically, you should:

1. Continue with marginal hands that you might fold in a small pot.

2.   Seize opportunities to knock out players, whether you have a made hand or a draw.

3.   Continue to draw even when you suspect that you might be drawing dead.

4.   Call liberally for one bet on the river, even when you are almost sure that you are beaten.

# Playing Aggressively With Marginal Hands

For example, say you have

in the big blind. Four players limp, and the button raises. The small blind folds. You call, as do the limpers (12.5 small bets). The flop is

You check, and everyone else checks to the button, who bets. You should raise. You have middle pair and a backdoor straight draw. You estimate its worth at about five outs (the two-flush and coordinated nature of the board lower the value of your hand

somewhat). For a five out draw you need the pot to lay about 8-to-1 to continue. Getting 13-to-1, you clearly should at least call.

But raising is better than calling. You may have a better hand than the preflop raiser. He could have a big pair or ace-ten, but he may also be automatically betting unimproved overcards such as ace-king.

More importantly, raising improves your winning chances. You would like to see many different hands fold. If you have the best hand, in this large pot, anyone with as little as one overcard to your pair of sevens threatens you.

Even without the best hand, you still want many hands to fold. Obviously, you would like anyone with a better hand to fold. If you raise, someone with a better seven, a weak ten, or pocket eights or nines may fear that your hand is stronger than just middle pair and fold. Even if it happens only rarely, this prospect is compelling; inducing a better hand to fold in a large pot is a coup. More subtly, you would also like anyone with a six or nine to fold. If you catch an eight on fourth street to make two pair, anyone with either of those cards will pick up an open-ended straight draw. With a hand this weak, your winning chances improve significantly with every player who folds. *When the pot is large, invest extra bets if doing so improves your chance to win.*

# Continuing When You Might Be Drawing Dead

In large pots you should often continue even if your winning chances appear grim. Poker folklore holds that drawing dead is a terrible mistake. As a result, many authors suggest that you fold straight and flush draws if the board pairs. Some even suggest that you fold straight draws if the board contains a two-flush. While this advice is generally incorrect in most situations, it is truly dreadful when the pot is large.

When you fold a live draw, you forfeit a percentage of the pot that corresponds to the likelihood of making your draw (and winning). If the pot holds twelve bets, and you will make your draw and win 30 percent of the time, by folding, you forfeit a share of the pot worth almost three bets. If you call, drawing dead, you forfeit one bet. Hence, drawing dead is usually not as expensive as folding a live draw. Consequently, if the pot is big, you should be relatively certain that you are drawing dead before you fold. Observing strong betting alone is not enough evidence. If the board is paired, a player betting strongly is more likely to have trips than a full house. You need additional, specific evidence of a full house to fold. Without such evidence, folding a flush draw in a large pot just because the board has paired is a big mistake.

For example, say you have

in middle position. Two players limp. You limp, and so does the button. The small blind raises. The big blind and all the limpers call (12 small bets). The flop is

giving you the nut flush draw and an overcard. The small blind bets. The big blind folds, and both limpers call. You raise. The button folds, and the small blind reraises. Both limpers call, as do you (12 big bets).[59] The turn is the J♠, pairing the board. The small blind bets, and the first limper now raises. The second limper folds (15 big bets).

There are fifteen bets in this large pot, and it is two bets to you, so you are getting 7.5-to-1 on a call. The board is paired, so you might be drawing dead. Nevertheless, you should call. Usually, the raiser will have no more than three jacks, and you will be drawing live. Because the pot is so large, you would have to be quite certain that you are drawing dead to fold. There is no way to be sure enough at this point, so you should call.

Also notice that if you make your flush, and your hand is good, you should collect at least one more big bet on the river. This compensates for those times that one of your opponents reraises the turn.

Continuing with the example, you call, and the small blind calls (18 big bets). The river card is the 6♥, completing your flush, but double-pairing the board. The small blind checks, and the turn raiser bets. The most likely hand for him to have had on fourth street was three jacks, so your completed flush is probably no good; if your read is correct, the river has given him a full house. Still, you should almost always call for one more bet in this huge, nineteen bet pot. He might have jacks full, but he also may have just a big pocket pair. He may have raised on the turn with a flush draw. Or the large pot may have encouraged him to try a desperate bluff.

None of these scenarios is particularly likely, but that is fine. If you win as little as five percent of the time, you profit by calling. It is almost impossible to read your opponent for a full house with 95 percent certainty. *Do not fold in large pots for one bet on the river if there is some chance you might win.*

---

[59] Raising again, especially if it is a cap, is also a strong option. You have position, a big draw, and three players calling. Your raise is probably for value, and it also might earn you a free card on fourth street.

# Final Thoughts

In small pots tend to fold marginal hands and draws like bottom pair and gutshot straight draws. You can bet once with weak hands or merely call with strong hands. But do not call with weak hands. In a loose game most of the money you make in small pots comes from opponents who call you down with weak draws and second-best hands. Make sure you do not miss bets in these spots.

In large pots play marginal hands and draws aggressively. Call liberally even if your winning chances are slim. In a loose game most of the money you make in large pots comes from forcing opponents to fold through aggressive play. Erroneously folding a live draw is costly. Folding the best hand on the river in a large pot is the single worst mistake you can make.

# Protecting Your Hand

The most costly error that you can make is to fold a hand that has a strong chance to win a large pot. This error is so costly because it theoretically costs you a large fraction of the pot when you make it. That is, if you have a forty percent chance of winning a ten bet pot, folding on the end for one bet rather than calling costs over three bets (3.4 bets to be precise, the four bets that constitute your forty percent share minus part of the bet you saved by not calling). Compare this to the error of calling when you should fold. Even with no hope of winning, calling costs at most one bet.

The fact is that most small stakes players rarely make this error. In a large pot most people instinctively see their decent hands and draws through to the end. Only players who believe that making "big laydowns" is the hallmark of expert play routinely make this mistake. They are doomed to wonder why they keep losing when they play so expertly.

Another error is almost as costly. It is so common that you will see someone make it on nearly every hand of a small stakes game. The error is *failing to protect strong hands in large, multiway pots*.

To "protect your hand," you bet or raise. Your bet should force players who hold weak draws to decide between folding and making an unprofitable call. When you make this play, any players with weak draws who call do so to their detriment.[60]

---

[60] When an opponent calls to his detriment, it usually also benefits you. Occasionally, an opponent can make an unprofitable call that costs you money as well (benefiting a third player). This relatively uncommon situation should not affect your general strategy much. Even when your opponent costs you money by calling, you should still protect your hand with a raise. You will lose more money in the long run if you let him call

153

As a simple example, you hold

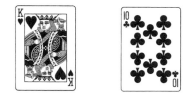

in the big blind. Two players limp, the small blind completes, and you check (4 small bets). The flop is

The small blind checks, and you bet. If the player next to act happens to hold

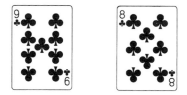

your bet protects your hand. He can choose to fold his draw, as he should. If he folds, your chance to win the pot improves. You will now likely win even if a six comes.

He can also choose to call. If he does, he pays one bet to win five (the size of the pot) plus any additional bets he gains on later rounds. Since he is over a 10-to-1 underdog to catch a six on the turn, this call probably loses money. Your opponent is in a lose-

---

only a single bet.

lose situation. No matter what he chooses to do, he loses. Protecting your hand is the art of placing your opponents in these lose-lose situations.

Sometimes, because merely betting out will not be enough, you have to work harder to protect your hand. Assume that you hold K♥T♥ in the big blind. Two players limp, and the button raises. The small blind folds. You call, as do the two limpers (8.5 small bets). The flop is again K♦7♥5♦. You bet. The player with 9♣8♣ now has a different decision. There are 9.5 bets in the pot instead of five. He is still over a 10-to-1 underdog to catch a six on the turn, but his situation is much better. If he calls and catches a six, he will almost certainly win the pot. He may also make two or three more big bets from you (plus, perhaps, some bets from other players) before you realize that you have been outdrawn. So when he completes his hand, he can expect to win the 9.5 bets in the pot plus at least four (two double-sized bets) more from you on fourth and fifth street. He is a 10-to-1 underdog to hit his card, but he will win at least thirteen bets on his one bet investment if he does get lucky. Since his call is profitable, your bet does not protect your hand.

To protect your hand here, you have to be more subtle. The player on the button raised before the flop. A player who raises before the flop will typically bet a ragged flop like this one. Many players will automatically bet with any hand; they need not have a king. You can exploit this tendency in order to protect your hand. If you check, and both limpers check, the button will probably bet. Now you should raise. To see fourth street, your opponent with 9♣8♣ must choose between folding and calling two bets. Since there are 11.5 bets in the pot, and it costs him two bets to see the turn, calling is again unprofitable for him. *A check-raise often protects your hand when betting out does not.*

# When Calling Cannot Be Right

Failing to protect your hand is almost always an error. Doing so allows an opponent to draw profitably who should have been forced to fold (or pay too much to draw). Sometimes he will draw out on you; when he does, you lose a whole pot that you should win. When the pot is big, losing it is devastating. A multiway pot magnifies your error further, as you often allow two or three opponents to draw instead of just one.

Because failing to protect your hand is such a significant error in large and multiway pots, you must usually play very aggressively on the flop. When the player directly on your right bets, you should almost always either raise or fold. If your hand is too strong to fold, raise. Calling is almost always wrong because it fails to protect your hand.[61]

For example, you are in the small blind in a loose $4-$8 game with

---

[61] Giving your opponents a cheap chance to draw out is not nearly as expensive if the pot is small. When the pot is three- or four-handed and unraised before the flop, you should sometimes call. We will not discuss this sort of scenario further, because it rarely occurs in loose, small stakes games. For more about this play, see p. 93 in *Hold 'em Poker for Advanced Players* by David Sklansky and Mason Malmuth. There are also two other important exceptions:

1.  You have a small straight or flush draw with no overcards. Since you will probably win only if you make your draw, but you will almost certainly win if you do, you do not need to protect your hand.

2.  The pot is so huge that a flop raise will be less effective than a raise on fourth street. See "When the Pot is Extremely Large" later in this section.

Six players limp, you call for $2 more, and the big blind checks (8 small bets). The flop is

giving you top pair, but with a poor kicker. You check, hoping to use the action behind you to help determine how likely it is that you hold the best hand. Everyone checks to the button who bets (9 small bets).

You probably have the best hand. If one of the limpers held a queen with a better kicker, say queen-jack or queen-ten, he typically would have bet. While the button could have one of those hands as well, he will often also bet weaker hands. He could just as easily have a hand like pocket nines or ace-eight. In fact, he could have an even worse hand; many players would bet in that spot with just a deuce, a gutshot draw, or even nothing at all.

There are nine bets in the pot. You have determined that it is reasonably likely that you have the best hand, so you should not fold. Since you have decided to continue with the hand, you should raise. There are six players behind you who may have weak draws. They may hold an eight or deuce (five outs), or a gutshot (four outs). If you call, you fail to protect your hand against these draws.

Sometimes, the button will have you outkicked. Occasionally, one of the players who checked the flop will have trapped you with a big hand. In those cases, you might regret your decision to raise, wishing that you had saved a bet. But always remember why you protect your hand: Raising when you should call can cost you a bet. Calling when you should raise, however, can cost you a whole pot. It is easily worth losing an extra bet here and there to save an occasional pot.

# Protecting Draws and Buying Outs

When the pot is big, you should similarly "protect" your strong drawing hands, especially when you hold a flush or straight draw with overcards to the board. You want to win if you spike a pair. Your pair is much more likely to win on the river if you force weak draws to fold on the flop.

For example, you have

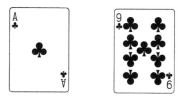

in middle position. Two players limp to you, and you limp. One player limps behind you, and the button raises. The big blind and all the limpers call (12.5 small bets). The flop is

giving you the nut flush draw and two overcards. The big blind checks, the first limper bets, and the second limper calls (14.5 small bets). You should raise.

Your raise is for value if two or more opponents call. With two overcards and a flush draw, you have fifteen outs to improve to top pair or a flush. Against two opponents you will win well over one-third of the time, so you make money on the extra bet when your opponents call.

Though you do not mind callers, since the pot is large you prefer that your opponents fold. If a nine comes on the turn, you will be glad that you thinned the field. With top pair you will often have the best hand. Your pair of nines will be very vulnerable, though. It is more likely to survive fifth street against a smaller field.

If an ace comes instead, you are less likely to be outdrawn on the river. But you are also less likely to have the best hand, especially if you had not thinned the field. Someone could hold a bigger ace (the preflop raiser could easily have one) or make aces up with ace-deuce or ace-four. You would like all of those hands to fold. For example, if your flop raise forces the preflop raiser with ace-king to fold, you will have "bought" two outs (the remaining aces). When the pot is large, invest an extra bet if it might buy a few more outs.

This concept is very important. Many players encourage their opponents to remain in the hand no matter the circumstances while they are still drawing. They figure that doing so maximizes their payoff if they make their hand. (They do not want to "lose any customers.") They are correct that *if they make the nut flush*, they would prefer many opponents. But they forget that they will often miss their flush, but improve to one or two pair. With such a hand you will win far more often with fewer opponents.

You should also sometimes raise when your draw is not as strong. Even if your raise is not for value, in a large pot improving your winning chances by just a few percent can make your raise profitable. For example, you have K♥Q♥ on the button. Three players limp, and you raise. Both blinds and the three limpers call (12 small bets). The flop is T♥9♣4♦ giving you two overcards, a gutshot draw to the nuts, and a backdoor flush draw. Everyone checks to the player on your right who bets (13 small bets). Again, you should raise. You have four outs to the nuts, six outs to top pair, and a backdoor flush draw. While a raise may not be for value, your three weak draws together give you a decent chance to improve to the best hand, especially if you can play heads-up. Since the pot is large, you should protect your overcard draw with a raise.

When you have a draw to a big hand (e.g., the nut straight or flush), the pot size determines how you should play it. If the pot is small, you should usually avoid eliminating players. You get more value from players paying you off with second-best hands than from winning what is already in the pot. In a large pot improving your chance to win is more valuable. *Protect vulnerable outs in large pots.*

# When a Raise Will Not Protect Your Hand

Sometimes, a flop raise will not protect your hand. When these situations occur, you should often just call on the flop. If the turn card is safe, you plan to protect your hand then with a bet or raise. This is especially true when the pot is large, *and* a lot of fourth street cards might cripple your hand. For example, you have

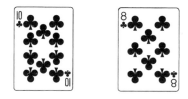

in the big blind. Two people limp, and someone in middle position raises. The button cold-calls, the small blind folds, and you call. The limpers call (10.5 small bets). The flop is

giving you bottom two pair. You check, and it is checked to the raiser, who bets. The button calls (12.5 small bets). You should just call.

A big, coordinated flop like this will give many players a draw. If you raise now, one or both limpers will often call anyway, and it will still be four or five players to the turn. Furthermore, your hand is only marginally strong, as a queen, jack, or nine cripples you, and any heart could also beat you. An ace or king is bad as well, as it might give the preflop raiser a bigger two pair or a pair and a straight draw.

The best plan is to call now, hoping for a safe card. If fourth street is a blank, plan to check-raise then. If fourth street ruins your hand, you should usually check and fold (though sometimes you should call depending on the specific card, the action, and the pot size). Either way, you are better off having just called on the flop: When a safe card comes, your opponents will not expect you to check-raise since you have yet to show aggression, and if you must check and fold, you will have lost less. With a very vulnerable hand that will often be ruined on the turn, and that you cannot easily protect, you should frequently wait to raise. There are two other common scenarios where a flop raise will not protect your hand. You should often wait for the turn in these situations as well:

1.  When the flop bet comes from your left.
2.  When the pot is extremely large.

# When the Flop Bet Comes From Your Left

Say you have

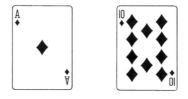

on the button. Two players limp, and you raise. Both blinds and limpers call (10 small bets). The flop is

The small blind bets. The big blind folds, but both limpers call (13 small bets). The pot is large, and your hand is vulnerable. You would like to protect your hand. But if you raise, there will be fifteen bets in the pot, and it will be one bet back to your opponents. Getting 15-to-1, all three of your opponents are almost certainly correct to call, no matter what they hold. Any straight draw, overcard, flopped pair, or flush draw can call the bet profitably.

Even if the small blind makes it three bets, you are still in trouble. Now the limpers must call two bets, but the pot will contain seventeen bets. Getting 8.5-to-1, the limpers are still correct to call with many weak draws. And if the small blind has a good enough hand to reraise, you may be far behind.

Since a raise will do nothing to protect your only moderately strong hand, you should just call. If the turn card is bad (e.g., an overcard to your pair, a straight card, or a spade), you may have to play the rest of the hand cautiously. If it is safe, consider raising on the turn. Your hand is more likely to survive with only one card to come, and the double-sized turn bet makes a raise far more effective.

# When the Pot is Extremely Large

Say you have

in middle position. Two players limp, and the player to your right raises. You reraise. The button cold-calls three bets, the blinds fold, and the two limpers call two more bets. Now the player to your right makes it four bets, which is a cap. Everyone calls (21.5 small bets). The flop is

It is checked to the preflop capper who bets. You raise. Everyone calls (15.5 big bets). The turn is the 2♠. Your opponents check, and you bet. Everyone calls (20.5 big bets). The river is the 8♠. Your opponents check again. Despite the scary river card, you bet because your opponents are likely to call with almost anything in this huge pot. The button raises. Everyone folds to you, and you call. The button shows

for the rivered gutshot.

This sort of hand frustrates many small stakes players. They correctly build a big pot before the flop with their premium hand. They raise the flop and bet the turn, only to lose on the river to one of several opponents chasing longshot draws. What they do not understand is that it is their poor postflop play, not their opponents' looseness, that costs them the pot.

After his atrocious preflop call, the player with jack-seven played his hand correctly. On the flop, the pot size was 24.5 bets when the action got to him, and it was two bets to call. He held a gutshot, which is about 11-to-1 to come on the turn. He was getting over 12-to-1, so he correctly called. On fourth street, the pot was 16.5 big bets when the action got to him. He still had an 11-to-1 chance to make his straight, and he was getting 16.5-to-1, so his call was again correct. The point is that the player with kings lost because he failed to protect his hand.

He went wrong when he raised the flop. The flop raise put 24.5 bets in the pot. It was two bets to call, so his opponents were getting over 12-to-1 to call. Offering 12-to-1 does not protect a hand against weak draws. In fact, there was essentially no way to protect his hand on the flop. No matter what he did, anyone with any reasonable chance to draw out on him would correctly call and see the turn.[62]

---

[62] Someone with a lone backdoor flush or straight draw could be an exception. He might be correct to call for one bet, but not two.

His best chance to protect his hand was on the turn. If he had faced the field with having to call two big bets cold on fourth street, he could have cut down the odds enough to make calling with weak draws like gutshots wrong.

Assume he just calls on the flop. Everyone else calls, so the pot is thirteen big bets. On the turn everyone checks to the flop bettor, who bets again. The player with kings raises. Now there are sixteen big bets in the pot, but the players behind him must call two bets to continue. The button is getting only 8-to-1 to call with his gutshot (plus he must worry about a reraise that would further cut his odds), which is still over a 10-to-1 underdog. A flop call and turn raise protected the pocket kings where a flop raise and turn bet did not.

Furthermore, this raise on the turn will often get hands like bottom and middle pair to fold. If players with these hands knew that the raiser had only a pair of kings (as opposed to a bigger hand like a set), getting 8-to-1, they would be correct to call even two big bets cold for their five outs. So not only does waiting for the turn to raise protect against people who should call one bet but not two, but it also sometimes induces folds from people with hands strong enough to call the raise.

By raising the flop you induce the flop bettor to check to you on the turn. When the pot is already so big, protecting your hand on the turn is more important than raising for value on the flop. *If the pot is extremely large, forgo a flop raise if doing so increases the chance you will be bet into on the turn.*[63]

---

[63] Some people disagree with this advice to wait for the turn to raise in huge pots. They argue that the kings have an edge in pot equity, and therefore raising the flop is profitable. They are correct; the kings make money on every additional flop raise. But we argue that, while raising the flop is profitable, waiting for the turn is *more* profitable. Sometimes you should forgo a small edge on the flop if doing so allows you to exploit a bigger edge on the turn. Raising the turn is *hugely profitable* in this hand, more so than getting only a single bet in. You should risk that

# Final Thoughts

When the pot is large, focus on winning it. Do not try to save bets with marginal hands. Do not play passively with strong hands and draws to "keep your customers." Develop a plan to protect your hand. If you are in early position, do you expect a player in late position to bet? If so, consider a check-raise. Is the pot on the flop so large that you expect no one to fold, even for a raise? If so, consider waiting for the turn. Force opponents with weak draws into lose-lose situations. When your opponents lose, you win.

---

immediate flop profit to maximize your chance to raise successfully on fourth street. (Even if you fail to get players to fold, waiting until the turn to raise will usually mean a bigger pot when you win it.)

# Raising for a Free Card

Poker players have a tendency to check to someone who raised on the previous round. If someone raises before the flop, some players will check no matter what comes on the flop. Instead of betting, they will check and call with top pair or an even better hand. Fearing the strength shown by the raiser, they instinctively check.

This effect is even stronger on the later betting rounds. Hand values change a lot between the first two cards and the flop. Many players recognize this and resist the urge to check to the preflop raiser. On later rounds, however, this tendency is pronounced. With only one new card, hand values change relatively little on fourth street. The person who is ahead on the flop will usually be the favorite on the turn as well. Players react to this fact by checking to the person who showed the most strength on the flop.

Even when someone improves on fourth street, he often does not bet. He anticipates that the flop aggressor will bet, so he checks, hoping to trap the bettor and anyone caught in between for two bets.[64]

You can exploit this tendency to check to the raiser. Say you are in late position with a drawing hand. You plan to call a bet on

---

[64] As a corollary, many players who bet unexpectedly on fourth street do not have what they represent. Say two players limp, the button raises, and both limpers call. The flop is J♦7♥4♠. Both limpers check to the raiser who bets. Only one limper calls. The turn is the 4♥. The limper bets. He probably does not have a four. If he had a four, his natural instinct would be to attempt a check-raise with his unlikely hand. He probably holds just two small pair or a draw. He may have a hand like T♥9♥, picking up a flush draw on fourth street. He is hoping that the preflop raiser has overcards and will fold fearing that he is drawing dead to trips. If the preflop raiser holds a big two pair like ace-jack or pocket queens, he should probably raise.

the flop and then another on the turn. Your total cost to see both cards is three small bets, one on the flop and two on the turn (because the bet size doubles).

But now instead of calling on the flop, you raise. The flop bettor will likely call and check to you on the turn. You can check behind if you miss and see the river card for free. This sequence costs only two small bets to see both cards.

Say you have

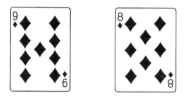

on the button. Three players limp, and so do you. The small blind calls, and the big blind checks (6 small bets). The flop is

giving you an open-ended straight draw. Both blinds check. The first limper bets, and both other limpers call (9 small bets). You should probably raise. If no one reraises, your opponents will likely check to you on the turn. You can check behind if you miss. This raise also has other value since you will be getting 3-to-1 (you have three opponents) on your raise, and you are only a little worse than 2-to-1 to make your hand.

# When to Use the Free Card Play

The free card play is most effective in passive games. The premise of the play is that your opponents will behave in a predictable and *passive* way if you raise the flop. The more likely your opponents are to just call your raise and to check to you on the turn, the more frequently you should attempt a free card play.

For instance, if you could be totally certain that your free card play would succeed (your opponents will *always* just call your flop raise and check the turn), you should raise virtually every time you have a draw that you would call with. If your draw is worth seeing one card for one small bet, it is almost always worth seeing two cards for two small bets.[65]

As the game gets more aggressive, you should become more selective with your free card attempts. When you raise for a free card, you risk being reraised, or called, and then bet into on the turn. With strong draws like flush draws and quality open-ended straight draws, this prospect should not concern you. Since these draws come in so often, you can often raise them for value; getting a free card on the turn is just a bonus. But when you hold a weak draw like bottom pair or a gutshot, you cannot raise with impunity. You must weigh the chance that your play will succeed against the chance that it will backfire. Paying three bets to see the turn when you could have paid only one is expensive. Even paying two bets on the flop is bad if someone calls, but bets into you on the turn.

Against passive players feel free to try free card plays with these weak draws. Your opponents will check the turn often

---

[65] There is a minor exception that involves hands with backdoor draws. With these hands you can be drawing live on the flop, but drawing dead on the turn most of the time (when you do not pick up your draw). For a backdoor draw, seeing fourth street is more valuable than seeing fifth street, so with a weak enough hand, you might want to see the turn for one bet, but not the turn and river for two bets.

enough to compensate for the rare times that someone flops a big hand and plays aggressively. However, when your opponents are aggressive, stop trying for free cards with your weak draws. It will fail too often and end up being less profitable than just calling.

For example, you have

on the button. One player limps. You raise. Both blinds and the limper call (8 small bets). The flop is

The small blind bets. The big blind folds, and the limper calls (10 small bets). You should raise if the initial bettor is passive, but call if he is aggressive. Your backdoor flush and straight draws and two overcards give you just enough hand to take one off. You will have to fold on the turn if you do not improve, and someone bets. If you are almost certain that a free card play will work, you should try it. A free card could win you the pot if the river is a queen or jack.

Against aggressive players you should just call. It is too likely that the flop bettor will reraise and bet the turn. You have the opportunity to call profitably and close the action. Take it.

If the flop were 9♠7♥3♥ (two hearts instead of one), you should certainly raise, even against aggressive players. A flush draw and overcards is a strong draw. You should no longer lament a reraise; your hand will improve to top pair or better over fifty percent of the time.[66]

In fact, if the reraiser is an aggressive player, you should probably make it four bets (especially if that is the cap). An aggressive reraiser could have as little as a pair or a straight draw. Your hand is very strong against those holdings. Your four-bet might cause your opponent to check the turn, allowing you again to take a free card if you miss.

To clarify, when your draw is *weak*, you prefer that the bettor be passive. When you have a very *strong* draw, though, you do not much care. In fact, an aggressive bettor is often actually better. Strong draws make money with each flop raise; you would like to be playing with someone who will often help you cap the betting. But if a passive player puts in three or four bets, he will often have a set (the one hand you fear with strong draws). An aggressive player has a much broader range of four-betting hands.

The more passive your opponents, the weaker your draw can be to try a free card raise. Against aggressive players try the free card play only if your draw is strong enough that you do not mind a reraise much.

# Hand Reading and the Free Card Play

One drawback to the free card play is that, when successful, it can give your hand away. Specifically, suppose you raise the flop, but then check the turn. If the flop contained a two-flush, it will be obvious to your observant opponents that you are likely to have a flush draw. If they are also on a draw, they may bet as a bluff if the river is a blank.

---

[66] You have six outs to top pair and nine to a flush — fifteen outs, twice, to improve. Also, you will occasionally improve to a straight.

For example, suppose you have

on the button. Two players limp, and you limp. The small blind folds, and the big blind checks (4.5 small bets). The flop is

The big blind bets, and both limpers fold. You raise, and he calls (4 big bets). The turn is the 8♠. He checks, and you take a free card (4 big bets). The river is the 8♦ (or any blank). If your opponent has a smaller flush draw, for instance Q♥J♥, he will probably bet as a bluff. You will fold, and he will steal the pot.

If you had instead just called on the flop and perhaps also called a bet on fourth street (assuming that he continued his bluff), he would probably have given up by the river. If he checks the river, you can check as well and win with king-high.

So if your opponent is an observant, thinking player, use the free card play with caution. Checking the turn exposes weakness and may allow someone to bet you off the best hand.[67]

Sometimes "giving your hand away" with a free card play can work to your benefit. This happens when you hold a draw that is

---

[67] This concept applies mostly to heads-up and three-handed situations. In a multiway pot you are very unlikely to have the best hand with ace- or king-high.

not the most obvious one (that being usually a flush draw). If the river completes the obvious draw, even though your draw missed, you can often steal the pot by representing the completed hand.

For instance, you have 9♦8♦ on the button. Three players limp, and you limp. The small blind calls, and the big blind checks (6 small bets). The flop is T♥7♥4♣ giving you an open-ended straight draw (but with two hearts on board). The small blind checks, the big blind bets, and one limper calls. You raise. The small blind folds, and the big blind and limper call (6 big bets). The turn is the 2♦. Your opponents check, and you take a free card (6 big bets). If your opponents understand the free card play and are trying to read your hand, they will probably think that you hold two hearts, not nine-eight. So if the river is the K♥, and your opponents check, you can often steal the pot with a bet.

This section assumes that your opponents are observant, competent players. If your opponents are loose, unobservant, illogical, or ignorant, none of this applies. They are not trying to read your hand, so you should not adjust your play based on what they might think you have. These ideas will be too advanced to use against the majority of small stakes players. Of course, you should be delighted if your opponents do not read hands. You can use the free card play again and again, and they may never catch on.

# Turning Down the Free Card

You should not always take a free card on fourth street despite making a free card play. Obviously, if you make your hand on the turn, you should bet. But sometimes you should bet even when you miss.

If you think there is some chance all your opponents will fold, you should consider betting. For instance, say you have

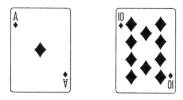

on the button. Three loose players limp, and you raise. Both blinds and all the limpers call (12 small bets). The flop is

It is checked to you, and you bet. Only two players call (7.5 big bets). The turn is the 2♠. If they check to you, you should probably bet again.[68]

Your opponents could easily be calling without a pair. Many small stakes players would call with hands like Q♥9♠ or K♣7♣. Some very loose players would call this ragged flop with literally any two cards. They hope pairing on the turn will be enough to win. Since this is a large pot, you should not give them a free card on fourth street.

---

[68] This example differs somewhat from the previous examples because you did not raise the flop; you merely bet after it was checked to you. While not technically "raising for a free card," this bet often has the same effect. It will induce your opponents to check to you on fourth street far more often than they would have had you checked the flop. Also, you can obviously expect your opponents' hands to be weaker on average when they all check than when someone bets.

Sometimes one of your opponents will have slowplayed a trey and will check-raise you on fourth street. Aggressive play causes many slowplay traps. Do not be embarrassed if you are fooled; continue to bet aggressively on future hands. When you fall for a slowplay, you lose an extra bet or two. When your opponents with weak hands all fold, you sometimes win a pot that you would have lost had you checked. In the long run it is much better to win more pots, even if it means being occasionally trapped for an extra bet.

In small stakes games you will often find weak opponents willing to call on the flop with almost nothing. *Against these players tend to bet your strong draws again on the turn instead of taking a free card.*

# The Cheap Showdown

Some players adapt the free card play as a method to obtain a "cheap showdown." They raise the flop with a pair. Then, if their opponents all check, they check behind on fourth street. They plan, if given the opportunity, to check again on fifth street. They are unsure whether they have the best hand, so they try to show their hand down cheaply. In a small stakes game employing this tactic is usually incorrect. If you raise the flop with a made hand, you should tend to bet on fourth street. To understand why, we must examine how a turn check affects the river action.

For example, you have

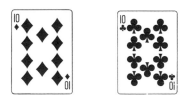

on the button. Two players limp, and you raise. The big blind and the limpers call (8.5 small bets). The flop is

It is checked to the second limper who bets (9.5 small bets).

You cannot be confident you have the best hand. The bettor could have a queen. The big blind or the first limper could also have a queen or better and be checking to the raiser. Conversely, the bettor could have a smaller pair or a flush or straight draw. There are over nine bets in the pot, so you would rather not fold; you may have the best hand. If the pot were smaller, you might consider folding. But since this is a raised pot, you probably should continue, unless the bettor would never bet a draw.

Since you have chosen not to fold, you should raise to protect your hand.[69] You should not allow a cheap card to the players who checked. So you raise. The big blind and first limper fold. The bettor calls. The turn is the 2♠. Your opponent checks.

If you check behind, your opponent will often bet on fifth street. He will usually have you beaten when he bets, but you should call anyway. Your show of weakness on fourth street may have induced a bluff. If you check behind on the turn, you lose one bet on the river when beaten.

If your opponent has a queen with a weak kicker, he has you beaten, but he probably does not like his hand either. If you bet the turn, he will probably call, not raise.[70] If he does not improve on

---

[69] See the section, "Protecting Your Hand."

[70] If your opponent is weak-tight, he may even fold a queen if his kicker is poor. Naturally, it is a coup to induce your opponent to fold a better

the river, he will typically check. You can show your hand down for free. When your opponent has a weak queen (his most likely hand if he has you beaten), you lose the same amount whether you check the turn and call his river bet or bet the turn and check the river.[71]

If however you have your opponent beaten, you are much better off betting the turn. Betting protects your hand; you do not give a free card to a hand like bottom or middle pair (5 outs) or overcards to your tens (6 outs). If you are behind, as long as you do not get check-raised, it does not matter whether you bet the turn.[72] If you are ahead, betting is important. Therefore, you should usually bet.

This is especially true if your opponent is a passive and predictable player. Passive players are unlikely to check-raise and virtually never do so as a bluff. When they do, it signifies a strong hand. You can fold your tens if check-raised by a predictable player. You are likely drawing to at most two outs. If your opponent is tricky and might check-raise you as a bluff, you need to be more careful about betting. You probably still should fold if he check-raises, but now, in addition to losing your chance to spike a set, you occasionally forfeit the whole pot to a bluff. This

---

hand. But do not expect this to happen often.

[71] Of course, you do not have to check behind on the river. Against players who play too many hands and automatically pay off with very weak hands, it may be better to bet your hand for value. See the section "Betting for Value on the River."

[72] The only time it matters is when you are check-raised *and* a ten would have come on the river *and* catching that ten would win the pot. This parlay occurs only rarely.

is true for all situations in poker: You should bet less often when you do not know how to handle getting raised.[73]

A similar situation arises when you have top pair with a weak kicker. Say you have A♥6♥ on the button. Two players limp. You limp. The small blind calls, and the big blind checks (5 small bets). The flop is A♣7♠5♥. It is checked to the player on your right who bets. You raise. The blinds and first limper fold. The bettor calls (4.5 big bets). The turn is the 2♠. Your opponent checks. What should you do?

This decision is actually quite different from the one in the tens hand. In fact, all the differences make betting less attractive. In a medium stakes game, where opponents tend to be trickier, you actually probably should check. Against the predictable opponents common in small stakes games, though, it is better to bet.

There are three important differences in this example:
1. No overcards can come to beat aces
2. If you are behind, you usually have more than two outs
3. The pot is smaller

Overcards could come to your previous pair of tens, giving your opponent a bigger pair. Since no overcards can beat aces, it is not as worrisome to give a free card. The river card is less likely to beat you.

If you are behind, you usually have more than two outs. You typically have at least three outs (3 sixes). You have six outs to beat ace-five (3 sevens and 3 sixes). You have eight outs to beat

---

[73] Another reason to check against tricky players is that they are more likely to bet the river as a bluff if you check behind on the turn. With a hopeless hand in a small pot, they might just check and fold the turn if you bet. But when you check, you will sometimes trick them into bluffing the river, and you can call, snapping them off and winning an extra bet. Again, use this play only in a small pot and only against *tricky, thinking* opponents.

seven-five (2 aces, 3 sixes, and 3 deuces). Being check-raised is more devastating when you have more outs. With only two outs you can just fold. With more you may have to call. Even if you do not call, you will wish you had taken a free card.

The pot is smaller. It is over six big bets in the tens hand, but only four and a half in this one. The smaller the pot, the less you need to protect your hand. Losing to a free card is a catastrophe in a big pot, but a mere unpleasantry in a small one.

If you think your opponent may be sandbagging, you should check (and call on the river). The disadvantages of being check-raised outweigh the advantages of betting. But if you do not fear a check-raise, bet. If you are ahead, betting protects your hand and gives your opponent the opportunity to make a weak call. If you are behind, it sets up a free showdown.

This section is complex because the decision whether to bet weak made hands again on the turn can be delicate. You must consider a large number of factors including the nature of your opponent, the size of the pot, the texture of the board, the number of outs you may have if you are behind, and the number of outs your opponent may have if you are ahead. Against good opponents this decision can be one of the toughest in limit hold 'em.

When your opponents play poorly, however, this decision is much simpler. A large percentage of your profit in small stakes games comes from opponents who call down with weak hands in small pots. If you habitually check the turn with medium-strength hands because you fear the worst, you miss out on these opportunities. Treat good players with respect, but value bet relentlessly against calling stations. If your opponent usually has a weak hand, he probably has one this time as well. He is not trying to outwit you; he is just hoping to get lucky. Against loose, weak opponents, *unless you have a specific reason not to, bet your medium-strength hands again on the turn.*

# Final Thoughts

The free card play punishes passivity. Timid opponents back down too quickly with top pair or other good hands. Raising with position exploits this mistake, allowing you to get the best of it on the turn. Against aggressive players this move is prone to backfire, especially when your draw is weak. But make liberal use of the free card play against passive opponents.

# Slowplaying

Slowplaying is playing a strong hand weakly, checking or calling instead of betting or raising, to deceive opponents. When successful, it has two effects:

1.  Players use the cheap cards you give to improve their hand to a better, *but still second-best*, hand. You hope to induce action on a later street from a worse hand that *would have folded* had you bet earlier.

2.  Opponents, suspecting a bluff, call your later bets with weaker hands than usual.

Slowplaying is a useful tool in small pots against players who play well after the flop. By design, it fails to protect your hand. (Thus you should almost never risk large pots by slowplaying.) It also helps you most against opponents who fold when they should. If your opponents are likely to call anyway, slowplaying just causes you to miss bets.

Many of your opponents habitually slowplay whenever they flop a strong hand: two pair, trips, a set, or a pat hand. They are usually wrong to do so. When the pot is large, many hands they slowplay are vulnerable. They give cheap cards in multiway pots when they should protect their hand.

Furthermore, even when their hand is strong enough to slowplay, they typically would get more action by betting. The same player who whines, "How can you call with that?" when a loose player hits a miracle draw walks on eggshells as soon as he flops a monster. "I didn't want to lose any customers. If I had bet, they all would have folded," he says, dragging a tiny pot with flopped quads.

Small stakes games feature players who go too far with their hands. These players do not know if you flop a monster; they call then just as they do when your hand is vulnerable. Do not miss flop and turn bets against these loose players. They will call you; that's what they always do!

In spite of the above, even against loose opponents, slowplaying is occasionally correct. If you have a very strong hand, the pot is small, and the player on your right bets, you should sometimes just call. If you raise, even very loose players will fold weak hands. For example, you have

in the big blind. Four players limp, the small blind calls, and you check (6 small bets). The flop is

The small blind checks, you check, and everyone else checks (3 big bets). The turn is the 2♠. The small blind bets. You should just call.

You have a set, and no flush draw is possible. You are way ahead; most of your opponents are drawing dead. The pot is small. If you raise, almost all of the players behind you are sure to fold. The bettor might even fold; he could be bluffing. If you just call, a suspicious player might assume the bettor does not have much and call with as little as a small pair or ace-high. If you are lucky, a weaker hand will raise, allowing you to reraise. The pot is small, and your hand is almost unbeatable. Allow people to make loose calls.

# Final Thoughts

You should not slowplay often. Slowplaying is a deceptive tool used to induce extra action from tight players. In small stakes games you usually do not need to give your opponents incentive to call. Your opponents' loose tendencies naturally build big pots for your best hands.

Against loose opponents you should almost never slowplay from late position by checking instead of betting.[74] They are willing to call single bets with many hands, so do not worry about everyone folding. Even if you flop quads, bet and hope they call. (Sometimes you should slowplay by calling instead of raising, though.) Before you slowplay, ask yourself three questions:

1.  If I give my opponents a cheap card, will it improve them only to a *second-best* hand or *unprofitable* draw, or will they sometimes beat me or catch a profitable draw? (Again, a draw is profitable only if its implied odds are greater than its odds of being completed.)

2.  Am I willing to risk losing the pot occasionally for a chance to win an extra bet or two?

3.  How likely are my opponents to call if I don't slowplay?

If a cheap card is not likely to beat you or give your opponents profitable draws, if the pot is small enough to risk losing, and if

---

[74] You may check from early position if you are going for a check-raise. But in late position, bet your strong hands.

your opponents will *fold* if you bet or raise, but might not if you don't, consider slowplaying.

# Two Overpair Hands

*This is a very difficult, but critical, section. Putting forth the effort to understand the concept presented here will improve your play significantly.*

Normally, if you determine that you have an edge, you should exploit it by betting or raising. The larger your edge, the more important it is to push. When your edge is small, however, you do not lose much if you pass on it. While you should not pass up small edges for no reason at all, consider passing on a small edge if doing so might allow you to better exploit a much larger edge later in the hand.[75]

Suppose your game is very loose. Your opponents all play in a similar way: before the flop, they play more than half of their hands (perhaps anything suited, any pocket pair, any two big offsuit cards, and any two connected offsuit cards). After the flop, they bet and raise with top pair or better or a good draw (and also sometimes some weaker hands if they feel lucky), otherwise they usually call. They will fold if they have no hand at all, or if it is painfully clear that they are terribly beaten. Typically, six or seven players see the flop, four or five see the turn, and three or four see the river.

---

[75] Many poker players routinely pass up small edges simply because they fear losing. This is *not* the way experts play and not what we are talking about here.

**185**

You are on the button with

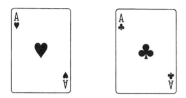

Four players limp, and you raise. The big blind and limpers call (12.5 small bets). The flop is

giving you an overpair and the backdoor nut flush draw. The big blind bets, and the first limper raises. Two of the three remaining limpers call (19.5 small bets). You should reraise.

You have four remaining opponents. No matter what you do, you probably cannot induce any of your opponents to fold; having already put money in on the flop, they will almost always call any future bets to see the turn card. If you just call, the likely turn bettor is on your left, so you will not be able to raise to face your opponents with calling two cold on fourth street. There is no good way to protect your hand.

Since you cannot protect your hand, you should push your edge with a value raise. You probably have the best hand; your betting and raising opponents could have you beaten, but they are much more likely to have flush or straight draws or top pair. Since they play so loosely, the callers could have anything: king-queen, jack-eight, trey-deuce, ace-four, or any number of other hands.

Not only do you probably have the best hand, but your pot equity is also quite high. You can probably expect to win this pot around fifty percent of the time.[76] With four opponents, you need only have twenty percent pot equity to make a raise profitable. With fifty percent, you have a huge edge. Build a big pot and hope your hand holds up.

Now, suppose you have the same preflop action and flop, but your hand is

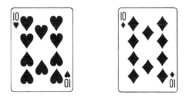

instead. Again the big blind bets, the first limper raises, and two of the three remaining limpers call (19.5 small bets). You should just call!

You are almost as likely to have the best hand with tens as you are with aces. It is unlikely, given the action, that one of your opponents has kings, queens, or jacks. But having the best hand does not necessarily mean you should raise. With the tens, your pot equity is much smaller: Any of four overcards can beat you, and, because you do not have the T♣, you are more vulnerable to the flush. Your opponents could collectively have as many as ten

---

[76] Fifty percent is obviously just an estimate. To see that it is reasonable, imagine a typical set of hands for your opponents. Perhaps they have a flush draw, top pair, a gutshot, and two overcards respectively. The flush draw has eight outs (you have the A♣, removing one out and giving you a potential redraw), top pair has four (one of his outs overlaps with the flush draw), the gutshot has three (again, one overlaps), and the overcards are drawing nearly dead. They have about fifteen outs collectively against you. A fifteen out draw comes in slightly more often than fifty percent of the time, so you dodge the draw a little less often than fifty percent. Add the four percent of the time that you catch your backdoor flush, and you will win about fifty percent of the time.

more outs to beat tens than they had to beat aces. These extra outs drive your pot equity down to around 25 percent.[77]

Even with 25 percent pot equity, you have an edge against four opponents (since 25 percent is better than 20 percent). The edge is relatively small, though. A value raise has a positive expectation, but not by much. When you have only a small edge on the flop, you should consider another option — waiting for the turn.

With the tens, no matter what comes on the turn, your pot equity will change drastically. If a bad card comes (e.g., the A♥), and an opponent outdraws you, you will likely be drawing nearly dead (giving you a pot equity near zero). If a good card comes, your pot equity will jump to fifty percent, giving you a big edge on all turn bets. Your opponents now have only the river with which to outdraw you, and at least half the deck is probably safe.

With the aces, the change is not nearly as drastic. If someone outdraws you by making two pair or a flush, you will still have seven or eight outs. With this redraw, you have a pot equity of fifteen or twenty percent. If a safe card comes, your pot equity increases, but only from fifty percent to around 65 percent.[78]

With the tens, the small edge on the flop combined with the large change in pot equity on fourth street makes waiting for the turn the better play. If you reraise the flop, your opponents will probably check to you on the turn. If you just call the flop, either the flop bettor or the flop raiser will probably bet the turn. When the turn card is favorable, you really want an opponent to bet so you can raise. Getting an extra double-sized bet from each opponent when your pot equity edge is large is *far* better than

---

[77] 25 percent represents having to dodge around half the deck, 23 outs, twice.

[78] The 15 out draw against you will come in 15/46 or around one-third of the time.

getting an extra single-sized bet when your pot equity edge is small. This play is a gamble. You are forgoing a raise with a small positive expectation, hoping to get one in later with a much larger expectation. Your opponents could decide to check on the turn even though you did not reraise the flop. Because you are risking a small amount of expectation to win a much larger amount, however, it need not succeed that often to be the better play.

With the aces the gamble is much riskier. Reraising the flop has a much higher positive expectation, and your edge on fourth street is not that much bigger than your edge on the flop. Since you are risking a larger amount to win a smaller amount, the play must succeed much more often to be correct. With aces, it is not worth the gamble; take the immediate payoff and reraise on the flop.

# Final Thoughts

Many players adopt a simple approach to postflop play. If they think they have the best hand, they raise whenever they get the chance. Frequently, this is the best strategy. It is not *always* the best strategy, however. Sometimes it is better to forgo pushing a small edge if doing so allows you to better exploit a bigger edge that might occur later. Specifically, you should sometimes wait for the turn to raise with a hand you think is probably best if the following criteria are met:

1.   Raising now has little chance to induce opponents to fold.

2.   Your hand is vulnerable, many cards (often up to half the deck) could beat you, and, thus, your edge is small.

3.   If a favorable card comes, your edge will be much bigger on the turn.

# Postflop Concepts

# Afterthought

Many small stakes players who take their games seriously get too bogged down in the minutia of starting hand strategy and neglect their play from the flop on. We see arguments like this on our Internet forums at www.twoplustwo.com all the time. If only these people would realize that small differences before the flop matter very little in their overall results and then concentrate on play from the flop on, their results would begin to improve.

But play on the later streets can be quite complex. As this section shows, it requires much strategic knowledge, good judgement of your opponents, and the courage to make plays that will usually cost an extra bet or two.

Perhaps that's why so many players concentrate only on the first two cards. It is a lot easier than playing well on the flop and the turn, and against the many terrible players who are present in the small stakes games, this fixation still does allow them to win a little.

But as we have already stated, this book is not aimed at those who just want to win a little. The information that it contains, plus some hard work on your part, should enable you to do much better.

So now let's move on to play on the river.

# Part Four
# River Play

# River Play

# Introduction

Many people seem to think that playing the river is straightforward. Some authors write whole books about hold 'em, but literally devote only two or three pages to this topic. Yet small stakes players make countless errors after all the cards are out, including the most costly error possible in limit hold 'em. This topic is so important that we will discuss it thoroughly.

Playing the river correctly is not easy. It can be tricky when you are heads-up, and it gets even more complicated when you have two or more opponents. And in small stakes games, you will often still have two or more opponents. In this section, we cover the most important principles for skillful river play.

# Betting for
# Value on the River

An aggressive player raises before the flop and is called by a loose, passive player in the big blind. The preflop raiser bets the flop, turn, and river when checked to, and the loose player calls all three bets. The bettor sheepishly turns over his unimproved ace-king, and the blind shows nine-trey for bottom pair. Then the aggressive player says, "They call with anything. How can you beat a guy who never folds?"

He is partially right. Many small stakes players play too many hands and go too far with them. They start with a weak holding, flop something like bottom pair, and call on the flop and turn, hoping to improve. Then, when they fail to improve, they call on the river (hoping that the bettor is bluffing).

But the aggressive player's conclusion is wrong! These players can easily be beaten. Yes, they can be frustrating at times, and they completely blunt one of your poker weapons, the bluff. But in defending themselves flawlessly against a bluff, they expose themselves to a different attack, because many hands that are too weak to bet for value against tighter opponents become much stronger against someone with low calling standards. You can exploit his bluff-catching strategy by *betting your marginal holdings for value on the river.*[79]

---

[79] This is even more true against opponents who are reluctant to raise without the nuts.

For example, you have

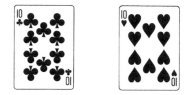

on the button. Three players limp, and you raise. The big blind and limpers call (10.5 small bets). The flop is

Your four opponents check, and you bet. The big blind and one other player call (6.5 big bets). The turn is the 2♣. They both check. You are worried about someone holding a king because your opponents are weak players who might not raise with top pair. You bet anyway, though, because the pot is large, and you must protect your hand (an ace, queen, or jack on the river could easily beat you). The big blind calls; the other player folds (8.5 big bets). The river is the 6♣. Your opponent checks again. If your weak opponent is also tight, you should check behind him. On the flop he could have a variety of hands with which he might call a bet. He might have a king that beats you, but he might also have two hearts, an eight, a four, or perhaps a hand like seven-six for a gutshot straight draw. On the turn, when he calls again after an innocuous deuce falls, his range of hands can be limited further. He now probably holds either two hearts or a king, as he would release his weaker holdings to the double-sized turn bet. Your weak-tight opponent will not call a river bet with a busted flush draw. So if you bet the river, and he calls, he will probably show you a king and take the pot. Since you will usually lose when your opponent calls, you should check. *Against a tight player you cannot bet your marginal hands for value on the river.*[80]

Now, let's assume your weak opponent is also loose, which is quite common at small stakes. Your thinking on the river should change. While you could narrow the tight player's holdings down considerably as the hand progressed, you will not be able to do so against the loose player. When he calls your bet on the turn, he could have a king, an eight, a four, a deuce, a pocket pair lower than your tens, a flush draw, a gutshot straight draw, ace-high, or even less. Now when a safe-looking card like the 6♣ comes on the river, and your opponent checks, you should bet. Since he will probably call you with any pair or even ace-high (typical of many calling stations), you will win an extra bet if he holds a deuce, four, six, eight, unimproved pocket pair, or ace. You will lose an extra bet if he holds a king, two pair, or better. It is much more likely that he holds one of the many hands that you beat than one of the relatively few hands that beat you. This value bet will show considerable profit in the long run.

As another example, you have K♥3♣ in the big blind and see the flop five-handed after four players call, including the small blind (5 small bets). Two of your opponents are clearly relatively new to casino hold 'em. Again, like many weak players, they play too many hands and go too far with them. They also do not raise often enough with stronger holdings like top pair or two pair. The flop is K♦8♥5♣. The small blind checks, and you bet. If you are raised, you plan to release your hand to a bet on fourth street if you do not improve. Only the two new players call (4 big bets). This is a great result for you since these two will call with almost anything, so it is likely that you hold the best hand. The turn is the

---

[80] Before the river, however, you should bet many of these hands to avoid giving a free card. For more on the conceptual difference between the last round of betting and the other rounds, see *The Theory of Poker* by David Sklansky.

6♥. You bet, and both players call (7 big bets). The river is the Q♣. You should bet your hand one more time against these loose opponents. Because you still have two opponents, there is a moderate chance that one either holds a king with a better kicker or has outdrawn you by making two pair. It is more likely, however, that your hand has survived the later streets and is still best. If you bet, you will often get called in one or both spots by worse hands. When this happens, you win an extra bet or two that you would have missed had you checked. Notice also that if you check and one of your opponents does have you beaten, he will likely bet, and you may lose a bet anyway (when you make a crying call).

Against predictable and passive opponents you should bet some very marginal hands when you are first to act. When you check, you allow your opponents to show down their weak hands, but bet their better hands. By betting, you lose the same amount when you are behind, but make more when you are ahead. Assuming they have shown no strength earlier in the hand, *if you plan to call a bet when you check, you should usually bet yourself against these players.*[81, 82]

---

[81] This is a very important concept. It is treated in greater detail beginning on p. 211 of *The Theory of Poker* by David Sklansky.

[82] This is not nearly as true against aggressive or tricky players, because you may have to pay off if they raise. Thus, you should probably check against them. Most of your small stakes opponents will not fit this description, though.

You should also check if your opponent will bet more hands than he will call with, that is, if he likes to bluff. You can exploit his overzealous bluffing by checking and calling with your marginal hands. This concept, an important one for medium and high stakes games, has been relegated to a footnote for this book. When they first learn this concept, many small stakes players begin checking far too many of their good hands on the river "to induce a bluff." In loose games with opponents willing pay off with so many weak hands, there are simply not

# Betting for Value
# when a Scare Card Comes

In the examples above, a relatively safe-looking card came on the river. Often, you will not be so lucky. When a scare card comes on the river, you will have to decide how likely it is that you have been outdrawn.[83] There are four major factors to consider when you make this decision:
1. How many opponents are left.
2. How many draws the card completes.
3. The likely range of hands your opponents might have.
4. How tight or loose your opponents are.

Obviously, the more opponents you have left, the greater the chances that a scare card will beat you. Say you are under the gun and hold top pair on the turn. You bet and are called by one loose opponent. If a card comes on the river that completes a possible flush, you should usually bet anyway. Sometimes your opponent will have a flush and raise. More often, he will have been calling with a weaker pair and pay off.

If instead three opponents call your turn bet, you should probably check the same river card. It is now much more likely that you have been outdrawn. Checking may save you a bet, as it might get bet and raised, allowing you to throw your hand away.

---

many situations where you should prefer to check instead of betting for value. So, while you should be aware that theoretically there are spots where you should check, in general you should bet your marginal hands for value. You can read more about these ideas on p.209 of *The Theory of Poker* by David Sklansky.

[83] A "scare card" is a card that may have helped your opponent outdraw you. If you hold an overpair to the board, then a card bigger than your pair, a card that puts three of a suit on board, or a card that pairs the board are all scare cards.

Some fifth street cards are more worrisome than others. Say you hold top pair or an overpair on the turn, bet, and are called in one or two spots. If the river is an overcard to your pair but does not complete a straight or a flush (e.g., you hold Q♦J♦, the board on the turn is J♠8♠4♦2♥, and the river card is the K♦), you should assume that you still have the best hand and bet. Except that if the overcard is an ace, you should be somewhat more concerned, as many players will automatically call to the river with ace-rag when they pair their kicker on the flop. Also, some extremely poor players will call to the river with any ace, hoping just to spike that one pair.[84]

In the same situation, if the overcard to your pair also completes a straight and a flush (e.g., you hold A♠9♠, the board on the turn is 9♥8♥4♣2♠, and the river card is the Q♥, completing both a potential heart flush and straight with jack-ten) then you should probably check. This card is much more dangerous because it opens three ways to beat you instead of one. It is especially bad because someone with queen-jack or queen-ten will likely call bets to the river looking to complete his gutshot or spike a pair.

If the river card is even worse, putting four to a straight or four to a flush (or both) on the board, you should usually refrain from betting for value unless, of course, you hold the straight or flush. An exception to this rule arises when you can narrow your opponents' holdings down to only those that cannot have improved to beat you on the river. For instance, you have

---

[84] There are two other reasons to check to an ace. You might induce a bluff. That is, your opponent might sense weakness when you check and try to bet you off your hand. Of course, you should always call this bet. Also, if you bet, an observant player might raise as a bluff, guessing that the ace is a scare card for you. Against opponents who have the potential to bluff-raise, you must play more cautiously. Fortunately, in small stakes games this is rare.

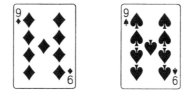

under the gun and limp. Three players limp behind you, the small blind folds, and the big blind checks (5.5 small bets). The flop is

giving you the best possible hand, a set of nines. The big blind checks, and you bet. Two players call, and the button raises. The big blind folds, and you reraise. The flop callers now fold, and the button raises again. You call, planning a check-raise on the turn (7.5 big bets).[85]

The turn is the 7♥. You check, your opponent bets, and you raise. Your opponent calls (11.5 big bets). The river is the 8♥. Normally, this would be a very scary card, as it makes a heart flush possible as well as puts four to a straight on board. Nevertheless, you can bet with virtual certainty that you hold the best hand. Your opponent's aggression on the flop indicated that he already held a strong hand. Most likely, your opponent flopped a smaller set or two pair. It is also possible that your opponent overplayed an open-ended straight draw, eight-seven, or even just top pair, ace-nine. But no matter what he has, he cannot have a ten

---

[85] Betting the turn would be okay here too.

or a five (unless he has the relatively unlikely pocket tens),[86] as any hand containing those cards would be far too weak to play so strongly on the flop. Likewise, he cannot have a heart flush unless he has specifically 6♥2♥. Therefore, despite the threatening board, you have a profitable bet.

Finally, you should be more willing to bet for value despite a scary card if your remaining opponents are very loose. As mentioned before, loose opponents can have a wide range of holdings, so the chance that they hold the one particular draw that was completed is small. Tight opponents are much more likely to hold the draw, especially if it was the only obvious draw available.

# Final Thoughts

There are three other factors that should make you more apt to bet the river for value. You should do it more against players who rarely try to check-raise on the river when they have a good hand. They bet those hands, perhaps feeling check-raising is impolite. Then their check is a sure sign of weakness.

You should do it more against opponents who would never bluff-raise than against those who might. For example, you are last to act against one opponent and hold what you think is the best hand on the turn. The river is a scare card that completes one or two draws. Your opponent checks. You should be more willing to bet if you think there is no chance your opponent would check-raise you as a bluff. If you can safely fold to a check-raise, you are always risking one bet to win one. If you are not sure how to proceed against a check-raise because your opponent is tricky, sometimes you will lose two bets in an attempt to win one (or fold the best hand, a huge mistake). You need a stronger hand to risk that extra bet.

---

[86] Many players would have raised with pocket tens before the flop, making that hand even less likely.

You should also bet marginal hands for value more when the pot is extraordinarily large. When the pot gets very big, your opponents will lower their standards for calling on the river. They might call you with ace-high after they miss their nut flush draw. They will look at the large pot, worry that you might be bluffing, and make a crying call. If the pot were smaller, they would throw those hands away.[87]

Betting more often in a large pot is contrary to how most players handle this situation. They actually bet less, sometimes reasoning that the pot is "big enough" or that they are "just happy to win what is out there." Do not be fooled by this logic; there is no point at which a pot is "big enough." A bet is either profitable or it is not. When the pot gets large, value betting on the river becomes more profitable, so do not miss the extra opportunities.

Many small stakes players constantly miss value bets. When they think they have the best hand, they bet the flop and turn. Then they often check the river and hope to win the pot. If you learn to bet the river aggressively in spots where your opponents do not, you will gain a significant edge over the competition.

---

[87] There is a caveat, however. When the pot is very large, it generally means that at least one of your opponents also holds a good hand. If someone put in several raises previously in the hand, you should make sure your hand compares favorably to the range of hands he might have before you bet.

# Playing the River
# When the Pot Is Big

The worst poker players display common characteristics: They play far too many hands, they do not fold enough after the flop, and they miss bets and raises with their marginal and strong hands. Studious players watch these calling stations and resolve to avoid their mistakes. They often decide to "fold when they are beaten."

While expert play requires that you often fold, some players, in their zeal to avoid the mistakes of their weak opponents, fold too much. They concentrate on making "good laydowns." They say things like, "Fit or fold," and, "A bet saved is the same as a bet won."

These ideas are not always bad. For many players this mindset may be useful *when the pot is small*. Unfortunately, the self-righteous folder often does not draw the size-based distinction. In small pots, making a good, early fold (especially before the flop) may save you a couple of bets. A bad (i.e., incorrect) fold costs relatively little. But when the pot is large, as it usually is on the river, a bad fold costs a fortune. *Even if you are almost sure that you are beaten, when the pot is large on the river, do not fold decent hands for one bet.*

For example, you have

on the button. Three loose players limp, and you raise. The big blind and limpers call (10.5 small bets). The flop is

giving you top set. Your opponents check, and you bet. The big blind and two limpers call (7 big bets). The turn is the 9♣. Your opponents check, and you bet. The two limpers call (10 big bets). The river is the K♦. The first limper bets. The second limper calls (12 big bets). You should call.

The K♦ is a very scary card; it puts four to a straight and three to a flush on board. The bettor probably drew out on the river. The caller could have a queen or small flush and be going for an overcall (or just be too timid to raise). Nevertheless, you should call. You are getting 12-to-1, so you need to win only eight percent of the time to profit. The bettor might be bluffing, or he might have improved to kings up. The caller could have two pair or a pair (or worse — some small stakes players make ridiculous calls). Usually, you will lose. You should win more than eight percent of the time, though, so call.[88]

---

[88] A bad laydown can cost even more than just the pot. Many players, even those who have generally strong discipline and emotional control, instantly go on tilt after making a terrible error. No matter how you handle it, tilt is costly. If you continue to play, you may make poor decisions. If you quit the game or sit out some hands, you lose your expected win for the hands you miss. It may be worth making a "loose" call if doing so ensures that you do not tilt. Another problem with folding here after being the aggressor the whole way is that it is very noticeable and may make otherwise passive players play trickier against you.

As another example, say you have Q♥J♥ in early position. A loose and aggressive player under the gun limps. You limp. Two calling stations limp behind you. The small blind calls, and the big blind checks (6 small bets). The flop is Q♣8♣4♦ giving you top pair. The blinds check, and the player under the gun bets. You raise. The calling stations both call. The blinds fold, and the original bettor reraises. You call, planning to raise on the turn to protect your hand in this large pot. The calling stations call (9 big bets). The turn is the 2♠. Unfortunately, the under the gun player checks. You bet, and everyone calls (13 big bets). The river is the A♥. The under the gun player bets. Call. Do not fold.[89]

Given the way he played the hand, it looks like the player under the gun had a flush draw. When people play aggressively on the flop, but check and call a blank on the turn, it frequently indicates a draw; clubs are most likely on this board. Obviously, if he had the nut flush draw, he outdrew you.

But there is no reason to give him credit for that. Loose players play many suited hands without an ace, even under the gun. Aggressive players bluff often. Do not assume that he cannot be bluffing because he bet into three opponents. Bad players often bluff too much, especially with a hopeless hand in a big pot like this one.[90]

The calling stations could have anything. You cannot narrow down a calling station's holding if he has just done what he does every hand — call.

There are fourteen bets in the pot. A call is profitable if you win more than seven percent of the time. You will almost certainly win more often than that.

---

[89] You should also consider raising. See the section, "When You Do Not Want Overcalls."

[90] Possible candidates are J♣T♣ or T♣9♣, straight flush draws that missed.

# Final Thoughts

Sometimes you will think that you cannot beat any hand that your opponent could logically have. But many of your opponents do not play logically. They call with hands you would never play. They bluff in obviously hopeless situations. Your opponents will constantly surprise you with bizarre holdings. To fold a good hand on the river, you often need to be over ninety percent sure that you are beaten. Against an illogical player, how can you ever be ninety percent sure about what he has?

Even against logical players, you often cannot safely lay down. There is almost always some chance that your opponent is bluffing. He may also have misread his hand (perhaps he thinks he has a straight when he actually has only a pair). Furthermore, good players will start bluffing more if they see you fold often in big pots. Even if you manage to find a good fold once, you cannot continue to fold without risking being bluffed out.

In loose games your opponents will often outdraw you on the river. Frustrated by a series of such losses, many people begin to *expect* to lose. Such players tend to fold too much on the river. "Why do I even bother? They river me every time!" they whine, folding their winning hand to a bluff. No one's hand-reading skills are keen enough to fold strong hands routinely in large pots. Calling with a second-best hand is not a big mistake. Folding a winner in a big pot is a catastrophe. Don't do it!

# Going for Overcalls

An overcall happens after a bet has already been called at least once. If Alex bets, Betty calls, and then Chris also calls, Chris has made an overcall. To make this play, you should have a stronger hand than you would need to be the first caller. There are two reasons:

1.  You must beat two hands instead of one.

2.  While a bettor can be bluffing, a caller cannot. If your hand can beat only a bluff, do not overcall.[91]

Many players do not understand this principle. They will overcall with any hand that they would have called with. Many times, these hands are very weak (e.g., ace-high) and have almost no chance to win against a bettor and a caller. Since many rivers are multiway in small stakes games, you should learn to exploit these dead-money overcalls.

If you have a strong hand with opponents yet to act, you should consider just calling instead of raising. You may make more money by encouraging players to overcall behind you. This is particularly true under the following conditions:
1.  There are several players to act behind you.
2.  Those players are loose and unsophisticated.
3.  Your hand is strong.
4.  The pot is not big.
5.  The bettor may have you beaten.
6.  The bettor may be bluffing.

---

[91] Do not take this idea too far. Many people will call with very weak hands. Folding the best hand because you gave the initial caller too much credit is a disaster. Watch your opponents to learn their calling standards.

Obviously, the more numerous and loose the players behind you are, the more you should play for overcalls. Your hand should be strong, though. If it is marginal, one of the players you let in might beat you. We will discuss this issue in the next section.

If you suspect that the bettor's hand might be unusually strong or weak, you should probably go for overcalls. When the bettor's hand is strong, just calling can save you a bet or two. Conversely, when the bettor is bluffing, he is unlikely to call your raise. In that situation, going for overcalls may be the only way to get extra value for your hand. By raising, you win only a portion of a bet (on average) from the initial bettor. You do not win a whole bet because sometimes he will have a better hand, and sometimes he will fold. Against loose opponents, playing for overcalls will often win more than just a portion of a bet.

For example, you have

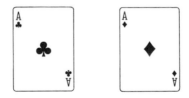

on the button. Two loose players limp from early position. A loose, but tricky, player limps from late position. You raise. Both blinds fold, and the three limpers call (9.5 small bets). The flop is

It is checked to the tricky player, who bets. You raise. Both passive players cold-call, and the tricky player calls (8.5 big bets). The turn is the 7♦. They check to you, and you bet. All three

players call (12.5 big bets). The river is the 4♦. It is checked to the tricky player who bets (13.5 big bets). You should just call.

This is an ideal situation to go for overcalls. There are two players to act behind you, both of whom are loose and capable of calling with weak hands. Since your hand, aces up, is strong, nobody with a better hand will fold, even for two bets.

The bettor is likely to have either a strong hand or a very weak hand. Though it seems strange, this combination often occurs when someone makes a *peculiar* bet. His bet represents a four. But does he have it? Since he is a tricky player, he might. He may have bet the flop with bottom pair, perhaps with a backdoor flush draw like A♠4♣. But he may also be bluffing. There were a flush draw and several straight draws possible on the flop. His play is consistent with drawing and missing.

If you raise, you are unlikely to make more than two bets. You could lose up to three if you are behind. If the bettor is bluffing, you will make only one if you are ahead.

If you call, you could make up to three bets on the river if both opponents overcall. If you lose, you will likely lose only one bet.

Going for overcalls is a gamble. Sometimes, everyone will fold behind you. If the bettor would have called a raise, you miss a bet by playing for overcalls. Nevertheless, going for overcalls on the river is often a strong tactic when your opponents are loose.

# Two Common Calling Situations

If you hold a one card straight, you should usually go for overcalls. For example, you hold

and the board is

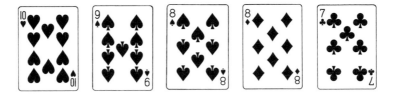

You are second to act with three opponents. The first player bets. You should just call.

You have a strong hand that will typically win at least half the pot. Unfortunately, you probably will win only half; someone willing to bet into three players on this board usually has at least a jack. You should not expect to win more money from the bettor.

If one of the players behind you has you beaten or tied, he will not fold even if you raise. On the other hand, any opponents you have beaten will be skittish. If someone holds a six (for the bottom end of the straight), an eight (for trips), or two pair, he may make a crying call for one bet. If it is a bet and a raise to him, he will probably assume (correctly) that someone has a jack or better and fold. Your only chance to win extra money on the river is to go for overcalls.

The same principle also applies when you have the second-nut one card flush. For instance, you have K♥Q♠, and the board is A♠T♣7♠6♠2♠. You have the second nuts, since anyone with the K♠ holds the nuts. A raise will never make someone fold the nuts. However, raising will scare out lesser hands that might call for one bet. This includes two pair, a straight, or a smaller flush. Someone betting into a field on this board will often have the nuts, so there is more value in calling than raising. Thus, if there are several players to act behind you, you should just call.[92]

---

[92] If you hold a smaller flush, the correct play is not as clear. With only the fourth- or fifth-nut flush, your raise might make a better hand fold. For instance, if you held K♥T♠ instead, you might choose to raise. You

# Final Thoughts

In a multiway pot on the river, always think before you raise. It may be better to go for overcalls even occasionally with the nuts. Consider the strength of your hand, the strength of the bettor's hand, and your opponents' tendencies. Just calling, in the right situation, will often win you one or more extra bets.

---

would be hoping to fold the J♠ or Q♠ behind you.

# When You Do
# Not Want Overcalls

You are playing $2-$4, and you are heads-up on the river. You have the button, and your opponent has just bet. You have

but unfortunately the final board is

You think he probably has you beat, but he might be bluffing. Should you call?

Hopefully, you realize that you do not have enough information to answer. To make the correct play, you must know how big the pot is and how likely you are to have the best hand.

So suppose the pot is $40 (including your opponent's $4 bet), and you judge that there is a ten percent chance that you will win a showdown.[93] Assuming your judgement is correct, if you call,

---

[93] Many people have pointed out that it is impossible to estimate the chance that you will win a showdown with such accuracy. We do not expect you to do so. Ignore the specific numbers, but make sure you

**211**

ninety percent of the time you will lose $4. The other ten percent of the time, you will win $40. The expected return on this call is $0.40.[94]

$$0.4 = (0.1)(40) + (0.9)(-4)$$

Since your expected return is positive, calling is better than folding. On the river, when you are heads-up, and your hand can beat only a bluff, but the pot is laying you 10-to-1 or more, it is often correct to call.

Now assume that you have a second opponent behind you. That is, your betting opponent acts first, you are next, and the second opponent is last. The pot is again $40, and you still estimate that there is a ten percent chance that you have the bettor beaten. You think the player behind you does not have much, but there is a twenty percent chance that he has you beaten. If he can beat ace-king, you expect that he will overcall. You think he probably will not call if he cannot beat ace-king, however. What should you do?

If you call, ninety percent of the time the bettor will have you beaten. The other ten percent of the time, you beat the bettor. But twenty percent of those times (two percent overall), the player behind you will overcall and win. So now 92 percent of the time,

---

understand the logic you should use when making these decisions. Then, at the table, make the best estimates that you can. Often they will be off, and you will choose the wrong action. But you will do much better if you understand the systematic approach to these problems than if you are just making decisions by the seat of your pants. In fact, many people who play by intuition alone never make the play described later on in this section. It never even occurs to them.

[94] This small expected profit comes from getting 10-to-1 pot odds while being only a 9-to-1 underdog.

you will lose $4. You win $40 eight percent of the time. The expected return on your call is -$0.48.

$$-0.48 = (0.08)(40) + (0.92)(-4)$$

Notice that with the player to act behind you, calling costs you forty-eight cents.

What about raising? Let's assume that the player yet to act will always fold for two bets. The bettor will fold to the raise if he was bluffing, but call if he can beat ace-king. The bettor will never reraise you. The raise forces out the player behind you, so you win the pot ten percent of the time again. But losing now costs you $8. The expected return for raising is -$3.20.

$$-3.2 = (0.1)(40) + (0.9)(-8)$$

Both calling and raising lose money, so folding is best.

The presence of an opponent behind you has turned a profitable call into a fold. Even though his hand was not very strong, he will take the pot with an overcall just often enough to force you to fold. *When your hand can beat only a bluff, you generally should fold if there are players behind you, even if you would have called heads-up.*[95]

Let us look at a slightly different hand. You are again heads-up on the river and have the button. The board is the same Q♥9♥7♣3♣3♦, and the pot is still $40. This time you have A♦9♦, so your hand is stronger. Your opponent bets. You now think there is a forty percent chance you have the best hand.

---

[95] This is true only if your hand is very weak, like unimproved ace-king. If you have a stronger hand, like a big pair, but you think you can only beat a bluff because the bettor is representing an even better hand, you need not be as concerned about overcalls. You will sometimes catch the initial bettor bluffing and still beat a player who overcalls.

214 Part Four: River Play

You should still call. Clearly calling is better than folding. If calling is profitable with only a ten percent chance of winning, it must also be profitable at forty percent. But raising is not correct.[96] Your opponent will have you beaten sixty percent of the time. So again, you should call when you are heads-up.

Now introduce the second opponent behind you again. Assume the same for him as in the last example: He will overcall with a better hand than yours twenty percent of the time, never overcall with a losing hand, and never call for two bets cold. Now what should you do?

If you call, you win 32 percent of the pots (eighty percent of forty percent). Your expected return for calling is $10.08.

$$10.08 = (0.32)(40) + (0.68)(-4)$$

If you raise, you win forty percent of the pots, but it costs you $8 when you lose. Your expected return in this case is $11.20:

$$11.2 = (0.4)(40) + (0.6)(-8)$$

You make eleven dollars and twenty cents when you raise — over a dollar more than when you call![97] Even though the bettor has you beat more than half the time, it becomes correct to raise because it shuts out the player behind you. *So when the pot is large, there are players behind you, and you have a mediocre*

---

[96] In tougher games a raise could be correct because it may make the bettor fold a better hand. This is not likely at small stakes, though.

[97] For this example we used simplified conditions. In a real situation sometimes you will be reraised, sometimes the bettor will call your raise with a worse hand, and sometimes the player behind you will call two cold (or reraise). Nevertheless, the principle demonstrated in the example holds for many real situations.

*hand, but there is a decent chance you can beat the bettor, you should consider raising instead of calling.*

Here is an example. You have A♠6♠ in middle position. Two players limp from early position, and you limp as well. The button limps. The small blind raises, and the big blind (an aggressive player) and all the limpers call (12 small bets). The flop is J♠6♥4♠ giving you middle pair and the nut flush draw, a terrific hand. The small blind bets, the big blind calls, and the two early position limpers fold. You raise. The button calls two cold, and both blinds call (10 big bets). The turn is the 8♥. It is checked to you, and you bet.[98] Only the button and big blind call (13 big bets). The river is the J♦. The big blind bets (14 big bets). You should probably raise.

There is a good chance the big blind is bluffing. He is an aggressive player, so you would expect him to have raised with top pair on the flop. A hand like A♥5♥, where he has missed his draws, is possible. He may have decided to use the top card pairing on fifth street as a bluffing opportunity. He could also have a range of other hands, perhaps a small pair.

The button has just called throughout the hand, so it is difficult to narrow down his holdings. He could have a jack. He could also have a busted draw, or, if he is very loose, also a four, six, eight, or an unimproved pocket pair like nines. If he has your pair of sixes beaten, he will almost certainly overcall for one bet in this big pot. But, when faced with calling two cold on the river, he is likely to fold a hand like eight-six (where his two pairs have

---

[98] There are two reasons to bet the turn. First, it is possible that your sixes are currently the best hand. And even if you do not have the best hand, you have fourteen outs (3 aces, 2 sixes, and 9 spades) to improve. You clearly have more than the 25 percent pot equity necessary to bet for value (assuming all your opponents call). Second, your bet may cause someone with a slightly better hand to fold. Specifically, someone with pocket sevens, nines, or tens might fold, fearing that you have a jack. While that will not happen often, your profit is huge when it does.

now been counterfeited), or pocket nines. Of course, he will still call with a jack.

There is a good chance that your sixes have the bettor beaten. The button could have anything, but a significant percentage of his possible hands have you beaten. He will probably (reluctantly) fold many of these hands to a raise. The pot is large — fourteen big bets. It is worth risking an extra bet to knock out the player behind you.[99]

# Final Thoughts

Most players go with their first thought when they play the river. Oblivious to the presence of players behind them, they make the intuitive plays, calling with their weak hands and raising with their strong ones. Proper strategy, however, frequently entails making the opposite and counter-intuitive plays. With strong hands, you should often just call, encouraging opponents with weaker hands to overcall. With marginal hands, you should sometimes raise, discouraging opponents with stronger hands from overcalling. When it is your turn on the river, remember that your action affects how your opponents will behave. A bad raise with a strong hand may cost you a few overcalls. A sloppy call with a weak hand could cost you the pot. *Never forget about the players behind you.*

---

[99] If you instead held A♠J♣, you should probably call, not raise. Since the bettor is often bluffing, and the player behind you will now never fold a better hand, you make more money going for an overcall. Also, if he has a jack, there is a good chance the player behind you will raise, allowing you to reraise.

# River Play

# Afterthought

For any book on hold 'em to be complete, it must discuss the river in detail. That's because errors on the river that cost you the pot every now and then can easily turn you from being a marginal winner into a significant loser. Likewise, the ability to snatch a pot away from a better hand occasionally can now turn you into someone who does much better than minimum wage.

Many relatively new players who are trying to play well learn that the best players seem to play tightly. Thus they are able to fold when they reason that it is most likely they are beaten. But strategy that fits this weak-tight model is flawed and sometimes very costly.

When playing poker, and hold 'cm in particular, it's important always to be aware of the size of the pot. You don't need to know the amount of money to the penny, but you should certainly recognize when the pot is big versus when it is medium-sized or small.

In small stakes games where many of your opponents will play too many hands and go to far with them, the pots will often be big. This means that hands that will win only a small percentage of the time are still frequently good enough to pay off on the river, and some questionable raises can also be correct.

Put another way, if early in a hand and you're not sure, it is probably best to fold (because the pot is small). But on the river, even though you frequently will not like the results, if your hand has some value, your chips will often need to go into the center of the table.

# Part Five

# Miscellaneous Topics

# Miscellaneous Topics

# Introduction

This section covers a few miscellaneous topics. While the chapters thus far have discussed mostly general strategic concepts, the topics covered in this chapter are somewhat more specialized. You should find them valuable.

# Playing Overcards

Many players complain that they have no idea how to play overcards. They raise preflop, the flop misses them, and they feel lost. But playing overcards is actually not much different from playing any other weak draw.

Like other weak draws, overcards vary greatly in strength. The first step to playing correctly is to evaluate their strength.

## Evaluating Overcards

Compare these four hands:

1. K♥Q♥ on a flop of T♥9♠4♣
2. A♠K♦ on a flop of T♠5♠2♣
3. Q♦J♦ on a flop of 7♥7♠6♣
4. K♠Q♠ on a flop of 9♣8♣7♣

Clearly Hand No. 1 is the strongest. In addition to overcards, you have a gutshot to the nuts and a backdoor flush draw. Using the approximations from the "Counting Outs" section, we assign 1.5 outs to each overcard, 4 outs to the gutshot, and 1.5 outs to the backdoor flush draw, making this draw worth about 8.5 outs total (as much as a good open-ended straight draw).

In Hand No. 2 you have two strong overcards and a backdoor nut flush draw on a relatively ragged flop. You can fairly ascribe about 1.5 outs to each overcard and 1.5 more outs to the backdoor draw, making this hand worth about 4.5 outs.

Hand No. 3 is much weaker. You have just two overcards, but the flop is paired[100] and contains a straight draw. If someone has

---

[100] That would be good if you had ace-king, but not queen-jack. A paired board leaves only five cards to match in other players' hands. Thus ace-

a seven, you are drawing essentially dead. Furthermore, spiking a pair on the turn could leave you open to a pair of aces or kings made on the river or still behind to someone who has you outkicked. Your overcards are probably not even worth 1.5 outs each. You might (generously) value them at 1.25 outs each, so your draw would be worth about 2.5 outs total.

Hand No. 4 is virtually worthless. You have no backdoor draws, and the board contains a three-straight and a three-flush. You could easily be drawing dead already, and if you aren't, you will often lose even if you happen to catch a king or queen.

In addition to the process we just used, apply these rules to help you evaluate your overcards:

1.   Overcards prefer ragged boards.
2.   Backdoor draws strengthen overcards.
3.   Overcards prefer few opponents.

# Overcards Prefer Ragged Boards

A ragged board helps overcards in two ways:

1.   Top pair is more likely to win when no straight or flush draws are available. With overcards, you are drawing, as over a 6.5-to-1 underdog on the next card, to make a single pair. One pair is the second-lowest-ranked poker hand, above only the lowly high-card hand. Drawing to one pair is *much* different from drawing to a straight or flush. You will often make your hand and still lose. Thus, a flop like

---

high could be the best hand. More on this later.

is far better than

if you are drawing to top pair.

2.  Ragged boards are less likely to have hit your opponents. You are much more likely to pick up the pot with a flop or turn bet on a ragged board than you are on a coordinated one. When the flop comes J♥T♥8♦, several of your opponents will usually find something to continue on for: hearts, a straight, a flopped pair, an overcard, etc. But ragged boards, especially paired boards that do not offer straight or flush draws, are hard to hit. When the flop comes J♦4♣4♥ it is likely that your A♦K♦ is the best hand, even against a few opponents. If someone has a four, you are in trouble, drawing to only your backdoor flush (or the even more unlikely running aces or kings), but otherwise you are in good shape.

# Backdoor Draws Strengthen Overcards

A backdoor flush or straight draw can turn your overcards from unprofitable to profitable. Obviously, they add outs to your draw. But having a backdoor flush draw can help you in a more subtle way. Compare the following two hands:

1.  A♣K♦ on a flop of J♥6♥3♣
2.  A♠K♦ on a flop of J♠6♠3♣

In the former hand, the two-flush is a distinct liability. Two of your outs to top pair (the A♥ and K♥) put three to a flush on board. Even if that does not make someone a flush, it almost certainly sets up a redraw for someone with a single heart.

In the latter hand, however, the two-flush is actually probably better for you than if the flop had been three different suits. Now only one of your outs (the K♠) puts three to a flush on board, and in that case, you are now the one with the redraw to the nut flush. So all six aces and kings are "good cards," whereas only four were clearly good in the other hand.

*If you have offsuit overcards, you are usually better off if the flop comes with two of one of your suits than if it comes three different suits.* This effect is strongest when you have the ace of the suit, but it is still positive even if you have only a king or queen.

# Overcards Prefer Few Opponents

As mentioned before, overcards are a draw to a medium-strength hand, top pair. Unlike draws to big hands like straights and flushes, overcards quickly drop in value as the number of opponents increases. Against one or two opponents, your unimproved overcards could still be the best hand, especially if they include an ace. Against three, you will probably be drawing, but top pair is likely to win if the board is not very coordinated. Against more than three, you will very often not have the best hand, and you may not win even if you hit your draw. There are two problems with having many opponents:

1.  The chance that you are "reverse dominated" increases. Reverse domination means that one of your opponents

flopped a pair, and his kicker matches one of your overcards.[101] If you have

the flop is

and one of your opponents has

you are in trouble. You will still lose even if you catch an ace. Reverse domination is most worrisome when one of your overcards is an ace, since so many people play ace-rag.

2.  The chance that someone will make a big hand increases. Even on a ragged board, top pair is the best hand far less often against seven opponents than against three. Your

---

[101] It's called "reverse" dominated because before the flop you had him dominated.

improved pot odds do not compensate for this drop in winning chances.

Overcard hands with backdoor draws retain more value against many opponents. The small chance to make a big hand is very valuable in that spot.[102] The exception is if your backdoor draw is a weak one, such as having A♥Q♠ on a T♠8♠4♣ flop. Your third-nut one card draw to the spade flush is much more likely to be good against few opponents. But the lone ace of trump on a two-flush flop, or a suited hand with one matching board card adds significant multiway value.

# Betting the Flop

Unfortunately, whether to bet or check the flop with overcards cannot be summed up by an easy formula. Some players use simple rules, such as "bet against two opponents, but check against three." Unfortunately, such rules are so oversimplified that they are essentially useless. The number of opponents affects the strength of overcards, but there are several other equally important factors.

Our approach will be to list the things to consider, and then provide a few examples. But again, once you understand how to evaluate overcards, you can consider them to be a weak draw and play accordingly.

When deciding whether to bet or check your overcards, ask these questions:
1. How big is the pot?
2. How likely are my overcards still to be best? That is, how likely is it that all my opponents missed the flop?

---

[102] A 5 percent chance to make a flush may improve your, say, 10 percent winning chances to 15 percent. Going from 10 to 15 percent is a 50 percent increase.

3. How strong is my hand? (Evaluate using the rules from earlier.)

4. How likely is betting to win the pot immediately?

5. Is betting likely to improve my winning chances significantly even if I do not win immediately?

6. Is betting likely to buy a free card on the turn if I want it?

Say you have

on the button. Two players limp, and you raise. Both blinds, and the limpers call (10 small bets). The flop is

Everyone checks to you. You should bet.

The pot is large, so you should tend to play aggressively if doing so will improve your winning chances. Even though you have four opponents, you are still a reasonable candidate to have the best hand on this ragged board. When the flop is paired, only five cards (2 nines and 3 fours in this example) connect with the board, instead of the nine cards that match an unpaired board. This makes it much less likely that someone made a hand.

As long as no one has a nine, your overcards are quite strong. Even if someone has a pair (either a four or pocket pair), all six of your outs, as well as your backdoor flush draw, will probably win. You are not subject to reverse domination either, as you still beat someone with ace-four if an ace comes.[103]

With four opponents, betting will not often win immediately. Many small stakes players will call with overcards like queen-ten. Some will call with any two cards, hoping that making a pair will be enough to win. *Nevertheless, betting will significantly improve your winning chances.* If you have the best hand, most of your opponents will have six outs. Even the lowly trey-deuce can pair and beat you. It is unlikely everyone will fold, but at least one or two probably will. These folds make it much more likely your hand will hold up unimproved and somewhat more likely that you will win if you spike an ace or king.

The pot is large, betting may improve your winning chances significantly, and even if you are behind, as long as no one has a nine, your overcard draw is relatively strong. Despite having four opponents, you should clearly bet.

Now say you have K♦J♦ in the big blind. Four players limp, the small blind calls, and you raise. Everyone calls (12 small bets). The flop is T♠7♣6♥. The small blind checks. You should check.

The pot is large, but there is almost no chance that your hand is best. Against five opponents king-high is almost certainly no good. Furthermore, your marginal overcards with no backdoor flush draw are very weak on this coordinated board. Several players probably have draws to straights and flushes, so even if you make top pair, your hand will be very vulnerable to redraws.

Betting will not win the pot immediately. Since this board affords many draws, someone will almost always have one and call. If you bet, you will probably be called in three or more spots. Betting may improve your winning chances, but not much.

---

[103] See the section "Hidden Outs" if you need an explanation.

Being out of position, you cannot try a free card play. You have a weak hand against many opponents on a board full of draws. Betting has almost no hope to win the pot or otherwise improve your situation. Despite the large pot, you should check.

Finally, say you have

on the button. Two players limp, and you raise. Both blinds fold, and the limpers call (7.5 small bets). The flop is

Your opponents check. This example is not as clear-cut as the first two, but you should probably bet.

The pot is again raised preflop, but it is smaller because you have only two opponents. It is possible that you have the best hand, but not as likely as if you had ace-high. Your overcards are of average strength: You have backdoor straight and flush draws, but your flush draw is a weak one card draw to the queen, and the board is somewhat coordinated, with possible flush and straight draws.

But unlike the first two examples, betting will sometimes win the pot immediately. If both of your opponents missed (which will happen a significant minority of the time), they may both fold. You are also in decent shape if one folds, and the other calls. He may be calling with a weak draw himself, planning to fold on the turn if he does not improve.

Sometimes both players will call. But when that happens, they will often both check the turn no matter what comes. If you do not improve, you can then take a free card. So even when both players call, betting may still help by buying a free card on fourth street.

Thus, betting helps you if no one calls (you win the pot), if one person calls (your winning chances improve), or if both call (you might get a free card). Even though you missed the flop, you should not abandon your stake in the pot just yet.

# Calling and Raising the Flop

When someone bets into you, and you have overcards, you should usually play them just as you would any other weak draw. When the pot is small, tend to fold. When it is large, tend to call or raise: Raise if it is likely to buy outs or win a free card; otherwise call.

What your opponents might have is more important when you have overcards than with some other weak draws, though. If you have a gutshot to the nuts, you do not much care what your opponent has. If you hit your draw, you will win. Not so with overcards. You are drawing almost dead if your opponent has two pair or a set, and your draw is also weakened if you are reverse dominated (one of your pair cards makes him two pair). Thus, in marginal situations, be more likely to continue with overcards if your opponent may be betting a weak hand or a draw than if he probably has a strong hand.

For example, you have

in the big blind. Two players limp, the small blind calls, and you raise. Everyone calls (8 small bets). The flop is

The small blind, an aggressive and thinking player, bets. You should raise.

Since you raised preflop, the small blind will assume that you have big cards or a pair and, therefore, based on card frequency,[104] you probably missed the flop. Being aggressive, he would bet many hands including flush draws, small pairs, and even wheel draws like ace-five. His bet is not likely to indicate a strong hand. In fact, because he would expect you to bet, he might have gone for a check-raise instead with a strong hand. So he is more likely than usual to have a draw.

The pot is large, and your overcards are relatively strong. The board is fairly ragged, and you have a backdoor flush draw. So you should continue.

Raising is better than calling because it improves your winning chances. If you have the best hand, each player behind you probably has at least six outs (any pair beats you). Raising may even get a better hand like a trey or four behind you to fold.

---

[104] See pages 118-126 of *Poker, Gaming, & Life* by David Sklansky for more discussion.

Now say you encounter a different flop with A♥Q♥ in the big blind. Again two players limp, the small blind calls, and you raise. Everyone calls (8 small bets). The flop is

The small blind, a loose, but timid player, bets. You should fold.

At first it may appear that you are better off in this hand. After all, the board is more ragged, with no flush draw and only an unlikely gutshot draw available. But this time the flop bettor is likely to have a *much* stronger hand (and/or have you reverse dominated). An aggressive player who bets a somewhat coordinated flop could have a wide range of weak hands. A timid player who bets a ragged flop cannot. He has at least top pair, maybe with an ace or queen kicker, and he might well have two pair or a set. You will be drawing slim or dead far more often in this hand than you were in the last one.

Overcards are often worth playing, but they are worthless against a monster hand. *Before you act, consider the likely range of hands that the bettor might have: The wider the range, the more willing you should be to continue.*

# Playing the Turn

If you bet the flop with overcards, get called, and the turn does not help you, you must decide whether to bet again. You should bet if you think there is a substantial chance (commensurate with the size of the pot — bigger pots need a smaller chance) to win immediately. Otherwise, you should usually check. On the flop you should sometimes bet even if you think there is little chance to win immediately. You are looking for a few people to fold to improve your winning chances. On the turn that idea is less useful, since the bet will cost you twice as much, and there is only one card to come.

How likely your opponents are all to fold depends on how many are left and the range of hands they might have. The fewer that are left and the weaker their possible range of hands, the more inclined you should be to bet.

For instance, say you have

on the button. Three players limp, and you raise. Both blinds fold, and the limpers call (9.5 small bets). The flop comes

Your opponents check, and you bet. If all three limpers call, and you do not improve, you should probably check the turn. If only one calls, though, you should bet. You are much more likely to win immediately against only one opponent.

In fact, if only one player calls, you could easily still have the best hand. He could have overcards or a gutshot draw like jack-nine. If all three call, though, you will rarely have the best hand and almost never pick up the pot with a turn bet. Take the free card.

But if the flop were

instead of T♣7♦5♠, you might check the turn even if only one player calls. On the queen-high flop, no draws are available. He cannot have called with a flush or straight draw, and the only hand with two overcards is ace-king. Thus, since he called, he is much more likely to have at least a pair than on the ten-high flop. (Remember, he could have called on that flop with a gutshot or overcards.) It is especially important to check here if your opponent always plays to the showdown whenever he flops a pair. He is likely to have a pair, and he is not going to fold it, so check.[105]

Thus, the best time to follow up on the turn is *when the flop was moderately coordinated.* If it was extremely ragged, any callers are quite likely to have at least a pair. If it was extremely coordinated, callers are likely to have strong draws or to be slowplaying big hands. But when the flop allows for plenty of gutshot or overcard hands, and the turn does not improve many of those hands, betting may well pick up the pot.[106]

---

[105] There are a small number of extremely loose players who almost always call on the flop, no matter what their hand is. If your calling opponent is of this variety, always bet again. You are too likely to have the best hand with ace-king to give a free card.

[106] An exception comes if the flop comes something like T♣7♦5♠, and the turn is something like the 9♣. Anyone who flopped a gutshot with the ten and seven now has at least a pair. You might check that card, as it is an example of one that improves many of the possible hands that could have called.

# Final Thoughts

Playing overcards correctly is tricky. Many players who have studied and played seriously for years still do not feel at ease with them. They find them particularly frustrating because, not only do you flop overcards frequently, but it also happens most often with your premium preflop hands. So on top of being disappointed by the flop, you must now navigate a difficult situation.

Trying to adopt a simple approach to overcards will leave you making many mistakes. If you resolve to check and fold, you abandon too many profitable opportunities and become too predictable to observant opponents. If you always play aggressively, you become harder to read, but you waste too many bets in hopeless situations.

On the flop, ask yourself the questions we listed before:

1. How big is the pot?

2. How likely are my overcards still to be best? That is, how likely is it that all my opponents missed the flop?

3. How strong is my hand? (Evaluate using the rules from earlier in the section.)

4. How likely is betting to win the pot immediately?

5. Is betting likely to improve my winning chances significantly even if I do not win immediately?

6. Is betting likely to buy a free card on the turn if I want it?

On the turn, narrow down your opponents' holdings. Were they likely "taking one off" with a weak hand, or do they probably have a pair or strong draw?

You will probably never feel comfortable playing overcards. But if you remember to evaluate everything before you act, you will make the most of a tough situation.

# Building Big
# Pots Before the Flop

Say you are in the big blind with

Five loose players, including the small blind, limp in. Should you raise or check? Many players argue that you should check. They typically reason along these lines:

> Raising gives my loose opponents odds to call to the river with gutshots and bottom pair. If I keep the pot small, I can play aggressively if I hit my hand and check and fold if I miss. Since the pot is small, if I flop top pair, my opponents are making a bigger mistake when they call with weak draws than they would be if I bloated the pot by raising. I'd like to see the flop cheaply and then outplay them after the flop.

The argument sounds plausible. After all, much of the profit in poker comes from your opponents' mistakes. Keeping the pot small certainly induces loose opponents to make more mistakes after the flop. Unfortunately, the argument is flawed and suggests the wrong conclusion. You should definitely raise.

This argument ignores the mistake that your opponents *have already made* by entering the pot. Your strong hand clearly has an edge in pot equity before the flop. You should expect to win significantly more often than your fair share of seventeen percent with five opponents. If you have a pot equity edge, at least one, and probably several, of your opponents must have a pot equity deficit. Money does not appear from nowhere; if someone is making it, someone else must be losing it. Several of these players have likely made a mistake by entering the pot in the first place. Exploit this mistake by raising.

Since you have a pot equity edge, raising now has a positive expectation. By checking you are *passing up a profitable opportunity*. Keeping the pot small helps you increase your postflop expectation, but at the cost of a smaller preflop expectation.

For some hands, making this tradeoff makes sense. For instance, if you held A♥3♥, K♠J♣, or maybe even ace-jack offsuit, instead of A♥J♥, checking might be better. These weaker hands usually have a modest preflop edge against five loose opponents, so a raise shows some profit. Your edge is relatively small, however, so when you check, you forfeit only a small amount. Your improved postflop expectation will usually compensate for this lost money. But A♥J♥ is *far* too strong to try this play. Missing raises to induce mistakes is useful when your decision is close. This decision is not close. Do not be afraid to gamble when you have much the best of it.

# Ace-King is Not Just A Drawing Hand

Some players advise that in loose games, you should play ace-king passively before the flop. They argue that ace-king must connect with the flop (usually by catching an ace or king) to win. That makes it a "drawing hand," and as such, you should just call with it. Most of the time the flop will disappoint you (an ace or king will flop only 32.4 percent of the time), so invest the minimum until you know whether or not you will flop a strong hand.

Any argument that does not mention a play's expectation is immediately suspect. When you make any decision, your goal should usually be to *maximize your expectation*. Labeling any hand a "drawing hand" and then making strategic decisions based on that label only obscures the important factors. To decide whether you should raise with ace-king, evaluate the expectation of the play and ignore labels.[107]

Even in a very multiway pot, ace-king has a significant pot equity edge.[108] Against many opponents you will probably have to connect with the board to win. But that condition holds for *every* hand except the biggest pocket pairs. You are not the only person who must hit the board to win; everyone must do it. The difference between ace-king and your opponents' hands is that ace-king can spike one pair and have a strong chance to win. Your opponent with 5♣2♦ does not have that luxury. He must get *very* lucky. In most cases he must hit the board at least twice to win.

Just like A♥J♥ in the previous example, in loose games ace-king offsuit has a large preflop edge. The postflop advantage you may gain by limping is a fraction of what you lose by missing the raise.

Thinking about preflop hands in terms of "drawing" hands and "made" hands is not helpful. Instead, especially in the multiway pots common in small stakes games, think in terms of pot equity and overall expectation. Will you win significantly more than your share of the time? If so, you should usually raise.

---

[107] In fact, labeling ace-king a "drawing hand" is not even accurate. If your raise limits the pot to a small number of players (which happens occasionally even in loose games), you will frequently win without improving.

[108] The only possible exception occurs in a *very* tight game that, for a single hand, is multiway. If several tight players have entered the pot, it may indicate that there are few aces or kings left for you to catch. This should *not* be a concern for small stakes players in loose games. We mention it only for the sake of completeness.

# Final Thoughts

While many players invent "logical" rationalizations to play passively with strong hands, their real motivation is usually to avoid bad beats. They eschew raising with their premium hands because they fear the emotional pain of losing a big pot. "Winning a small pot is better than losing a big one." Obviously that is true, but it is just as true that winning a big pot is better than winning a small one. More importantly, neither of those platitudes evaluates the expectation of raising versus calling. Do not allow your emotions to make poor poker decisions for you. In loose games all your premium hands have a large edge. You cannot recoup your lost preflop expectation simply by keeping the pot smaller.

If your goal is to win the maximum, you must build big pots with your best hands. Do not say, "But I'm out of position," or "Maybe if my ace-king were suited," or "My big pairs never hold up." If you get an edge, push it. Poker is a gambling game; timid play is not rewarded. When you have much the best of it, be willing to put the chips in.

# "Loose" Flop Calls

You have

in the big blind. Three passive players limp, and the small blind calls. You check (5 small bets). The flop is

giving you top pair with no kicker and a backdoor flush draw. The small blind checks, and you bet. The first two limpers fold, but the third one raises. The small blind folds (8 small bets).

Since he is passive, your opponent's raise means he probably has at least a king with a fairly good kicker. Even passive players surprise you sometimes, though, so he could have only a flush draw or an open-ended straight draw.

You will probably make the best hand if the turn is a trey, and a diamond will give you a strong draw. While kings and treys is a strong hand, you could make it and still lose. So instead of three outs, perhaps count the remaining treys as 2.5 outs. Count the backdoor flush as 1.5 outs. Thus, you estimate that your hand has about four outs. Getting only 8-to-1 to call, you might conclude that you should fold.

Folding is reasonable, but we suggest that you call for several reasons.

1.   Since your opponent is passive, he may check the turn even if he has a king. Passive players tend to give too many free cards. You can exploit this error by making some marginally loose calls on the flop — calls that would be wrong if you could see only one card, but that become correct when you might see two cards for the same price.

2.   Your opponent might be on a draw. If he is, because he is passive, he will typically check on fourth street if he misses. He is not likely to try to bluff you out: If your opponent bets again, he probably has a hand he thinks is best. When a later bet is unlikely to be a bluff, you can loosen up on the flop a little bit.

3.   When it is otherwise close, refrain from betting and then folding to a raise on the same round. Doing it too often may encourage your more observant opponents to throw in an extra raise with a draw or weak made hand. You would prefer that they continue to play in a straightforward manner.[109]

So you call the raise. The turn is the J♠, giving you K♦3♦ on a K♣8♦6♣J♠ board. You check, and your opponent bets (5.5 big bets). You should now fold. You are probably beaten. It will cost two big bets to call on the turn and river, and the pot contains only 5.5 big bets now. The combined chance that you are behind now and that your opponent will draw out on you even if you currently have the best hand is great. You will not win often enough to make calling down in this small pot profitable.

But just because you do not plan to call to the showdown does not necessarily mean you should throw your hand away on

---

[109] Only call when it is close, though. If you should clearly fold, do so.

the flop. Do not be afraid to make a "loose" flop call occasionally in the right situations.

# Using Tells

A "tell" is a specific behavior, mannerism, or aspect of an opponent's demeanor that transmits information about the nature of his hand. You might notice that a typically boisterous player always clams up when he flops a monster, that a slouching opponent sits subtly more upright in his seat if the newest board card helps his hand, or that two opponents on your left have their cards in hand, prepared to fold. Small stakes games are usually rife with tells.

We do not intend to teach you what to look for or how to interpret it. Plenty of material on this topic is already available elsewhere. We will give you two tips for using the information once you have it:
1. Attack weakness.
2. Use tells cautiously in large pots.

## Attack Weakness

Many of your opponents often expose the weakness of their hands through tells. They may agonize for several seconds before calling a flop bet or appear genuinely disappointed by the river card. Attack these weak hands with extra bets and raises.

You should bluff more often when your opponent demonstrates weakness. For example, say you have in late position. Everyone folds to you, and you raise. Only the big blind calls (4.5 small bets). The flop is

missing you completely. Your opponent checks, and you bet. Your opponent hesitates several seconds and calls, tossing his chips in a manner that says, "What the heck." If your opponent checks again, bet the turn no matter what comes.

Without the demonstration of weakness, after being called twice already you would usually give up your bluff on fourth street. But when your opponent exposes weakness, you should continue to attack him.

When someone makes an "agonizing" flop call, he usually has a very weak draw. For instance, he may have in this example a hand like Q♦6♦ for undercards and backdoor flush and straight draws. He knows his hand is poor, but he calls anyway to see if he pairs or picks up a draw. He plans to fold on the turn if he does not improve. Since he is an underdog to help his hand, always follow up with a turn bet no matter how poor your holding.

You should also value bet more aggressively on the river when your opponent is weak. For instance, say you have

on the button. One player limps, and you raise. The big blind and the limper call (6.5 small bets). The flop is

giving you bottom pair. They check to you, and you bet. The big blind folds, and the limper agonizes and calls (4 big bets). You suspect he has a very weak hand. The turn is the 4♥. He checks, you bet, and he surprises you by calling immediately.

His call indicates that the turn card helped him. He likely has either a four or a wheel draw such as ace-trey or ace-deuce. (You can narrow his hands down so well because the 4♥ puts one of each suit on board, so he could not have picked up a flush draw. If the turn card had been the 4♣, you would not know the rank of his cards so specifically because he could have any club draw.)

The river is the K♦. Your opponent checks, slightly disappointed. You should bet for value. Normally you would check this river, but your opponent's tells have allowed you to narrow his possible hands down to a much weaker range than normal. It is far more likely than it otherwise would be that your opponent has specifically a four. So you should bet, hoping he has exactly that and calls.

# Use Tells Cautiously in Large Pots

If you detect a tell that indicates that your opponent has a stronger hand than usual, you can use it to save bets, but only when the pot is small. For instance, if you had a marginal hand and were unsure whether to call down, a tell that indicates strength could tip your decision to a fold.

But when the pot is large, be *very cautious* acting on a tell. When considering a big laydown, you should know *precisely* what the tell means. Most tells are, by their nature, imprecise. If your opponent's hand is shaking for the first time all session (sometimes an indication that he holds a stong hand), it could simply be past time for his medication. To fold a decent hand in a large pot, you often must be well over ninety percent sure that you are beaten. Few tells are remotely that accurate.

Similarly, do not become passive in multiway pots because you think you have detected a tell. For example, you have

in the small blind. Three players limp, and the button raises. You call, the big blind calls, and the limpers call (12 small bets). The flop comes

giving you top pair and a backdoor flush and straight draw. You check, planning to raise if the button bets. It is checked to the button, and he bets. When he puts his chips in the pot, he uses a much more deliberate motion than usual, which you interpret as a sign that his hand is strong.

You should raise anyway. Your hand is vulnerable, the pot is large, and you must protect it. If you are wrong about the tell, not raising is a big mistake that could cost you this large pot. Hand reading (of which interpreting tells is a subset) becomes less valuable the larger and more multiway the pot. You often become "slave" to large pots; the money in the pot, the number of your opponents, and the vulnerability of your hand dictate your action. A mere suspicion that you are beaten is worthless if the pot is big.

# Final Thoughts

On top of granting you a mathematical advantage by playing so many weak hands, small stakes players often let you know exactly how weak they are through tells. Focus on detecting tells that indicate weakness, and attack ferociously when you see one. These tells allow you to pick up pots and value bet hands you otherwise wouldn't. Your opponents will wonder why they never seem to get free cards and showdowns, and your results will improve.

# Image

In many competitive endeavors, people cultivate a serious, intense, or intimidating image to help them succeed. Football players try to look and act "mean" to get a psychological edge on their opponents. Baseball pitchers sometimes throw at or near batters to keep them off balance. Even in non-athletic competitions, like vying with colleagues for promotions or raises at work, people try to appear serious, studious, and intense to impress their managers.

Many poker players who are trying hard to succeed, consciously or unconsciously, project the same intense image. They would be better off if they did not, however, as *appearing serious and intimidating is counter-productive to winning at small stakes hold 'em.*

The money you make comes from your opponents' mistakes. The players who make the most mistakes, and therefore who are the most profitable for you, almost invariably do not take the game seriously. They do not view poker as a battle of wits, as a mathematical and psychological test; they view it as an enjoyable way to spend a few hours. They know that they are a favorite to lose, but they play anyway because it is fun.

If you project an intense or intimidating image, these ideal opponents will likely react in one of three ways:

1.  They will take the game more seriously when you are in the hand. They usually do not think too much while they play, but when playing against you, they will try to play their best. Bad players do play better when they try.

2.  More likely, they will simply tend to avoid you. They are not here to play "serious" poker, and they do not want to be the patsy for someone who does. So when you enter the pot,

instead of calling with 8♣6♦ as they normally would, they will just toss the hand to avoid you.

3.   They may even leave the game. If the atmosphere of the whole game turns intense, usually because several players are taking things too seriously, weak players often simply leave. They may go find another table, or they might decide that they have a better place to spend the afternoon than at the card room.

Thus, looking too serious will tend to make poor players leave, or at least play better and more tightly, all of which cost you money.[110] Here are several specific things that some players do that make them seem to take the game too seriously:

1.   When you enter a game, you usually have the option either to post an amount equal to the big blind and take a hand immediately or wait for the big blind to come to you. Mathematically, the choice you make does not much matter. (Nevertheless, people seem to like to debate this picayune topic.) But psychologically, the way you handle this situation can be important. Some players will sit down, refuse to post, and wait almost a whole round for their blind. They sit there, arms folded, watching the action for up to fifteen minutes before playing. Don't do it. If you do not feel comfortable posting immediately, put your chips down and leave the table for a few hands. Get a drink, or go talk to someone. Come back to the table only when you have one or two hands left to

---

[110] In a poker *tournament*, it may well be advantageous to project an intimidating image precisely because it achieves those effects. You often *want* your opponents to play more tightly against you than they would otherwise. But this is virtually never the case in a small stakes cash game.

wait. If you sit out seven hands before you play, you will appear too serious.

2. Do not wear wrap-around sunglasses, hooded sweatshirts, or other clothing intended to obscure your face. You are playing small stakes hold 'em, not training for covert operations. You do not need full camouflage gear to beat the array of tourists, recreational gamblers, and retirees at your table. They are not sweating your every facial tick to "see into your soul." These items only hide things that your opponents are not looking for. They do, however, may make you look intimidating and overly intense.

3. No matter how good you are, some opponents will occasionally criticize your playing decisions (often employing outlandish and absurd logic). Defending your actions is the natural tendency, but avoid doing so. Do not explain how you were correct to call because of the implied odds, or that you raised your draw correctly because of your pot equity edge. Just smile and change the subject. You have little hope of convincing your critic that you actually play well (which is good), but your technical discussion will make other players at the table feel ignorant and outmatched. Poker is a terrible game for those who compete primarily to earn the respect of their peers. Some of your opponents will think you play terribly, and there isn't anything you can do to convince them otherwise. Why would you want to anyway?

4. Similarly, *never criticize an opponent's play*. In addition to angering the target of your criticism, it makes you look like a jerk and intimidates every recreational gambler at the table who will now worry that he may be the next recipient of a verbal tirade. One ill-timed bout of criticism can send your most profitable opponents home and turn a terrific game into a terrible one. As a poker player and a decent human being,

252 Part Five: Miscellaneous Topics

there is simply no excuse for criticizing any of your opponents.

When most new players think of their "image," they worry about how their opponents perceive their play. Should they play a few junk hands to shake a tight image? Should they make a crazy bluff and show it to "advertise"? If they have raised before the flop several times recently, should they just call if they are dealt another "raising" hand? Should they behave in a ridiculous and obnoxious manner to appear loose and wild?

In a small stakes game, the answer to these and many similar questions is almost always, "No." For the most part, your opponents do not pay attention to your playing tendencies.[111] Even most of those who are vaguely aware usually do not bother to adjust their play based on their observations. Someone may say, "Man, you haven't played one hand in the last hour," as he calls your under the gun raise with K♣9♦. It does not much matter if your opponents think you are tight or loose, passive or aggressive.

If you want to build an image, build a friendly and laid-back one. Small stakes hold 'em is a company softball game, not the World Series. It is not the place for "war paint" or brush back pitches. Do not charge the mound if a pitch hits you; just take your base with a smile. If you behave like you are just playing to enjoy the game, your opponents will have more fun, and you will make more money.

---

[111] The exception, as previously noted, is if you often fold for a single raise on the same round you have bet. Try to avoid doing that too much, or your opponents will take shots at you.

# Miscellaneous Topics

# Afterthought

Once you become an excellent player and can beat hold 'em games at a pretty good clip, you should discover that there are a few additional skills that can enhance your win rate. These include tells and image.

On the other hand, being an expert at picking up tells and having an image that encourages your opponents to play incorrectly against you won't do any good if you play the wrong starting hands, don't understand postflop strategies, and make errors on the river. If this is the case, expect all of your money to disappear, no matter how good your tell-reading is or how strong your image might be.

When playing limit hold 'em, you need to realize that the best way to play, which maximizes your expectation, is not always the most fun way to play. Of course tells and image are a fun aspect of poker, and they do have a little bit of value. But keep in mind that too much emphasis on these skills, especially if you neglect other more important areas, will allow for a good time only in the short run. That's because it's much more enjoyable to win than to lose.

# Part Six

# Hand Quizzes

# Hand Quizzes

# Introduction

In this chapter, you can put the concepts that you have learned into practice. Working through these hands will develop your ability to determine the correct play at the table. You will encounter situations similar to those in our quizzes, recall our analysis, and identify the correct play.

Furthermore, these quizzes act as a diagnostic to tell you how well you have understood the material we have covered so far. We have carefully constructed these examples both to illustrate specific concepts and to have unambiguously correct solutions. In some poker situations, two plays will be so close in value that experts will disagree about which one is better. *You will find no such situations in these quizzes.* We have intentionally avoided them. In each of these quizzes, we believe that one play is clearly superior to the others. Thus, if you disagree with our answers more than once or twice, you should take it as a sign that you do not fully understand some concepts.

# Hand Quizzes — Preflop Play

**1. You are on the button with the K♣J♠. One player limps, and an aggressive player on your right raises. What should you do?**

> **Answer:** Fold. King-jack is often a fairly good hand, but its expectation generally becomes negative against a raiser. You will often be dominated, which devastates any offsuit holding. Those times that you are not dominated (e.g., if the raiser has ace-ten), king-jack shows a modest profit. But when you are dominated, it is a big loser. Even against an aggressive raiser who will raise many hands, you cannot risk calling. The losses when you are dominated outstrip the wins when you are not. Having the button is not enough to make this call profitable. And while a reraise might be a good play if it could get the limper and blinds all to fold, that rarely happens in small stakes games. Thus, if you have an offsuit hand (except ace-king and sometimes ace-queen), you simply must fold if someone raises in front of you.

**2. Your game is loose and aggressive with many players who habitually misplay their hands after the flop. Your opponents are raising and calling before the flop with a wide range of hands. You are on the button with A♣7♣. The player under the gun raises, and four people cold-call. What should you do?**

> **Answer:** Call. You could be dominated here as well, but it is not nearly so devastating as it was in Hand No. 1. Your hand is suited, so you do not depend as heavily on winning with top pair. Also, there are four callers, many of whom are likely to have weak hands. These loose calls provide dead money, and they practically assure that you will get action after the

257

flop if you do flop a flush draw. You have a solid hand, position, and many weak opponents who lose money after the flop. This hand should show a modest profit.

**3. The player under the gun raises, and everyone folds to the small blind who calls. You have A♦9♥ in the big blind. What should you do?**

> **Answer:** Fold. The threat of domination is so menacing in this situation that you cannot call profitably even for one bet. After the flop you will be out of position for three betting rounds against someone who may have a bigger pair if you flop a nine or a better kicker if you flop an ace. Even if your opponent plays poorly, you cannot overcome such an overwhelming disadvantage.
>
> Another concern should dissuade you from playing. When the pot is short-handed, the effect of the rake is greatly magnified. In small stakes games often as much as a full small bet (sometimes even more) is removed from each pot. For example, a four dollar rake is common in many $4-$8 games. When the game is loose with six players seeing each flop and lots of action after the flop, the effect of the rake is relatively small. Many pots in such a game are more than $100, so the rake removes four percent or less. Your opponents' myriad mistakes compensate for the loss.
>
> The high rake is overwhelming in small pots, though. Often it removes up to ten percent of the pot. Many hands that would be playable without a rake become costly. For example, say you played a pot heads-up, and at the end both you and your opponent had contributed $20. A typical rake might remove $4 from the pot, so the winner gets $36. But his profit is only $16, because he invested $20. In effect, both players are laying 5-to-4, betting $20 to win only $16. In this example your hand is nowhere near strong enough to overcome the situation and rake.

**4. You are on the button with J♥J♦. Two players limp, and someone in middle position raises. The player on your right cold-calls. What should you do?**

**Answer:** Reraise. Many people play pocket jacks timidly. They fear an unfavorable flop, such as one or two overcards and no jack. Since these bad flops occur relatively frequently, they conclude that they are better off waiting until they know the flop is favorable before they gamble.

They are wrong. Pocket jacks are a premium holding, and they usually win *far* more than their share against four loose opponents. While unfavorable flops come relatively often, so do favorable flops. You will flop three undercards about a third of the time and a set an additional twelve percent of the time. Those times that you flop a set, your pot equity will often be over seventy percent (against four players). Sets come infrequently, but when they do come, they are extremely profitable.

Remember, when you raise for value against four players, you are not betting that you will win a majority of the time. You are basically betting that you will win more than twenty percent of the time. Unless one of your opponents has a bigger pair, you will almost always win more often than that with jacks. When one of your opponents does have a bigger pair, you will still sometimes outflop him. Your edge is big. To maximize your winnings, you simply must gamble in favorable spots like this. The upsides of waiting to see the flop do not compensate for your failure to make the pot bigger.

**5. You have A♣T♣ in the big blind. Six players limp, including the small blind. What should you do?**

**Answer:** Raise. Your hand figures to win far more than its share against a big field. Again, many timid players dislike gambling with hands like these before the flop. They would check, planning to spring to life on a favorable flop. That strategy is profitable, but it is *less profitable* than raising now. A big suited ace is a terrific hand in a seven-handed pot. Expect to win significantly more often than the fourteen percent of the time that is your share against six opponents. Being out of position should make you somewhat less willing to raise, but not when you have such a strong hand. You must take advantage of an edge this big. In fact, not raising here is *terrible*. It might be a bigger mistake than raising with seven-deuce offsuit!

**6. Two very loose and passive players limp. If they perceive that they have any reasonable chance to draw out, they will call to the river regardless of the size of the pot. They rarely raise after the flop and never as a bluff. You are on the button with J♦4♦. What should you do?**

> **Answer:** Fold. Under normal circumstances, even from the button, you would fold jack-four suited without a second thought. When your opponents play this poorly, however, many marginal hands become profitable. You will win a lot when you make the best hand and lose only a little when you do not. Unfortunately, jack-four is still a little too weak. Against these opponents you will have to make the best hand to win. Jack-four simply does not make the best hand often enough to be profitable. The decision is close, though; for instance, you should definitely play with K♦4♦. A pair of kings will win significantly more often than a pair of jacks, enough difference to make the hand profitable. J♠8♠ would also be worth a play in these circumstances.

**7. Two tight, tricky, and aggressive players limp. They play at least as well as you do after the flop. You are on the button with K♣T♥. What should you do?**

**Answer:** Fold. Hands derive their value from two sources:

1.  Their comparative strength against the range of hands your opponents play.

2.  The frequency and magnitude of mistakes that your opponents are prone to make after the flop.

That is, the weaker the hands your opponents are willing to play, and the more mistakes they make playing them, the more valuable your hand becomes.

Many hands are profitable when played against weak hands and weak players, but unprofitable when played against strong hands and strong players. King-ten offsuit is such a hand. With offsuit hands you make most of your profit against loose players by flopping top pair and letting them call you down with a smaller pair or weak draw. For instance, if the flop comes K♥7♠2♠, and your opponent calls you down with T♣2♣, you make a bundle. He is drawing to only two outs. When your opponents are prone to mistakes like this, even weak hands like king-ten show a profit.

Against tough opponents this will not be the case. Your tight and tricky opponents may limp with hands like K♦Q♦ and A♠A♣, but surely not T♣2♣. They will not call you down with bottom pair, but they will punish you when you are dominated. For instance, say the flop comes K♥7♠2♠, and one of your opponents check-raises you. He may have king-queen or a set, leaving you drawing very thin. But he may have a spade draw. Your choices are to call, paying off a better hand, or to fold, allowing a flush draw to steal the pot. No matter what decisions you make, you will often find yourself taking the worst of it when you play these "trap" hands against a good player.

Therefore, in this example, you would call on the button against two loose, weak limpers, but you should fold against tough opponents.

**8. An aggressive player raises from early position. Three players cold-call, and the small blind folds. You are in the big blind with 9♣6♣. What should you do?**

**Answer:** Call. When the pot is multiway, and it is one bet to you in the big blind, you can call liberally, *especially with suited hands*. This situation is particularly favorable for your hand:

1.   Since the raiser is aggressive, he will often have two big cards instead of a pocket pair. If so, you will sometimes win with only a pair of nines.

2.   The raiser is on your left. This gives you a desirable *relative* position on the flop. If you flop a weak draw like a gutshot or bottom pair, you can check, and he will likely bet. Your other three opponents must then act on the bet before you, giving you an advantage that having absolute position (i.e., the button) usually has: You get to see what your opponents do and how many bets it will be before you act. Having a bet on your right and opponents yet to act presents a problem when you have a weak draw. Sometimes you will call the bet, and it will be raised (and even reraised) behind you. This possibility reduces the value of your hand because you will sometimes be forced to fold profitable draws (or pay too much for them). That is unlikely to happen when you have good position relative to the preflop raiser.

When the raiser is on your left, and there are already several callers, you can call from the big blind with many suited hands. The good relative position, the multiway advantage of being suited, and the one bet discount from the big blind makes hands like K♦2♦, 9♣6♣, and even 5♠2♠ worth playing.

**9. Three loose and passive players limp. You are in the small blind (which is half the size of the big blind) with 6♠2♠. What should you do?**

**Answer:** Call. When deciding whether to play from the small blind, you should always consider implied odds. You are calling the half bet now, not just to win the 4.5 bets currently in the pot, but also to win all the bets that will be made after the flop. From the small blind your implied odds are roughly double what they would be if you called a full bet. Instead of calling one bet for the chance to win twenty after the flop (if that is your estimate of postflop action), you call only half a bet to win the same twenty bets.

The doubled implied odds allow you to loosen up drastically from the small blind. Hands like six-deuce suited are usually too weak to play from outside the blinds because they do not get lucky often enough. That is, though they are quite profitable when you hit your hand (usually by making two pair or better), you do not make a hand this good often enough to compensate for the one bet preflop investment. You do make it often enough to compensate for half a bet, though. Thus, while you would fold from outside the blinds, you can call from the small blind. (Warning: The above advice assumes that you can play well if you flop a mediocre hand like bottom pair or a gutshot. If you understand the postflop concepts in this book, that should not be a problem for you. But hands like six-deuce suited in the small blind, while slightly profitable for a good player, will lose money if played poorly.)

**10. You are playing in a card room with a cap of a bet and four raises (a maximum of five bets on each betting round). Your opponents are very loose and somewhat aggressive. Four players limp. You have K♥Q♥ on the button, and you raise for value. The big blind and the first three limpers call, but the fourth limper reraises. What should you do?**

> **Answer:** Reraise. You raised the first time because you have a very strong suited hand that has a big edge in pot equity against four loose players and the blinds. The player on your right reraising you does not change anything. Sometimes players limp-reraise with strong hands like pocket aces or kings or ace-king. They usually do this because they want action on their big hand. They fear that if they raised immediately, most players would fold. So they limp, hoping to encourage several limpers and a raise behind them. But that is not the case here. It is unlikely that the player on your right has a big hand; three players had already called when he acted. If he held a big hand, he probably would have raised immediately. There is no need for him to limp to get action; there was already plenty of action. He probably has a speculative hand like J♥T♣, 8♦6♦, 5♠5♣, or A♣4♠ and decided to reraise because he thought building a big pot would be fun. This behavior is quite common, particularly in aggressive small stakes games.
>
> Since you have little to fear from your reraising opponent, you should raise again. You have a very strong hand in a multiway pot. Push your edge.[112]
>
> If the cap were a bet and three raises instead, reraising would usually be even more correct. You should almost always be more willing to raise if it caps the betting. Unless you have the nuts, raising exposes you to a reraise from a better hand. Though it is unlikely that the limp-reraiser in this

---

[112] See "Building Big Pots Before the Flop."

case has a big hand, no read is perfect; he can always surprise you. If you cap it, you do not risk a reraise from a superior holding.

In this example, though, it does not matter what the cap is. Worry about it in borderline situations. If your read is correct (and it probably is), your edge is large. Build the pot.

# Hand Quizzes — Flop Play

**1. You have A♣7♣ in middle position. Two players limp, and you limp. The button limps, the small blind calls, and the big blind checks (6 small bets). The flop is A♦T♦9♠, giving you top pair. The small blind bets, the big blind calls, and the first limper raises. The next limper folds (10 small bets). What should you do?**

> **Answer:** Fold. You have top pair with a weak kicker and no redraws. Either the bettor or the raiser could already have you beaten, perhaps with an ace with a better kicker or aces up. If that is the case, you are drawing nearly dead (you'd have to catch a seven, probably not the 7♦, to have any chance to win). Even if you do have the best hand, you are still in bad shape. Any card eight or higher counterfeits your kicker, leaving you no better than tied against any other ace.[113] Furthermore, the three high cards and two-flush are very dangerous. This type of board makes it easy for someone to make a flush, straight, or two pair by the river. If you are behind, you are drawing almost dead. If you are ahead, you will often be outdrawn and usually just tie when you are not outdrawn. The pot is not very large. This is a *clear* fold.

**2. You have 9♥9♠ on the button. Four players limp, and you raise. The big blind and limpers call (12.5 small bets). The flop is 9♣7♣3♠ giving you top set. The big blind bets, and the first limper raises. Two of the three remaining limpers call. What should you do?**

---

[113] See "Hidden Outs."

**Answer:** Reraise. You may recognize this hand as similar to the examples presented in the "Two Overpair Hands" section. The flop and action are identical, except you have a set now instead of an overpair.

In that section, we argued that you should reraise with a pair of aces (with the A♣), but just call with a pair of tens (without the T♣). With the aces you will win probably fifty percent of the time, so your expectation with four opponents on the flop was large. With the tens your hand was more vulnerable, so your flop equity was much smaller.

With a small edge sometimes you should just call and wait for the turn. You do not lose much expectation by missing the flop raise. If the turn card is a blank, your advantage will be much greater (with only the river left that can beat you) and your raise more profitable.

With a large edge you lose a lot of expectation when you miss your flop raise.[114] You can skip the small edges if doing so may give you a tactical advantage later in the hand. But you should bet or raise immediately when that action will show a large return. Thus, you should reraise with the aces.

When you have a set (as in this example), your edge is even larger. You will win the overwhelming majority of the time. Missing this flop raise gives up way too much.

Notice that many players would automatically just call to slowplay this hand (as they do every time they flop a set). This is wrong, not because there is a two-flush on board (you will never force a flush draw to fold no matter how many flop raises you put in), but because your flop edge is too big. You expect everyone to call if you reraise. Take their money now while you have the chance!

---

[114] An exception occurs when you are quite sure a reraise on the flop will result in everyone just calling and then checking to you, while a call on the flop on your part is almost certain to result in another bet and calls on the turn. Only then is it worth waiting for the turn to raise.

3. You have Q♥T♥ in the big blind. Three players limp, and the button raises. You call, as do the limpers (10.5 small bets). The flop is T♠8♣4♥, giving you top pair and a backdoor flush draw. What should you do?

> **Answer:** Check with the intention of raising a bet from late position. Betting out does not protect your hand. If you bet, any prospective caller will be getting over 11-to-1, making it correct to call against your hand with weak draws like bottom pair, gutshots, or even as little as A♠3♠ (an overcard and backdoor flush draw). Since the most likely bettor, the preflop raiser, is on the button, it is likely that your check-raise will make three opponents face two bets cold.[115]
>
> Missing your check-raise (because everyone checks behind you) would be unpleasant. You have a vulnerable hand, and giving a free card is dangerous. But remember, you are check-raising because betting does not protect your hand. Someone with a decent chance to draw out would usually not fold for one bet. So missing the check-raise only rarely costs you the pot. (Though it will cost you a few bets if you go on to win the pot.)
>
> On the other hand, succeeding with the check-raise is frequently the difference between winning and losing. Since the pot is large (raised preflop), you should follow those strategies that improve your winning chances. The button will probably bet, and that is enough reason to try a check-raise.
>
> Some players, fearing that the preflop raiser has a big pair or ace-ten, might be too timid to check-raise. Do not always fear the worst. If the preflop raiser has a big pair, your aggressive play will cost you an extra bet or two. If he does not have a big pair, however, passive play allows weak draws to call profitably. That could cost you the pot. Those times your check-raise wins you the hand more than make up for

---

[115] See "Protecting Your Hand."

the extra bets you lose when behind. Hold 'em generally rewards aggressive play. This is a good example.

**4. You are in a game full of loose and passive opponents. You have K♦4♦ on the button. Four players limp, and you limp. The small blind calls, and the big blind checks (7 small bets). The flop is J♠7♥4♣, giving you bottom pair. Everyone checks to you. What should you do?**

Answer: Bet. Betting is right for two reasons:

1.  It improves your winning chances. If you have the best hand, betting is obviously correct. Even if you do not, you still want people with hands like queen-ten to fold. If you catch a king on the turn, queen-ten picks up an open-ended straight redraw. Betting might even get a better hand like pocket sixes to fold.

2.  Against passive opponents, betting will likely buy a free card on the turn. Your draw is not strong, but the pot is big enough that it is worth investing a small bet to try to get a free look at the river. Against passive opponents (when the free card play is most likely to succeed), if you are on the button, you should usually try for a free card with any hand that is worth calling one bet. Since you definitely would have called here (getting at least 8-to-1), you should probably try for a free card on the turn by betting the flop.

If the game were aggressive, our recommendation would change to a check. Aggressive players check-raise more and give free cards less often. For a bet to be right, your free card play has to work most of the time. Since it will against passive opponents, you should bet.

**5. You limp under the gun with 7♥7♠.** Two players limp behind you, the small blind calls, and the big blind checks (5 small bets). The flop is J♣6♣4♠. The small blind bets, and the big blind calls. What should you do?

> **Answer:** Fold. The pot is small. Two players like their hands enough to bet and call. Two more are yet to act. If anyone has a jack, you are drawing to at most two outs. You could be drawing to only the 7♦, since the 7♣ makes a flush possible. Even if you have the best hand now, your hand is very vulnerable, since so many overcards can beat you. Your predicament here is relatively common. Specifically,
>
> 1. You have a marginal made hand that may not be best.
>
> 2. You have little chance to improve if you are behind.
>
> 3. Your opponents have many opportunities to outdraw you if you are ahead.
>
> 4. The pot is small.
>
> In general, when these conditions apply, you should fold. If you return to Hand No. 1 of these quizzes, you will see that these conditions also apply to that example. We recommended that you fold that hand, and we recommend that you fold this one as well. (Important: There is a big difference between betting and calling. Pocket pairs just above the second highest flop card exemplify this point. In this example if the hand had been checked to you, you should definitely bet.)

**6. You are in a very loose and aggressive game. Your opponents are prone to raise and reraise on the flop with draws and pairs as well as big hands like sets and two pair.**

You are on the button with A♥8♥. The player under the gun raises, and four people cold-call. You call. Both blinds also call (16 small bets). The flop is T♥9♥2♠, giving you the nut flush draw. The small blind bets, the big blind calls, and the preflop raiser raises. Two more players call, and the other two fold (24 small bets). What should you do?

> **Answer:** Reraise. You have a big draw to the nuts. By the river, you will make the nut flush 35 percent of the time, and you will also sometimes win just by spiking an ace. With five remaining opponents, you will win far more often than seventeen percent of the time, so you have a huge pot equity edge. Reraise for value.
>
> Also, since you have position, reraising may allow you to take a free card on the turn if you so choose.[116]

**7. You have A♣4♣ on the button. Three players limp, and you limp. The small blind raises, and the big blind and everyone else call (12 small bets). The flop is K♦5♣2♥, giving you a gutshot, an overcard, and a backdoor flush draw. The small blind bets. The big blind calls, and the first limper raises. The next two limpers fold (16 small bets). What should you do?**

> **Answer:** Reraise! Individually, each of your draws is weak. Taken together, however, you have a relatively robust hand with decent winning chances. Getting 8-to-1, folding is clearly wrong. The pot is almost big enough that you would call with only a gutshot (e.g., six-four). You are just under

---

[116] Do not automatically take the free card, though; betting may be better. It may induce someone to fold a hand like ace-queen, buying you two important outs in this huge pot. Even if no one folds, you will be getting 5-to-1 on your bet (because you have five opponents), and you will be only a 4-to-1 underdog to make your flush. If the turn card weakens your hand, though (for example the T♠), you should take the free card.

11-to-1 to complete your straight on the turn. In a pot this big, if you make your straight, your opponents are almost certain to pay you off for several big bets. Since you should probably call with just a gutshot, you should definitely play with your gutshot, overcard, and backdoor flush draw. Thus, the only question is whether you should call or reraise.

Reraising has two important advantages over calling:

1.  If you reraise, the small blind might fold a better ace. Since he raised preflop, he could easily have a hand like ace-queen or ace-jack. If he folds, it could buy you two more outs. For only one more bet, even with those weak hands, he will probably call. For two bets, he might fold.

2.  Since you have the button, reraising could buy a free card on the turn. If you do not improve, you should almost certainly take it if you get it. The player who raised this ragged flop likely has a king. Do not expect him to fold.

So, unless you are very unlikely to get a free card, you should probably invest the extra small bet and reraise.

**8. You have J♣9♣ in middle position. Two players limp, and you limp. The button limps, the small blind calls, and the big blind checks (6 small bets). The flop is K♥T♦4♣, giving you a gutshot and a backdoor flush draw. The blinds check, and the first limper bets. The next limper raises (9 small bets). What should you do?**

Answer: Fold. You are getting only 4.5-to-1, you are unlikely to win by spiking a pair, and there are several players still to act. The previous example (Hand No. 7) showed that, even if it is two bets to you, there are some times that you should play a gutshot. This is not one of them.

In fact, more often than not, you should fold a gutshot if it is two bets to you.

**9. You have A♥J♣ on the button. Two players limp, and you raise. The big blind and the limpers call (8.5 small bets). The flop is 9♠6♠5♦, giving you two overcards. The blind and the first limper check. The second limper bets (9.5 small bets). What should you do?**

> **Answer:** Fold. You have just the overcards with no backdoor draws. You have six outs to improve, but those can be counted only as partial outs. If you catch an ace, you will sometimes still be behind to someone with ace-nine, ace-six, or ace-five — ace-rag hands are commonly played. If you catch a jack, two overcards can beat you on the river. The A♠ or J♠ may make a flush for someone, or at least set up a river redraw for anyone with a single spade. These considerations devalue your draw; it is probably worth no more than a clean three-outter.
>
> Getting 9.5-to-1, the pot is not big enough to draw to such a weak hand. There are two other factors that should dissuade you from continuing:
>
> 1. The board is coordinated. While unlikely, if someone flopped a straight, you are drawing dead. More importantly, a seven or eight puts four to a straight on board, which is very dangerous.
>
> 2. The bettor is on your right. The players who checked may have strong hands. You will sometimes call the first bet only to run into a check-raise. A check-raise is particularly likely since you raised before the flop and players tend to check to the raiser.

**10. Three players limp to you, one off the button, with Q♠Q♣. You raise. Both blinds and the three limpers call (12 small bets). The flop is J♦6♦4♦, giving you an overpair. Your opponents check to you, and you bet. The small blind check-raises, and two players cold-call (19 small bets). What should you do?**

> **Answer:** Call. Getting 19-to-1, the pot is far too big to fold. While it is possible that one of your opponents has a flush, you cannot be certain. *Do not fold decent hands in big pots on mere suspicion of the worst.* To fold, you must be quite certain with specific, compelling evidence that you are drawing dead. In this hand the small blind could easily have just top pair or the A♦. If the cold-callers are loose, they could have almost anything. You absolutely cannot fold.[117]
>
> With three players against you, your hand is quite vulnerable. There is almost certainly a flush draw (if not already a made flush), and each of your three opponents probably has at least a few other outs against you as well. If you are ahead at this point, your winning chances are probably no better than thirty percent. If behind, you are drawing almost dead. This is certainly not a good spot to reraise. Call now, planning to evaluate all three options (raise, call, or fold) on fourth street.

**11. You have 7♣6♣ in the big blind. The player under the gun raises, and three players cold-call. You call (10.5 small bets). The flop is K♣8♥4♣, giving you a gutshot and a flush draw. What should you do?**

---

[117] At least you cannot fold yet. If the turn is a diamond or another dangerous card, or if one of the flop callers wakes up and raises on the turn, you can seriously consider folding.

**Answer:** Check with the intention of raising a bet from *early* position. You have a big draw that will often win. With small cards you do not have much chance to win by pairing, so eliminating opponents will not significantly improve your winning chances.

Since your draw is so strong, you should bet or raise for value. If you bet, one of two things will likely happen:

1. The preflop raiser will raise (usually with a king) and face the field with cold-calling two bets.

2. The preflop raiser will just call, and a couple of others will call behind him.

Neither of these scenarios is optimal. The first scenario eliminates players, leaving you against an opponent with top pair. This does not maximize the value of your big draw. The second scenario will often only get one bet in on the flop.

If you check, the preflop raiser (on your left) will usually bet a relatively ragged flop like this no matter what he has. Loose players behind him will call the single flop bet with many hands. Then you check-raise, trapping everyone for two bets. *Use the position of the likely flop bettor to help you choose between betting and check-raising with your strong hands and draws.*

**12. You have 2♥2♦ in the big blind. A very loose and aggressive player limps under the gun. Three more players limp, the small blind completes, and you check (6 small bets). The flop is K♥7♣2♠, giving you bottom set. The small blind checks, and you check, hoping to raise a bet from the aggressive player on your left. Unfortunately, he checks, and it is checked to the button who bets (7 small bets). The small blind folds. What should you do?**

**Answer:** Call. While you should rarely slowplay in loose games, you should here. You checked, hoping to trap the field for two bets, but your play backfired; the player on your right bet.

Remember the three questions we told you to ask yourself at the end of the "Slowplaying" section:

1.  If I give my opponents a cheap card, will it improve them only to a *second-best* hand or *unprofitable* draw, or will they sometimes beat me or make a profitable draw? (Again, a draw is profitable only if its implied odds are greater than its odds of being completed.)

2.  Am I willing to risk losing the pot occasionally for a chance to win an extra bet or two?

3.  How likely are my opponents to call if I do raise?

When the flop is this ragged (no straight or flush draws possible), almost no one will have a decent hand or draw. Even so, loose players are often willing to call one flop bet to see if their hand develops on fourth street. For instance, many players would call a bet with queen-jack to see if they pick up a straight draw or a pair on the turn. If it is two bets to them, though, they fold.

Your hand is so strong that most of your opponents are already drawing nearly dead. You may have over an eighty percent chance to win, even if all four of your remaining opponents see the river. The pot is small, so you do not risk too much by encouraging your opponents to remain in the hand.

For instance, say the player with queen-jack calls one bet on the flop, and a jack comes on the turn. Now he is drawing totally dead (on the flop his only chance to beat you was his backdoor straight draw). Yet he will likely pay you off for at least one big bet on both the turn and river. If he gets "lucky" and makes two pair or trips on the river, he will probably raise, and you can reraise, winning two extra big bets from him.

If you raise him (and the others) out now, you improve your chance of winning from, say, 85 percent to 95 percent. But in a pot this small, improving your winning chances by ten percent (assuming no more betting action) is worth less than one small bet (10 percent of the seven bet pot is 0.7 bets). Allowing your opponents to draw nearly dead against your monster hand is worth far more.

By the way, even though you just called on the flop, you should probably *bet out* on the turn, no matter what comes. Slowplaying on the flop does not obligate you to try for a check-raise on fourth street. If you check the turn, one of two things will probably happen:

1. Everyone will check to the button, who will bet. You will again have to choose between calling, missing the chance to get value for your monster hand, and blowing away the field with a raise.

2. Everyone will check to the button, who will check. Obviously, that is even worse than the first scenario.

Betting out is better than either of these scenarios. It will confuse your opponents, making them more likely to call even if they are drawing dead. Someone with a lesser hand may even raise. Betting out also ensures that you do not give a free card. Your attempt to trap the field for two bets failed on the flop. On the turn it is even less likely to succeed. Abandon it and use a different plan.[118]

---

[118] This hand is an example of an important general principle. If you check and call with a monster when the bettor is on your right, you

This hand exemplifies a concept that appears repeatedly throughout this book. To win the most possible playing hold 'em, you must *maximize your expectation for the whole hand*. Usually this means that you bet or raise immediately with your good hands. But sometimes it means that you play your hand in a different manner.

In this hand, two important factors shape your strategy: the size of the pot and your position relative to the other players (particularly the aggressive player). If we had made the pot bigger, you should raise. If we had moved the aggressive player to your right, you should bet out instead trying for a check-raise. In either of these cases the aggressive strategy becomes best. But given the specific parameters of this example, a passive strategy maximizes your expectation.

Average players usually play the same way no matter what. They might always check and call to slowplay. They might always bet and raise. Expert players take all the parameters into account and choose the optimal strategy.

**13. You have 8♦7♦ on the button. Two players limp, you limp, the small blind calls, and the big blind checks (5 small bets). The flop is K♠T♥9♣, giving you an open-ended straight draw. The small blind bets, the big blind calls, and the first limper raises (9 small bets). The second limper folds. What should you do?**

> **Answer:** Fold. Your draw is open-ended, but it is quite weak. If a jack comes, anyone with a queen beats you. If a six comes on the turn, you may lose anyway if a jack or queen comes on the river. In fact, sometimes you will be drawing dead already to someone with queen-jack. You have no backdoor flush draw and almost no hope of winning by

---

should not go for a check-raise on the next round if players called behind you. That play should be considered only when the bettor is on your left.

spiking a pair. Getting 9-to-2 is not enough in this spot. You should not fold many open-ended straight draws on the flop, but you should fold this one.

**14. You have A♥A♦ in middle position. One player limps, and you raise. Two players cold-call, the small blind folds, and the big blind reraises. The limpers call, and you cap. Everyone calls (20.5 small bets). The flop is Q♥9♥9♠. The big blind bets, and the limper raises (23.5 small bets). What should you do?**

**Answer:** Call with the intention of raising on the turn. This board is scary, and you might be beaten already. Still, you cannot fold. The pot is way too big. When you build enormous pots preflop with big pairs, you generally *commit yourself to a showdown*. While there are occasionally exceptions if things go very badly, this is definitely not one of them. Even if someone does have a nine, you have two outs to aces full and a backdoor nut flush draw that will sometimes bail you out.

Calling is probably better than raising. Putting in a third bet is unlikely to protect your hand; the only hands that will fold are hands that you have badly beaten. Also, the flop raiser is on your immediate right. He is likely to bet the turn as long as he is not reraised on the flop. If you call and let him bet the turn, you can then raise to force the field to call two big bets cold.

On this board your main target is someone with a gutshot. People with four-flushes and jack-ten (an open-ended straight draw) will not fold, no matter how many raises you put in. The pot is too large; you just have to hope that they miss. Someone with a queen or pocket pair has only two outs against you. A gutshot has four outs and is a legitimate threat. On fourth street the pot will probably be around fifteen big bets. A gutshot can call profitably for one bet, but not two. Thus, you should strongly consider raising the turn.

When the pot is this large, focus on maximizing your winning chances. Do not try to save bets, and do not try to squeeze an extra bet out of someone drawing thin. Protect your hand! The best chance to do that is to call now, planning to raise the turn.[119]

**15. You have Q♠Q♣ in middle position. One player limps, and you raise. Two players cold-call, and the big blind calls (10.5 small bets). The flop is K♠9♥7♠, giving you a pair much higher than middle pair. The big blind bets, and the limper folds (11.5 small bets). What should you do?**

**Answer:** Raise. It is a little unnatural to bet a king from the big blind into four players, including a preflop raiser. Most players would check: Passive players might check and call for fear that you have ace-king, and aggressive players might check, planning to check-raise. While the bettor could have a king anyway, he could also very well have a flush or straight draw or even a weaker hand that he decided to bluff.

Since the pot is large, you probably should not fold. Your winning chances are too strong. If you did not have the Q♠, your decision would be closer. Having the Q♠ improves your hand in two ways:

1. If you spike a set, an opponent cannot make a flush using the same card.

2. It gives you a backdoor flush draw.

*Without* the Q♠ you might fold against a particularly straightforward opponent who wouldn't bet a draw or middle pair. You should almost certainly not fold *with* it, though.

---

[119] See the sub-section "When a Raise Will Not Protect Your Hand" in the section "Protecting Your Hand."

Since you are continuing, you should raise to protect your hand. Anyone with a gutshot or middle or bottom pair can profitably call one bet on the flop (getting 12-to-1), but not two (getting 6.5-to-1). Even though you are not sure whether your hand is best, you should still force people with weak draws to choose between calling unprofitably and folding.[120]

**16. You are in a loose and very aggressive game. You have A♠J♠ in the big blind. Four players, including the small blind, limp. You raise. Two limpers call, and then the button reraises. The small blind calls, and you cap. Everyone calls (20 small bets). The flop is K♥Q♣7♠, giving you a gutshot, an overcard, and a backdoor flush draw. The small blind checks, and you bet. The first limper raises, the second limper reraises, and the third limper caps. The small blind folds (30 small bets). What should you do?**

Answer: Call. You are getting 30-to-3 or 10-to-1 immediate pot odds with no chance to be reraised. Three more bets (the two impending calls) are almost certain to go in as well, lifting your odds to 33-to-3 or 11-to-1. You have a gutshot to the nuts, as well as an overcard (admittedly it is probably not good, given the action), and a backdoor nut-flush draw. Folding, even though your draw is weak, would be a blunder. The pot is too big.[121]

---

[120] See "Protecting Your Hand."

[121] For an explanation of the preflop action, raising and then capping from the big blind with A♠J♠, see Hand No. 10 in "Hand Quizzes — Preflop Play." To maximize your expectation in small stakes games, you must become comfortable with building huge pots with your premium hands. You give up a lot if you insist on keeping the pot small.

**17. You have Q♠5♠ in the small blind. Three players limp, and you call. The big blind checks (5 small bets). The flop is K♦T♦5♣. You check. The big blind and first limper check. The second limper bets, and the button calls (7 small bets). What should you do?**

> **Answer:** Fold. You are getting 7-to-1 to call, which is close to the threshold for a five out hand that also has a small chance to be best at the moment. A few factors tip this hand to a fold:
>
> 1.  There is a two-flush. Catching the Q♦ or 5♦ will sometimes give someone a flush and will almost always set up a redraw for anyone with a lone diamond.
>
> 2.  Any queen puts three Broadway cards on board. Straights and two pair (bigger than queens and fives) are more likely than usual with three high cards. Also, a queen gives anyone with an ace or nine a gutshot and anyone with a jack an open-ended straight draw.
>
> 3.  You must count on improving to win. Even if your pair of fives is the best hand right now (which is relatively unlikely), you have to dodge flushes, straights, overcards, and bluffs you cannot call to win.

**18. You have 4♣3♣ in the big blind. Three players limp, and someone in middle position raises. The button cold-calls, the small blind calls, and you call. Both limpers call as well (14 small bets). The flop is A♥J♥4♠, giving you bottom pair. Everyone checks to the preflop raiser who bets. The button calls (16 small bets). What should you do?**

> **Answer:** Call. Your draw is very weak. There is a two-flush. There are two Broadway cards on board. You could be

drawing almost dead against a set or to two outs against ace-jack. Catching the 4♥ or 3♥ could give someone a flush. Even if you catch one of your magic cards on fourth street, someone could outdraw you on the river. If you make two pair on the turn, any ace or jack on the river counterfeits your hand. You do not close the action; someone could check-raise.

Despite all this, you should call. The pot is just too big. Your draw is dubious, and you could lose even if you get there. But that is not quite enough reason to fold a potential five-out draw getting 16-to-1. Put the money in and hope for the best.

**19. You have A♠K♦ on the button. Three players limp, and you raise. Both blinds and all the limpers call (12 small bets). The flop is K♠9♠6♣, giving you top pair and a backdoor, nut flush draw. Everyone checks to you, and you bet. The small blind check-raises, and three people cold-call (21 small bets). What should you do?**

**Answer:** Reraise. You probably have the best hand, and you have a backdoor nut flush draw just in case. No overcards can beat your pair. With flush and straight draws available your hand is somewhat vulnerable, though. Even so, this hand is strong enough to win significantly more than its share (twenty percent against four opponents).

Notice that something a little unexpected happened. The small blind check-raised, probably hoping that your other opponents would fold. Instead, three out of four called. Normally, you could count on the flop check-raiser to bet the turn. Here you cannot; the unwanted callers might scare him into checking.

You have too much equity to miss a raise. If you knew the small blind would bet the turn if you just called, then you would prefer waiting until then to raise. But do not wait unless you are confident your opponent will bet. Here you are better off taking the sure thing.

**20. You have 6♥6♦ on the button. Five players limp, and the player on your right raises. You cold-call, both blinds call, and all the limpers call (18 small bets). The flop is T♠6♠6♣ giving you quads. Everyone checks to you. What should you do?**

> **Answer:** Bet. Checking is absurd. Your opponents are clearly very loose (tight players do not make nine-handed pots). Since the pot is large, they will find any excuse they can to call: a flush draw, a gutshot, two overcards, one overcard, a backdoor straight draw, a backdoor two pair draw, etc. Do not be surprised if all eight of your opponents call. They do not know you flopped quads. They do not know they are drawing dead. Even if they did know, half of them would probably call anyway.
>
> Your pot equity is nearly 100 percent. That edge is *way* too big not to push. If you would bet pocket aces here (and you should), then definitely bet quads as well.
>
> Slowplaying is useful only if the pot is small, and you expect most or all of your opponents to *fold* if you bet. In this example expect six or seven of your eight opponents to call. *But they can't call if you don't bet!*

# Hand Quizzes — Turn Play

**1. You have A♠K♠ on the button. Four players limp, and you raise. The big blind and limpers call (12.5 small bets). The flop is T♠6♠4♣, giving you the nut flush draw and two overcards. Everyone checks, and you bet. Three players call (8 big bets). The turn is the 2♦. Everyone checks. What should you do?**

> **Answer:** Bet. You should not take a free card. There are a few reasons. First, you could still have the best hand. Since the pot is large, many players would call on the flop with almost any two cards. The flop calls do *not* necessarily indicate that someone has a reasonable hand. Remember, your opponents are loose and do not have the same calling standards that you do.
>
> Several good things could happen because you bet. If some of your opponents fold, your chances to win unimproved or by spiking a pair increase. For example, someone might fold a hand like 9♥7♥, a gutshot straight draw, even though it has seven outs to beat you (excluding the spades that give you a flush, there are 2 nines, 3 eights, and 2 sevens that beat you). You also obviously want a hand like A♦4♦, bottom pair with an ace kicker, to fold. That could buy you two outs (the remaining aces). In a large pot like this one, improving your winning chances even a little bit is worthwhile.
>
> If everyone calls, that is fine as well. You have fifteen cards to make top pair or the nut flush, making you slightly worse than a 2-to-1 underdog to improve. If everyone calls, you will get 3-to-1 odds on your bet. While you might not win with just top pair, there is still enough overlay to bet for value.

Even if the worst happens — you get check-raised — it is not so bad. You have seven outs to the nuts, and a few more of your outs may be good as well. But you will not be check-raised on this ragged board very often. Usually some of your opponents will just call, and others will fold. Every player who folds potentially improves your winning chances. *But they can't fold if you don't bet.*

**2. You have 9♥9♦ on the button. Three players limp, and you raise. The small blind calls, and the big blind reraises. Two of the limpers fold, but one calls. You call, and so does the small blind (14 small bets). The flop is J♥3♦3♠. The small blind checks, and the big blind bets. The limper calls, you call, and the small blind calls (9 big bets). The turn is the 4♣. Everyone checks to you. What should you do?**

**Answer:** Bet. You *must* bet here. The pot is large, and you may have the best hand. Except for the big blind's preflop reraise, no one has shown much strength so far. When the big blind checks the turn, he probably has two big cards, like ace-king, rather than an overpair or a jack. He could have pocket tens, but otherwise you probably have him beaten.

Likewise, you probably have the limper beaten. He has done nothing but call so far, and he checked the turn. If he had a jack or trey, he probably would have bet. He likely has two unpaired cards (that may be overcards to your nines).

The small blind could have you beaten. He might have checked a trey twice, planning to check-raise on fourth street. He also may have played a jack timidly. But there is no good reason to give him credit for a good hand. He has done nothing but call so far, which usually means that he has little.

Your hand is vulnerable. Any of four additional overcards to your nines could beat you. You should bet to protect your hand.[122]

**3. You have A♠A♣ on the button. Three players limp, and you raise. Both blinds and all the limpers call (12 small bets). The flop is Q♥7♦3♣. Everyone checks, and you bet. Three people call (8 big bets). The turn is the 9♣. Everyone checks, and you bet. The first player folds, the second calls, and the third check-raises (12 big bets). What should you do?**

Answer: Call. You are probably behind. A player who check-raises the field on the turn (i.e., check-raises after one or more players have already called) is rarely bluffing. This board is also relatively ragged, so the chance that he is pushing a draw is reduced.

Still, you cannot fold. The pot is too big. You are getting 12-to-1 to call, and your opponent could have two pair. You have eight outs to beat any two pair (2 aces, and 6 cards that pair the board but do not give him a full house), making you only a 4.75-to-1 underdog.[123]

---

[122] Even though, in this particular case, you are quite likely to have the best hand, you need not feel that you have the best hand anywhere near fifty percent of the time for betting to be correct. There are two reasons for this:

1.   Those times you do have the best hand, betting might save the whole pot because someone with overcards folds who would have made a higher pair on the river.

2.   Betting will often allow you to take a free showdown. So you invest an extra bet on the turn, but you frequently save a bet on the river.

[123] See the section "Hidden Outs."

Your other opponent does pose a small threat, as he could have flopped a pair other than the two that the check-raiser might have (e.g., the check-raiser might have nine-seven and the caller queen-ten). In that case, you have only five outs against two pair if the caller remains in the hand. Even so, five outs is plenty when you are getting 12-to-1 to call.

Also, do not assume that you must be behind. Your opponent is probably not bluffing, but he could have just top pair. Folding is a monumental mistake if you still have the best hand. While he probably has at least two pair, the chance that he could have only top pair helps make calling profitable.

Reraising is also a strong option. It might buy you two outs by knocking out the caller. In fact, if you plan to call a bet on the river (and you probably should), then reraising is better than calling *if* the check-raiser will call your reraise and check the river. Calling the turn and river costs two more bets, and so does reraising the turn and checking the river.

But reraising exposes you to an expensive four-bet. So consider reraising only if your opponent is passive, ideally so passive that he would not four-bet without the nuts (pocket queens). Definitely do not reraise against an aggressive player who might four-bet you with only two pair.

Either way, folding is very wrong. When the pot is large, as it often will be when you have a big pocket pair, *you typically cannot fold your overpair on fourth street for one bet even if you are sure you are behind.*

**4. You have T♣7♠ in the big blind. Three players limp, the small blind calls, and you check (5 small bets). The flop is Q♥9♦4♦. The small blind checks, you check, and it is checked around (2.5 big bets). The turn is the 7♥. The small blind bets. What should you do?**

**Answer:** Fold. The small blind could be bluffing, but you should still fold in this small pot. In addition to the small blind, who could have you beaten, there are three more players yet to act. If you are behind to any of them, you are drawing slim. There are five cards that will improve you, but of these only the 7♣ does not put three cards to a straight or flush on board. Even if you are ahead, your hand is quite vulnerable to redraws. You are drawing slim if behind, your opponents may be drawing quite live if you are ahead, and the pot is small. Fold.

**5. You have A♦9♦ in the big blind. The player under the gun raises, two players cold-call, the small blind calls, and you call (10 small bets). The flop is T♥4♠4♦. The small blind checks, you check, and it is checked around (5 big bets). The turn is the 9♣. The small blind bets. What should you do?**

**Answer:** Raise. The small blind may be bluffing, but unlike in Hand No. 4, you should take a stand in a raised pot. He could have a ten or a four, but he might also bet with a variety of other hands including a nine with a weaker kicker than yours, a small pocket pair, a straight draw, or a total bluff.

The paired board makes it less likely that a better hand is out against you. There are only five cards (3 tens and 2 fours) that can beat you, whereas in Hand No. 4, six cards (3 queens and 3 nines) as well as any seven with a better kicker had you beaten.

Furthermore, this board has fewer draws, so your opponents will draw out on you less often when you are ahead, while you will draw out on an opponent with a ten more often when you are behind — your partial outs are stronger on a non-coordinated board. So, compared to Hand No. 4, your hand is stronger, and the pot is larger. These differences mean you should not fold.

Raising is better than calling because it protects your hand. Someone may have picked up a straight draw. You should force these possible holdings to call two bets. Furthermore, your raise may occasionally cause someone with a ten to fold, as your play may appear to others as a slowplayed four.

Raising will occasionally cost you an extra bet when you run into a four or a full house. Nevertheless, you should not play passively in a multiway pot with a vulnerable hand. *Play aggressively and protect your equity.*

**6. You have K♥K♦ under the gun. You raise. Two players cold-call, and both blinds call (10 small bets). The flop is J♥6♦3♥. The blinds check, you bet, and everyone calls (7.5 big bets). The turn is the Q♠. The small blind bets, and the big blind calls. What should you do?**

Answer: Raise. The turn card is a little scary, as now anyone with queen-jack has two pair. Still, the pot is large, and you should not let a funny, unexpected bet stop you from protecting your hand. If the small blind has made two pair, you have eight outs. If he hasn't, you still probably have the best hand. In that case, it is crucial that you raise.

Getting in a raise on fourth street is extremely valuable with a vulnerable hand in a large pot. Almost no weak draw can call two bets cold on the turn profitably. *You cannot afford to let a strange bet freeze you up and miss this raising opportunity.*

**7. You have 8♥7♥ in the big blind. Two players limp, and the button raises. The small blind calls, you call, and the limpers call (10 small bets). The flop is K♦9♥5♠, giving you a gutshot and a backdoor flush draw. Everyone checks to the button, who bets. The small blind calls, you call, and one limper calls (7 big bets). The turn is the 2♠. Everyone checks to the button,**

who bets. The small blind folds (8 big bets). What should you do?

Answer: Fold. You are a 10.5-to-1 underdog to catch a six, and the pot lays only 8-to-1. It is very unlikely that you could make up the three extra bets on the river, so your implied odds are not favorable enough to call. Furthermore, while relatively unlikely, someone behind you could check-raise, which would make your call very costly. Also, the 6♠ does not give you the nuts, since it completes a backdoor flush. *You should frequently call on the flop with a weak draw, but abandon it when you miss to the double-sized turn bet.*

8. You have A♥Q♥ on the button. Four players limp, and you raise. The small blind folds, the big blind calls, and the limpers call (12.5 small bets). The flop is Q♠T♠7♥, giving you top pair and a backdoor nut flush draw. The big blind bets, the first limper calls, and the second one raises. The next player cold-calls, and the final limper folds. You call. The big blind and the first limper call (11 big bets). The turn is the 3♣. It is checked to the flop raiser who bets. The next player calls (13 big bets). What should you do?

Answer: Raise. The reason you just called the flop raise was to get a raise in on fourth street if a blank fell. The 3♣ is a great card for you; follow through with your plan. The pot is large, and you could well have the best hand.[124]

We have had several examples where you have had a marginal, vulnerable, one pair hand, and we have advocated raising the turn. This raise is a critical play that most small stakes players miss. Some people are unwilling to raise the

---

[124] Again, it is not necessary that your hand be best even close to fifty percent of the time for raising to be correct. Your raise could save you the pot, and it could also buy you a free showdown if you want it.

turn with one pair. They freeze up completely on the big bet streets when someone else shows strength by betting into them. Not everyone who bets the turn has two pair, even when the bet is unexpected or comes from a new opponent.

In fact, many times an unexpected turn bet actually indicates weakness, not strength. When someone checks and calls the flop with bottom pair and improves to two pair or trips on the turn, he often naturally tries for a check-raise rather than betting out. So when you see someone check and call the flop, but bet the turn, for many players, his chances of bluffing or betting a weak made hand have gone up. Perhaps he picked up a flush draw, or maybe he has just a small pair and wants to gauge your reaction to his bet. *Either way, if the pot large and multiway, do not play cautiously; protect your hand.*

**9. You have 8♣6♣ on the button. Three players limp, you limp, the small blind calls, and the big blind checks (6 small bets). The flop is J♣9♣4♥, giving you a flush draw. The small blind checks, the big blind bets, and two of the three limpers call. You raise. The small blind folds, and the big blind and limpers call (7 big bets). The turn is the Q♦. Everyone checks to you. What should you do?**

Answer: Check. Take the free card. You are relatively unlikely to win the pot with a bet against three opponents. A pair of eights or sixes will probably not be enough to win, even if you thin the field a little by betting. You cannot bet for value because you are over a 4-to-1 underdog to make your flush, and you have only three opponents. Furthermore, the turn card is one that could have made someone a straight or two pair, and he could be planning to check-raise. This is a straightforward application of the free card play.

10. You have A♥6♥ on the button. Two players limp. The player on your right, a loose and weak player new to poker, limps. You limp, the small blind calls, and the big blind checks (6 small bets). The flop is A♦Q♣4♥, giving you top pair. Everyone checks to the player on your right, who bets. You raise. Everyone folds to the flop bettor, who calls (5 big bets). The turn is the 4♦. Your opponent checks. What should you do?

> **Answer:** Bet. Your weak opponent is unlikely to pull any tricky moves. If he check-raises, you are likely badly beaten and can safely fold in this small pot. Having said that, you are probably no worse than tied. Your opponent could have bet the flop with an ace, but he also could have a queen, a pocket pair, or some strange holding he decided to bluff with. If he has an ace, the four pairing solves your kicker problem unless he has ace-king, ace-queen, or ace-four. So there are only a few possible hands that beat you.
>
> The pot is small, and if you are ahead, your opponent likely has only a couple of outs to beat your aces up. So you do not need to protect your hand; this bet is for value. You are hoping that your poor-playing opponent will call you down with a dubious holding.
>
> Winning small stakes poker often involves isolating and attacking confused players. Your strategy against them should be to wait for decent made hands and then value bet every time you get the opportunity. Do not give free cards and free showdowns. This is a perfect, low-risk, value-betting opportunity.

11. You have 7♦6♦ on the button. Two players limp, you limp, the small blind calls, and the big blind checks (5 small bets). The flop is Q♦8♦5♣, giving you a huge draw — an open-ended straight draw plus a flush draw (fifteen outs, twice). The small blind bets, and all three players call. You raise. The small

blind reraises. Everyone calls again. You four-bet. Everyone calls (12.5 big bets). The turn is the 3♦, completing your flush. Everyone checks to the player directly on your right, who bets. What should you do?

> **Answer:** Raise. It is a little scary that this player woke up with a bet when the flush card came. If he has a flush, it is probably bigger than your seven-high flush (leaving you drawing dead). Nevertheless, you must raise. The pot is large, and you should protect your hand against bigger one card flush draws. Obviously no one with the A♦ will fold (but you should still usually charge that person two bets). A player with the K♦ may not fold either, but someone with the lone J♦, T♦, or 9♦ may well fold to two big bets. *Again, do not assume the worst just because someone bets the turn, and protect your hand when the pot is large.*

**12. You have A♣Q♣ on the button. Four players limp, and you raise. Both blinds fold, and the limpers call (11.5 small bets). The flop is J♦9♣5♣, giving you the nut flush draw and two overcards. Everyone checks to you, and you bet. The first limper check-raises. Two of the three remaining limpers cold-call. You reraise. Everyone calls (11.5 big bets). The turn is the J♥. The first limper (and flop check-raiser) bets. One player calls, and then the next raises (15.5 big bets). What should you do?**

> **Answer:** Call. The pot is too big to fold. The board is paired, so someone could have a full house, leaving you drawing dead. But you are getting almost 8-to-1 on your call. That is too much overlay to abandon for the times you are drawing live. When you jam the flop betting with a big draw (as you usually should), you generally also tie yourself to the pot even if the turn card weakens your draw. You must be fairly sure that someone already has a full house to consider

folding, and so far there is no reason to give anyone credit for more than just three jacks.[125]

**13. You have J♥5♦ in the big blind. Two players limp, the small blind calls, and you check (4 small bets). The flop is J♣8♣3♥, giving you top pair. The small blind checks, and you bet. The first limper folds, but the second raises. The small blind folds, and you call (4 big bets). The turn is the 9♠. You check, and your opponent bets. What should you do?**

**Answer:** Fold. You bet the flop because there was a strong chance that you had the best hand. While you did not have a strong kicker, any top pair will often be the best hand in a four-way, unraised pot. When raised, you cannot like your hand much anymore. It is likely that you are behind to a jack with a stronger kicker. Even if you are ahead, your opponent probably has a decent draw (e.g., a flush draw, perhaps also with an overcard to your jacks). So you will rarely outdraw your opponent if behind, but he will outdraw you relatively often if you are ahead.

You might fold immediately to the flop raise, but there are a few reasons to call.

1.   You could catch a five and improve to the best hand.

2.   Your opponent might be raising with a draw. In that case, he may check behind on the turn when you check. When that happens, you will win the pot most of the time.

3.   Sometimes you should make a somewhat "loose" call when you are raised on the flop. That is, if you bet and

---

[125] See the subsection "Continuing When You Might Be Drawing Dead" in the section "Large Pots vs. Small Pots."

are raised, you should not always fold immediately even if you think you do not have odds to continue. If you always fold, your opponents may begin to play their weak hands more aggressively, knowing that you will often give up instantly. Many small stakes players are completely unaware, but some will pick up on your folding pattern and test you.

These three considerations combined can make calling the flop raise correct. But no matter what, you should usually give up on the turn when you do not improve, and your opponent bets. *Calling down with probable second-best hands in small pots is not profitable.*

**14. You have 6♣5♣ in the big blind. Four players limp, and the button raises. The small blind folds. You call, and the limpers call (12.5 small bets). The flop is Q♦7♣3♥, giving you a gutshot and a backdoor flush draw. You check, and it is checked to the button, who bets. You call, and three other players call (8.5 big bets). The turn is the 4♠, completing your straight. What should you do?**

Answer: Bet. Most players would instinctively try for a check-raise, but that is probably not the best play. You have the nuts, and no flush draw is available. Your goal should be to get as much action as possible from your remaining opponents.

If you check, two scenarios are more likely than any other:

1.  It is checked to the button, who bets. Your check-raise would then face the other players (who are probably drawing dead) with calling two bets cold.

2. It is checked to the button, and he checks behind. He is likely to do that if he has unimproved big cards like ace-king.

Either way, you do not get the most from your hand. Check-raising blasts everyone out of the pot because the likely bettor is on your right. And you may not even land that check-raise because it could easily get checked through. *This is a very important concept, so make sure you understand it.* If you bet, you will often get called in several places. If you are lucky, you may get raised, allowing you to reraise. You will almost certainly get more action by betting out, so that is what you should do.

**15. You have 6♣5♣ in the big blind. Four players limp, and the button raises. The small blind folds. You call, and the limpers call (12.5 small bets). The flop is Q♦9♣5♥, giving you bottom pair and a backdoor flush draw. You check, and it is checked to the button, who bets. You call,[126] and three other players call (8.5 big bets). The turn is the 6♠, giving you two pair. What should you do?**

Answer: Check, planning to check-raise. This situation is very different from Hand No. 14. While the action is the same, you have bottom two pair instead of the nut straight. This hand is far more vulnerable; a queen or nine counterfeits your two pair, and anyone with one big pair can also beat you by pairing his kicker. Furthermore, anyone with a lone seven or eight has a gutshot straight draw, and plenty of hands like king-jack make a gutshot draw with the queen and nine.

The pot is large, and you are quite vulnerable. Your chief concern should be to maximize your chances of winning the pot. The best way to do that is by check-raising the button,

---

[126] A raise would be okay also.

facing the field with calling two cold. Now you *want* to blast everyone out of the pot.

Again, it could be checked around, but it is so beneficial to protect your hand that you must run that risk. Betting out does not achieve this. After all, the point of betting with the nuts was to encourage people drawing dead to call. Many of those same hands are now drawing live and can call one bet profitably.

You may find it counter-intuitive to bet out with the nuts, but check-raise (normally a stronger move) with a much weaker hand. When choosing a betting sequence, do not automatically play your strong hands strongly and your weak hands weakly. *Instead, decide what result you would like to obtain* (lots of callers or no callers, for instance), *and then choose the action that maximizes your chance to achieve the desired result.*

# Hand Quizzes — River Play

1. Two players limp, and you raise from one off the button with Q♥Q♦. The big blind and the limpers call (8.5 small bets). The flop is T♥8♥4♣, giving you an overpair. Your opponents check, and you bet. They all call (6 big bets). The turn is the 4♦. Your opponents check, and you bet. The big blind calls, but the limpers fold (8 big bets). The river is the A♥. Your opponent bets (9 big bets). What should you do?

> **Answer:** Call. The river is scary, and your opponent could recognize that. Many players, even some typically passive ones, decide to try a bluff when an ace comes. While your opponent could easily have outdrawn you, you are getting 9-to-1 to call, so you need win only ten percent of the time to break even. Expect to catch a bluff significantly more often than that. Unless you have very strong evidence that you are beaten, do not fold decent hands for one bet on the river. An out-of-the-blue bet at a scare card is anything but.

2. You have A♥T♥ in the small blind. Three loose and straightforward players limp, and you raise. The big blind folds, and the three limpers call (9 small bets). The flop is K♣T♣4♥, giving you middle pair and a backdoor flush draw. You bet, and two limpers call (6 big bets). The turn is the 2♥, giving you a flush draw. You bet, and both limpers call again (9 big bets). The river is the 7♣. What should you do?

> **Answer:** Bet. You probably have the best hand. You have second pair with an ace kicker, and no one has shown any strength thus far. One of your opponents may have a king (probably with a weak kicker) or may have drawn out with a hand like T♦7♦ or 7♥7♣. Remember, though, that they are

299

*loose.* Since they call with all sorts of hands, do not fear the worst. Being straightforward, your opponents would have raised already with a big hand; most players do not slowplay to the river.

Since they have just called the whole way, you cannot use their actions to define their hands. You can use the underlying distribution of hands (i.e., weak hands are much more common than strong hands) to aid you. Your opponents' holdings, in rough order of likelihood, are:

1. A weak made hand (A♣4♦, 5♥5♣, T♣8♠, etc.)
2. A busted flush or straight draw
3. A king
4. Two pair or trips made on the river

It is not that unlikely that both of your opponents have weak made hands, and that they will both pay you off, producing two extra bets.

Furthermore, if you are behind, you cannot necessarily save a bet by checking. Your opponent may value bet his hand, and you will have to call to defend against a bluff. Checking allows your opponents to value bet their better hands and show down their weak ones. This is a very important concept. Think about it.

Finally, since your opponents are straightforward, you can probably fold if someone raises. Most players would never consider a bluff-raise in this situation.[127]

---

[127] Obviously, if you suspect your opponent might bluff, you should call a raise. In fact, if one of your opponents is very bluff-happy, checking may be better than betting. Since he bluffs so often, you make more money by allowing him to do so and then picking him off. Most players do not fit this description, though. So unless you have are up against a habitual bluffer, bet.

Betting usually makes you more when you have the best hand, but loses the same when you are behind. Exploit your opponents' looseness. *Value bet your marginal hands.*[128]

**3. You have K♥K♦ on the button. Four players limp, and you raise. Both blinds and the limpers call (14 small bets). The flop is Q♥8♦3♦, giving you an overpair. Everyone checks to you, and you bet. Five players call (10 big bets). The turn is the J♠. Everyone checks to you, and you bet. Three players call (14 big bets). The river is the 5♠. Everyone checks to you. What should you do?**

**Answer:** Bet. The large number of callers should not discourage you from value betting. Many players with two pair or better on the turn would have check-raised you. Thus, you probably had the best hand then. The river card is a blank; it completes no straights or flushes, and there is no reason to suspect that it made two pair for anyone. If you had the best hand on the turn, you are a big favorite to hold the best hand still.

Anyone with a pair will be reluctant to fold in a pot this large. They will hope you were bluffing the whole way with ace-king (or maybe they will not even think at all) and call. In fact, you could get two or three weak calls from smaller pairs.

If someone did draw out, you will probably be check-raised. Since the pot is so large, you should probably call. You will lose two bets if you are beaten. On the other hand, you may very well win two calls if your hand is best. Your hand will be good and paid off much more often than you will be beaten. Therefore, betting will be profitable over the long run.

---

[128] See "Betting for Value on the River."

302 Part Six: Hand Quizzes

Some players routinely check here. They perpetually fear
that someone may have outdrawn their big pair. They
consider it a miracle when their hand survives to showdown
with so little resistance, and they gratefully check the river
down and take the pot.

Do not think this way! Big pairs win a lot of multiway
pots, even unimproved. This ragged board is terrific for your
hand. Loose players will pay you off. *Do not be afraid! Bet
for value.*

**4. You have A♥Q♣ in middle position. One player limps in,
and you raise. Two players cold-call, the blinds fold, and the
limper calls (9.5 small bets). The flop is K♥9♦4♣. The limper
checks, and you bet. All three players call (6.5 big bets). The
turn is the 4♦. The limper checks, you check, and it is checked
around (6.5 big bets). The river is the 2♥. The limper bets (7.5
big bets). What should you do?**

Answer: Fold. It is possible that your ace-high is still the best
hand. If there were no one behind you, you might call getting
7.5-to-1. You would have to win only twelve percent of the
time to show a profit. With players behind you, though,
calling is out of the question. Even though you may
occasionally have the bettor beaten, someone will overcall
with a weak, but slightly better hand too often.

You could raise. Neither player behind you likely has a
strong hand. They checked the turn, and the river was a
blank. They could have a small pair, perhaps a nine, a deuce,
or a pocket pair. Even loose players would usually fold those
hands for two bets cold. Thus, if the river bettor is a habitual
bluffer, raising might be profitable.

But against most bettors you should fold. Unlike the
players behind you, he could have checked a strong hand on
fourth street intending to check-raise. Typical players do not
bluff often, first to act, into three opponents. For a raise to be

profitable, you must win over twenty percent of the time (risking two bets to win 7.5). An average opponent will not be bluffing that often.

Above all, you should recognize that this is a raise or fold situation. Calling is essentially never correct because a weak hand will overcall too frequently. When your hand is vulnerable, you must usually take decisive action if there are players behind you. Raise to improve your prospects, or fold when your chances are too remote.[129]

**5. You raise from under the gun with A♠K♥. Only the loose small and big blinds call (6 small bets). The flop is J♥7♥2♦. Your opponents check, and you bet. The small blind folds; the big blind calls (4 big bets). The turn is the 3♠. Your opponent checks, and you bet. He calls again (6 big bets). The river is the 3♦. Your opponent checks. What should you do?**

**Answer:** Check. Believe it or not, there is a good chance that you still have the best hand. Many loose players call to the river as long as they retain some hope of drawing out. On this board your opponent could have a busted gutshot draw (e.g., T♣9♠), a busted flush draw, or overcards (perhaps only one overcard). He may have picked up a gutshot draw on fourth street with a hand like A♦4♦. You can beat many hands that he might have.

Even so, you should not bet against most loose players. While he may call with a few of the hands you beat (like A♦4♦), he will fold most of those hands (like T♣9♠). On the other hand, he is quite likely to call if he flopped bottom or middle pair. So even though you will win a fair percentage of the time, you will almost always lose *when he calls you*, and you will not get him to fold a better hand.

---

[129] See "When You Do Not Want Overcalls."

There is a (very lucrative) exception. A few players will call on the flop and turn with any pair, but always fold on the river with less than top pair (when they do not improve). This strategy is terrible on all streets; they call with weak draws in pots that are too small, but then they fold on the end for one bet when the pot is large. These opponents are uncommon, and when they exist they do not last long, but their mistakes are so bad that you should look out for them. If you see someone play a lot of pots to the river, but fold often to the last bet, suspect that he is in this class.

To exploit his mistakes, loosen up preflop when he has entered the pot, particularly if he is the only player to have entered so far. Once you are heads-up with him, bet the flop, turn, and river almost no matter what you have (provided he does not raise you, of course). It is hard to make top pair or better; your opponent will shake his head and fold far more than fifty percent of the time. The pots you steal plus the pots you win by making the best hand will give you a very healthy profit.

**6. You raise from under the gun with T♠T♥. Only the loose small and big blinds call (6 small bets). The flop is J♥7♥2♦. Your opponents check, and you bet. The small blind folds; the big blind calls (4 big bets). The turn is the 3♠. Your opponent checks, and you bet. He calls again (6 big bets). The river is the 3♦. Your opponent checks. What should you do?**

> **Answer:** Bet. This is exactly the same hand as in Hand No. 5, except you have a pair of tens instead of ace-high. You now beat all the deuces, sevens, and small pocket pairs your opponent may have. Your opponent will have a smaller pair far more often than he will have a trey or a jack (a jack with a strong kicker is relatively unlikely, as he may have raised you already with that). This is a clear value bet.

Interestingly, if you are against the player who calls the flop and turn with any pair, but folds on the river, you should now *check*. Since he folds anything less than top pair, he will never call with a worse hand. You cannot bet for value, and there is no need to bluff since you can beat any hand he might fold. Hold 'em is sometimes counter-intuitive. Always approach poker decisions logically; otherwise, you will miss important subtleties.

The player who folds too much on the river is an aberration, though. You should routinely value bet here against typically loose opponents. Players who go too far with their hands are making big mistakes, and you must learn to value bet aggressively to exploit them. By doing so you will consistently win extra bets on the river that most people miss. Confident value betting distinguishes expert players.

**7. You have Q♣Q♦ under the gun. You raise. Four people cold-call, and both blinds call (14 small bets). The flop is Q♥Q♠T♥, giving you quads. The blinds check, and you bet. Everyone except the small blind calls (10 big bets). The turn is the T♠. The big blind bets. You call, hoping others who are drawing dead will call behind you. Three players do call (15 big bets). The river is the J♥. The big blind bets (16 big bets). What should you do?**

Answer: Call. It is hard to figure out what your opponents are betting and calling with, since you have had all the cards worth having since the flop. Nevertheless, you still had four opponents on the turn. While they could not have had much, they probably had at least something. Some probably had tens, flush draws, straight draws, or ace-high. In very loose games expect players to draw to hopeless hands despite scary boards, especially if they can do so for only one bet.[130]

---

[130] See "Slowplaying."

The river card is good for you, that is, as long as no one made an unlikely straight flush. It completes many potential straight or flush draws; someone behind you may have completed his hand. Even so, he probably knows that he is a long shot since the board is so scary. He will overcall one bet, praying for a miracle, but reluctantly fold if it is two bets to him.

If the river card had been the 2♣ (or any other blank), you should probably raise instead. The situation is changed in two ways:

1.  It is much less likely that someone behind you will overcall. Now the only hands someone might overcall with are tens full, a pocket pair of jacks, kings, or aces, or possibly ace-high.

    When you decide whether to go for overcalls, you must compare the money you expect to make from the bettor (if you raised) to the money you expect to make from the overcallers (if you called). With the J♥ two or even all three opponents might overcall. With the 2♣ overcalls are unlikely, since one or two of them at least were probably on a draw.

    Furthermore, one of the most likely potential overcalling hands now is tens full. A loose opponent might even call two bets cold with that hand. If so, obviously raising is better.

2.  You have the nuts. Though unlikely, it is possible that the bettor has quad tens. If so, you might be able to win a lot of bets from him (provided there is no cap heads-up). He might think you have just queens full and reraise you indefinitely. Against the right opponent you can sometimes win twenty bets or more in a situation like this. While it is rare, it can be so profitable when it happens that you must consider it.

The J♥ makes a straight flush possible. You can no longer reraise your opponent with quad tens indefinitely, because you must now fear a better hand.

It may feel strange to flop quads and never raise. While you usually make more money with your strong hands if you raise them at some point, always consider every option. Think about the range of hands your opponents may have and anticipate their actions. Then choose the play that will maximize your profit. In this case that means keeping the bet small to induce weak overcalls.[131]

**8. You have A♥A♦ in middle position. One player limps, and you raise. Everyone folds to the big blind, who calls. The limper calls (6.5 small bets). The flop is J♥9♥4♠. The big blind checks, and the limper bets. You raise. The big blind and limper both call (6 big bets). The turn is the 7♠. Both players check, and you bet. The big blind check-raises. The limper cold-calls. You call (12 big bets). The river is the 2♦. The big blind bets, and the limper calls (14 big bets). What should you do?**

Answer: Call. The big blind probably has at least two pair. You will probably lose. Nevertheless, you should call. Since the pot lays 14-to-1, you need to win only one time in fifteen to make calling profitable. Sometimes the big blind will have something like A♠J♠ or even 9♠8♠ and have taken a shot on fourth street after picking up a draw. Sometimes he will have a hand that makes little logical sense. Occasionally you will win, and that is all you need to make calling profitable.[132]

Despite what many people think, paying off is the *correct strategy*. Some people call, but think that if they

---

[131] See "Going for Overcalls."

[132] See "Playing the River When the Pot is Big."

"played better" they could make the "correct" fold. Folding is wrong. Do not feel guilty about calling. Paying off is not a sucker play. It is part of the game. This is true in small stakes games because the pots are large, and many people play illogically. It is just as true in high stakes games where people play aggressively and frequently try to push you off hands. Consistently folding is the sucker play. Pay off with confidence.

**9. You have A♣K♣ on the button. Two loose players limp, and you raise. The blinds fold, and the limpers call (7.5 small bets). The flop is K♦9♦6♠. Your opponents check, and you bet. Both limpers call (5 big bets). The turn is the 7♣. Your opponents check, and you bet. Both limpers call (8 big bets). The river is the 6♦. Both limpers check. What should you do?**

**Answer:** Bet. The river is a scare card, but you should bet anyway. One of your opponents could have diamonds or a six, but they could just as easily have a nine, a seven, a weak king, a busted straight draw, a pocket pair, ace-high, or something else.

If one of your opponents has drawn out, he might have decided to bet instead of go for a check-raise. That is, it is more likely that you are still ahead *after* your opponents check than it is before they check.

Here is a simple example to clarify this concept. Say you have the button, and your opponent is drawing to a better hand than yours. You know there is a fifty percent chance that he will make his hand. The other fifty percent of the time, he will not improve, but still call your bet. If he makes his hand, you also know he will bet fifty percent of the time and check-raise the other fifty percent. Thus, half the time, he will check and call. A quarter of the time he will bet, and the other quarter he will check-raise. Before he acts there is a fifty percent chance he drew out. After he checks there is only a one-third chance that he drew out! If he checks, he is twice as likely to call as raise (he check-calls fifty percent of the time and check-raises only 25 percent). Thus, two out of three times after he checks, he will call, not raise. Even if you suspect he might check-raise, you are better off after he checks than you are beforehand.

Against one or two loose opponents you should bet your good hands even if a scare card comes. Being loose, their possible range of hands is broad. The broader this range, the less likely they are to have a specific draw like a flush draw or bottom pair, and the more likely they are to have a weak pay-off hand. Frequently up to half of the possible river cards will complete some draw. Since your opponents have only two cards, they cannot have every possible draw. Usually the completed draw will not be *their* draw. Do not let every river card scare you. *Bet!*

# Hand Quizzes

# Afterthought

The best hold 'em players have the ability not only to make the correct decisions in the heat of battle, but also to make them almost instantly. This alone gives them a significant advantage.

Others, who have to stop and think, will often get confused and make costly mistakes. And these mistakes will sometimes turn a long-term winner into a long-term loser.

So how do the experts do it? Is their hold 'em experience so extensive and their thinking process so fast that their opponents don't stand a chance? Or is there another possibility?

We believe it is something else, and that something else is thinking about poker hands away from the table. At least it was that way with us, and it's also the case with all the expert players we know.

The hand quizzes in this section are a great start towards this process. They not only show how many hands should be played, but the thinking behind those decisions.

To become expert, you should go over these quizzes many times, as well as additional hands that you remember from the games you play. So in the future, when a tough situation develops, you will recognize it from your study away from the table and instantly make the correct play.

# Part Seven

# Questions and Answers

# Questions and Answers

# Introduction

We have covered a great deal of material in this book. However, for many people, reading and learning can be two different things. Consequently, to help you retain some of the more significant ideas, we have reiterated them in a question-and-answer format.

We suggest that after you have read and studied the text, you try to answer the following questions. You probably will want to go over them many times. In addition, we suggest that you cover the answer that immediately follows each question. Only look at the solution after you have answered the question to the best of your ability.

Also, we want to point out that what follows is not a substitute for the text. In fact, some of the ideas in the text are not contained here. But enough material is included so that after you have thoroughly digested the text, the questions should help keep your hold 'em game sharp.

Finally, the questions and answers are organized by topics covered in the text, so you can easily return to the appropriate section for a fuller explanation.

# Preflop Concepts

1. When selecting starting hands, which hands should you choose?
   Only those that have a positive expectation.

2. Which hands lose in the long run?
   The slightly above average, average, and below average hands.

3. If your opponents limited themselves to only those hands that are profitable, what would most pots look like?
   They would be contested heads-up or three-handed.

4. By definition, an unprofitable hand expects to recover how much from the pot?
   Less than its original investment.

5. Why should you often raise with your better hands?
   Not to limit the field, but to increase your overall expectation.

6. What are the three hand types?
   Top pair hands, speculative hands, and powerhouse hands.

7. What type of hand is A♠J♣?
   A quintessential top pair hand.

8. On which betting rounds do top pair hands make lots of money?
   On the early betting rounds, preflop and the flop.

9. Do the best top pair hands — ace-ten, king-jack, and better — make more or less money against an increasing number of callers with bad hands?
   More.

313

10. What type of hand is 4♥4♦?
    A speculative hand.

11. Do speculative hands play better against many or few opponents?
    Many.

12. What type of hand is A♦Q♦?
    A powerhouse hand.

13. How should you play powerhouse hands?
    You should raise with them.

14. When is playing a dominated hand before the flop especially costly?
    When the pot is short-handed.

15. When is domination not as dangerous?
    In multiway pots.

16. What is the second most important component of hand value? (Your own and your opponents' cards arc the most important.)
    Position.

17. Name three valuable attributes of non-pair hands.
    High card strength, suitedness, and connectedness.

18. To be worth playing, how many categories must a non-pair hand usually be strong in?
    At least two of the three.

19. What is the most important attribute?
    High card strength.

20. Why are hands with two big cards much stronger than those with only one?
    1.  They can make top pair with either card.
    2.  When they make top pair, they always do so with a good kicker.

21. If you hold two suited cards, exactly three more cards of your suit will appear by the river how often?
    A little less than six percent of the time.

22. If you are in doubt about whether to play a hand, how should you decide?
    Be inclined to play it if it is suited, but fold it otherwise.

23. What are the two major mistakes that most players make that are so costly that no one prone to making them has a long term win?
    1.  Playing weak hands out of position, particularly weak offsuit hands.
    2.  Cold-calling raises with mediocre and potentially dominated hands.

24. You have A♥T♥ in middle position. The player under the gun, a tight, unimaginative player, raises. Everyone folds to you. What should you do?
    Fold.

25. What if he might also raise with some slightly worse hands like king-queen?
    You should still fold.

# Preflop Hand Categories

1. Which hands are the monsters?
   AA and KK.

2. How should you play the monsters?
   Almost always raise and reraise, no matter the action.

3. Which hands are the big pairs?
   QQ, JJ, and TT.

4. In light of the fact that an overcard could beat you, how should you play these hands before the flop?
   Not timidly. You should typically raise with these hands from any position if it has not yet been raised. It is also usually right to reraise if it has been raised once.

5. Which hands are the medium pairs?
   99, 88, and 77.

6. In which two situations do these pairs shine?
   1.  When you are two- or three-handed, and your opponents are likely to have weak hands.
   2.  Against five or more opponents.

7. When you have a set, what type of game do you prefer?
   A loose and aggressive one.

8. Which hands are the small pairs?
   66-22.

9. Under what game conditions do small pairs play best?
   When it is loose and somewhat aggressive.

10. From which positions can you usually play small pairs?
    In most games you can play these hands profitably from any position if it has not yet been raised.

11. Which hands are the big suited Broadways?
    AKs-ATs, KQs, and KJs.

12. If the pot is unraised, how should you usually play these hands?
    Raise with any of them.

13. Which hands are the little suited Broadways?
    QJs, KTs, QTs, and JTs.

14. If the pot is unraised, how should you play these hands from early or middle position?
    Limp. You would like to encourage loose limpers behind you.

15. Which hands are the suited aces?
    A9s-A2s.

16. What type of hands are suited aces?
    They are fundamentally speculative hands.

17. For these hands, is the size of the kicker important?
    Yes. A9s is a much better hand than A2s.

18. How should you play suited aces if it is raised in front of you?
    Usually fold.

19. Which hands are the suited kings?
    K9s-K2s.

20. What is the main reason suited kings are weaker than suited aces?
   A pair of aces is stronger than a pair of kings.

21. How should you play these hands from early position?
   Fold.

22. What hands are the suited connectors?
   T9s-54s, J9s-64s, Q9s-96s, Q8s, and J7s.

23. Under what game conditions do suited connectors play best?
   Loose and passive.

24. Which hands are the big offsuit Broadways?
   AK, AQ, AJ, and KQ.

25. What should you do if someone raises in front of you?
   Be prepared to fold all offsuit hands except AK.

26. Which hands are the little offsuit Broadways?
   AT, KJ, QJ, KT, QT, and JT.

27. In middle position, how should you play AT and KJ?
   If one or two loose players have limped, you should usually raise.

28. To what category do offsuit aces (A9-A2) and offsuit connectors (T9-54) belong?
   Junk offsuit hands. Do not play them.

# Preflop Recommendations

1. What adjustment should you make if your game is very passive?
   Play more of the weaker suited cards from early and middle positions.

2. What are the four fundamental principles of preflop play?
   1. Play tightly in early position, more loosely in late position.
   2. Raise with your better hands.
   3. Play only the strongest offsuit holdings.
   4. Play *very* tightly if someone has raised in front of you.

3. When do small pairs thrive?
   When they get lots of action if they flop a set.

4. How often should you cold-call a preflop raise?
   No more often than once every three hours (on average).

5. If someone raises after you act, how should you play?
   Call with any hand if it is one bet back to you.

6. If it is two bets back to you (i.e., raised and reraised), how should you play?
   Tighten up almost as much as you would if cold-calling a raise.

7. What is an important reason we zealously suggest raising with big suited cards?
   They hit the flop so frequently that you will often want to play on whether the pot was raised or not.

8. What advantage does early position afford in loose games that middle position does not offer?

The opportunity to check-raise to protect your hand or to build a pot when you flop a monster.

9. When you are first to enter a pot from middle position, what adjustments should you make?
1. You should fold some small pairs and small suited connectors like 2♥2♣ that should usually be played.
2. You should tend to raise some hands that you might ordinarily just limp with.

10. When you are first to enter a pot from late position, what adjustment should you make?

You should almost always raise.

11. How should you play from the small blind if it is less than half the size of the big blind?

We suggest that you play only those hands from the small blind that you would play on the button.

# Large Pots vs. Small Pots

1. When should you begin to consider the pot to be large?
   If one of the following is true:
   1. It is six-handed or more preflop.
   2. It is raised preflop and four-handed or more.
   3. It is three-bet or more preflop.
   4. At least two of your opponents will usually go to the river.

2. When the pot is small, and you bet a marginal hand on the flop to try to pick up the pot, but are raised, how should you play?
   Usually release your hand immediately or on fourth street if you do not improve.

3. In a small pot, if an opponent is betting or raising, what do you need to be fairly confident of to call?
   You have the best hand or a strong draw.

4. In a small pot if you think you have a close decision between continuing and folding, what should you do?
   Tend to fold.

5. When the pot is large, what major adjustment should you make?
   Maximize your chance to win it.

6. Specifically, how should your plays change?
   1. Continue with marginal hands that you might fold in a small pot.
   2. Seize opportunities to knock out players, whether you have a made hand or a draw.
   3. Continue to draw even when you suspect that you might be drawing dead.

4.    Call liberally for one bet on the river, even when you are almost sure that you are beaten.

7. If the pot is large, what must you be relatively certain of before you fold a draw?

You are drawing dead.

8. Is strong betting alone enough evidence?

No.

9. What if there is some chance you might win, and it is one bet to you in a large pot on the river?

Do not fold.

# Protecting Your Hand

1. What is the most costly error that you can make?
Folding a hand that has a strong chance to win a large pot.

2. Who are the only players who routinely make this mistake?
Only those who believe that making "big laydowns" is the hallmark of expert play.

3. Another error is almost as costly. It is so costly that you will see someone make it on nearly every hand of a small stakes game. What is it?
Failing to protect strong hands in large, multiway pots.

4. How do you protect your hand?
You bet or raise, forcing players who hold weak draws to decide between folding and making an unprofitable call.

5. Sometimes simply betting out does not protect your hand. What must you do in those circumstances to protect your hand?
Check-raise.

6. When the player directly on your right bets the flop, how should you play?
Almost always either raise or fold.

7. Why should you liberally raise to protect your hand?
Raising when you should call can cost you a bet. Calling when you should raise, however, can cost you a whole pot. It is easily worth losing an extra bet here and there to save an occasional pot.

8. When the pot is big, how should you play a flush or straight draw with overcards to the board?
    You should protect those hands.

9. In a large pot, how much must you improve your winning chances to make a raise profitable?
    Often just a few percent.

10. When you have a draw to a big hand, how should you play it if the pot is small?
    Usually avoid eliminating players.

11. What about if the pot is large?
    Protect your vulnerable outs with a raise.

12. When will a flop raise not protect your hand?
    1.   When the pot is large, and a lot of fourth street cards might cripple your hand.
    2.   When the flop bet comes from your left.
    3.   When the pot is extremely large.

13. What is the best play in that case?
    Call on the flop, hoping for a safe card. If fourth street is a blank, plan to raise there.

14. When the pot is extremely large, when should you forgo a flop raise?
    When doing so increases the chance you will be bet into on the turn.

# Raising for a Free Card

1. What do poker players tend to do if someone else raised on the previous round?
    Check to him.

2. When someone improves on fourth street, what does he usually do?
    He often checks, hoping to check-raise.

3. How do you exploit this tendency to check to the raiser?
    Raise the flop in late position with a drawing hand, intending to check behind on fourth street if you miss to see the river card for free.

4. In what kind of games is the free card play most effective?
    Passive games.

5. As the game gets more aggressive, how must you adjust?
    You should become more selective with your free card attempts.

6. What if you have a strong draw like a flush draw or a quality open-ended straight draw? Should you stop trying for free cards with these draws?
    No. You should not worry about being reraised, or called, and then bet into on the turn.

7. What draws should you stop trying for free cards with against aggressive players?
    Weak draws like bottom pair or a gutshot.

8. Against what kind of players should you attempt free card plays with weak draws?
    Passive ones.

9. What is one drawback to the free card play?
    It can give your hand away.

10. How can "giving your hand away" work to your benefit?
    If you happen to hold a draw that is not the most obvious one.

11. Should you always take a free card on fourth street if you make a free card play?
    No.

12. When should you bet?
    If you make your hand on the turn, obviously you should bet. You should also bet if you think there is some chance all of your opponents will fold.

13. How should you play strong draws on the turn against weak opponents willing to call on the flop with almost nothing?
    You should bet them again on the turn.

14. When should you raise the flop for a "cheap showdown"?
    In small stakes games employing this tactic is usually incorrect.

15. Where does a large percentage of your profit in small stakes games come from?
    Opponents who call down with weak hands in small pots.

16. How should you play the turn against these calling stations?
    Value bet relentlessly.

# Slowplaying

1. What is slowplaying?
   Playing a strong hand weakly, checking or calling instead of betting or raising, to deceive opponents.

2. When successful, what are its effects?
   1. Players use the cheap cards you give to improve their hand to a better, *but still second-best* hand. You hope to induce action on a later street from a worse hand that *would have folded* had you bet earlier.
   2. Opponents, suspecting a bluff, call your later bets with weaker hands than usual.

3. When is slowplaying a useful tool?
   In small pots against players who play well after the flop.

4. Against opponents likely to call, what does slowplaying do?
   It just causes you to miss bets.

5. Against loose opponents, when is slowplaying correct?
   When you have a very strong hand, the pot is small, and the player on your right bets. In that situation, you should sometimes just call.

# Two Overpair Hands

1. Normally, if you determine that you have an edge, what should you do?

Exploit it by betting or raising.

2. When should you consider passing on a small edge?

If doing so might allow you to better exploit a much larger edge later in the hand.

3. If you choose to pass on a small edge, how should you play?

Wait for the turn to raise.

4. Under what specific conditions should you wait for fourth street?

1. When raising now has little chance to induce opponents to fold.
2. When your hand is vulnerable, many cards (often up to half the deck) could beat you, and, thus, your edge is small.
3. When, if a favorable card comes, your edge will be much bigger on the turn.

# Betting for
# Value on the River

1. What poker weapon does a player who plays too many hands and goes too far with them blunt?
   Bluffing.

2. In defending themselves flawlessly against a bluff, what attack do they expose themselves to?
   Betting your marginal hands for value on the river.

3. What hands will many calling stations often call on the river with?
   Any pair or even ace-high.

4. If the board is K♦8♥4♥2♣6♣ on the river, and you have T♣T♥ on the button, what should you do on the river if a tight player has called you on the flop and turn?
   Check behind.

5. What about if loose player has called you down instead?
   Bet for value.

6. When you are first to act against predictable and passive opponents, how should you adjust your strategy?
   You should bet some very marginal hands. If you plan to call a bet when you check, you should usually bet yourself against these players.

7. What are the four major factors to consider when you decide how likely it is that you have been outdrawn when a scare card comes on the river?
1. How many opponents are left.
2. How many draws the card completes.
3. The likely range of hands your opponents might have.
4. How tight or loose your opponents are.

8. If the river card is very scary, putting four to a straight or four to a flush (or both) on the board, how should you play?
Refrain from betting for value unless, of course, you hold the straight or flush.

9. What is the exception to this rule?
If you can narrow your opponents' holdings down to only those that cannot have improved to beat you on the river.

10. Should you be more or less willing to bet for value if your opponents are very loose?
More.

11. At what point is a pot big enough that you should no longer bet for value?
There is no such point. No matter how big the pot is, you should bet for value if you feel it will show a profit.

# Playing the River
# When the Pot Is Big

1. What characteristics do the worst poker players display?
   They play far too many hands, they do not fold enough after the flop, and they miss bets and raises with their marginal and strong hands.

2. What mistake do some players make in their zeal to avoid playing this way?
   They fold too much.

3. When might a folding mindset be useful?
   When the pot is small.

4. When the pot is large, which mistake is worse, a bad call or a bad fold?
   A bad fold is much worse.

5. If you are almost sure that you are beaten, should you fold for one bet on the river when the pot is large?
   No. You must be absolutely sure you are beaten.

6. If you are getting 12-to-1, closing the action, how often must you have the best hand for a call to be profitable?
   Eight percent of the time.

7. Should you assume an aggressive player has you beaten if he bets into three players on the river?
   No. Bad players often bluff too much, especially with a hopeless hand in a big pot.

8. If you cannot beat any hand that your opponent could logically have, should you fold?

> Not necessarily. Many of your opponents do not play logically. They will constantly surprise you with bizarre holdings.

# Going for Overcalls

1. To overcall on the river, you should have a stronger hand than you would need to be the first caller. Name two reasons:
   1. You must beat two hands instead of one.
   2. While a bettor can be bluffing, a caller cannot. If your hand can beat only a bluff, do not overcall.

2. How do many players play when they overcall?
   They will overcall with any hand that they would have called with.

3. If you have a strong hand with opponents yet to act, how should you consider playing?
   Consider just calling instead of raising.

4. Under what conditions is this particularly true?
   1. There are several players to act behind you.
   2. Those players are loose and unsophisticated.
   3. Your hand is strong.
   4. The pot is not big.
   5. The bettor may have you beaten.
   6. The bettor may be bluffing.

5. What does a peculiar bet often mean?
   The bettor has either a very strong or a very weak hand.

6. Name two common situations where going for overcalls is often correct.
   1. When you have a one card straight.
   2. When you have the second-nut one card flush.

# When You Do
# Not Want Overcalls

1. If there are players behind you and your hand can beat only a bluff, how should you play?

You should generally fold even if you would have called heads-up.

2. When the pot is large, there are players behind you, and you have a mediocre hand, but there is a decent chance you can beat the bettor, what should you do?

Raise instead of calling.

# Playing Overcards

1. Playing overcards is not much different than playing what type of hand?

   A weak draw.

2. What three rules help you evaluate the strength of overcards?
   1. Overcards prefer ragged boards.
   2. Backdoor draws strengthen overcards.
   3. Overcards prefer few opponents.

3. Name two reasons why overcards prefer ragged boards.
   1. Top pair is more likely to win when no straight or flush draws are available.
   2. Ragged boards are less likely to have hit your opponents.

4. Which hand is stronger: A♠K♦ on a flop of J♥6♥3♣ or A♣K♦ on a flop of J♠6♣3♣?

   The latter hand is stronger because the A♣ in your hand gives you a backdoor flush draw.

5. If you have offsuit overcards, are you better off with a board having three different suits, or one having two of one of the suits of your cards?

   You are usually better off with two of one of the suits of your cards.

6. What are two problems with having many opponents?
   1. The chance that you are reverse dominated increases.
   2. The chance that someone will make a big hand increases.

7. How correct is the rule, "Bet overcards against two opponents, but check against three?"

It is so oversimplified that it is essentially useless.

8. What questions should you ask when you decide whether to bet or check your overcards?
1.  How big is the pot?
2.  How likely are my overcards still to be best? That is, how likely is it that all my opponents missed the flop?
3.  How strong is my hand? (Evaluate using the rules from earlier.)
4.  How likely is betting to win the pot immediately?
5.  Is betting likely to improve my winning chances significantly even if I do not win immediately?
6.  Is betting likely to buy a free card on the turn if I want it?

9. If betting the flop has little chance to win the pot immediately, should you check?

Not necessarily. Even if you have no chance to win immediately, betting can improve your winning chances enough to be worthwhile.

10. If someone bets into you and you have overcards, how should you play?

Usually play them as you would any other weak draw.

11. How should you play them in a small pot?

Tend to fold.

12. How about when the pot is large?

Tend to call or raise: Raise if it is likely to buy outs or win a free card; otherwise call.

13. In marginal situations, what should you consider when deciding whether to continue with overcards?

Be more likely to continue if your opponent may be betting a weak hand or a draw than if he probably has a strong hand.

14. Should you be more or less willing to continue if the bettor has a very wide range of possible hands?

More.

15. If you bet the flop with overcards, get called, and the turn does not help you, when should you bet again?

When you think there is a substantial chance to win immediately.

16. What kind of flop provides the best prospects for betting the turn with overcards?

A moderately coordinated flop.

17. Why is a very coordinated flop bad?

Because callers are likely to have strong draws or to be slowplaying big hands.

18. Why is a very ragged flop bad?

Because callers are quite likely to have at least a pair.

# Building Big
# Pots Before the Flop

1. Say you are in the big blind with A♥J♥. Five loose players, including the small blind, limp in. Should you raise or check?
   Raise.

2. Does keeping the pot small before the flop cause your opponents to make more mistakes?
   Yes.

3. If so, why is it correct to raise?
   Because your opponents have already made a mistake by entering the pot.

4. Is just checking with A♥J♥ an acceptable alternative?
   No. It is far too strong.

5. Since you must usually catch an ace or king to win, should you usually just call with ace-king in a very multiway pot?
   No. It has a significant pot equity edge.

# "Loose" Flop Calls

1. Name three reasons to call a flop raise (after you have bet) with a weak made hand even if you are fairly confident that you are beaten.
   1.   Your opponent may check the turn even if he has you beaten.
   2.   Your opponent might be on a draw.
   3.   When it is otherwise close, you should refrain from betting and then folding to a raise on the same round.

2. Why should you refrain from betting and then folding to a raise on the same round?
   Doing it too often may encourage your more observant opponents to throw in an extra raise with a draw or weak made hand.

# Questions and Answers

# Afterthought

Again, these questions are not designed as a replacement for the material in the text. Their purpose is to help keep you sharp between complete readings of *Small Stakes Hold 'em: Winning Big with Expert Play*. We recommend that when you believe you have become a winning small stakes hold 'em player that you reread the text material every other month and review the questions about once a week. Also, remember to cover the answers and to think through those questions that you have trouble with. In addition, attempt to relate the questions to recent hands that you have played, and try to determine which concepts were the correct ones to apply.

# Conclusion

For many years people have been writing a steady stream of "low-limit," "small stakes," and "beginners'" hold 'em books. Most of them advise similar conservative, "stay out of trouble" approaches. These strategies are fine for new players who need simple guidelines to avoid immediately dumping their bankrolls. But we have encountered innumerable players who continue to play this weak-tight style for years. Their thinking is so molded by these books that they refuse to take the steps necessary to improve. As far as they are concerned, they play "by the book," and their mediocre results reflect bad luck rather than bad play.

We propose a very different strategy. We advise playing a more daring, aggressive, and attacking style than any "small stakes" book ever written. We do not want to turn rank beginners into successful recreational players. We want to turn eager students of the game into experts. We want you to play well enough to earn $50,000 a year or more playing $3-$6 online. We want to provide you with the skills necessary to move up to $30-$60 games and higher. We do not want you to beat small stakes games. We *want you to crush them!*

# Glossary

**Action:** The betting in a particular hand or game. A game with a lot of action is a game with a lot of betting. The player who starts the action is the player who makes the first bet.

**Active player:** A player still in the pot.

**All-in:** Having all one's money in the pot.

**Back door:** Three cards to a flush or a straight after five cards have been dealt. In general, the term is used for a hand made on the end which a player was not originally trying to make.

**Bad beat:** Having a hand that is a big favorite defeated as the result of a lucky draw, especially when the person drawing was playing incorrectly by being in the pot in the first place.

**Bad game:** A game in which your opponents are too good for you to expect to win; a game in which you're an underdog.

**Bankroll:** The amount of money you have available to wager.

**Belly buster:** A draw to an inside-straight. Also called a gut shot.

**Best of it:** A situation in which a wager can be expected to be profitable in the long run.

**Bet:** To put money in the pot before anyone else on any given round.

**Bettor:** The person who first puts money in the pot on any given round.

343

**Bet for value:** To bet in order to be called by a lesser hand. You are betting to make money, not to make your opponents fold.

**Big slick:** Ace-king.

**Blank:** A card that is not of any value to a player's hand.

**Blind:** A forced bet that one or more players must make to start the action on the first round of betting. The blind rotates around the table with each new deal. The person whose turn it is to bet is said to be in the blind.

**Bluff:** A bet or raise with a hand you do not think is the best hand.

**Board:** The community cards in the center of the table.

**Bottom pair:** Pairing the lowest card on board.

**Broadway:** An ace-high straight.

**Broadway card:** Any card that could be used to make Broadway (i.e., any ace through ten).

**Busted hand:** A hand that does not develop into anything of value.

**Button:** When there is a house dealer, as in the card rooms of Las Vegas, the *button* is a round disc that rotates around the table to represent the dealer for the purposes of indicating which player is to be first to act.

**Buy in:** The minimum amount of money required to sit down in a particular game.

**Card room:** The area in a casino where poker (and sometimes panguingue) is played.

**Call:** To put in the pot an amount of money equal to an opponent's bet or raise.

**Call a raise cold:** To call a double bet — that is, a bet and a raise.

**Caller:** A person who calls a bet or raise.

**Chase:** To continue in a hand trying to outdraw an opponent's hand you are quite sure is better than yours.

**Check:** To decline to bet when it is your turn.

**Check-raise:** To check and then raise after an opponent bets.

**Chip:** A round token in various denominations representing money. Among many professional gamblers it is also called a check.

**Chop:** To tie, splitting the pot; also, to take back your blinds if no one opens the pot.

**Cinch:** The best possible hand, given the cards on board, when all the cards are out.

**Cold-call:** To call two or more bets (e.g., a bet and a raise) at the same time.

**Come hand:** A hand that has not yet been made, with more cards still to be dealt. Thus, a four-card flush would be a come hand.

**Community cards:** The cards dealt face up in the center of the table that are shared by all active players.

**Counterfeit:** To "improve" a hand in such a way that one or both hole cards no longer play, and the relative strength of the hand is reduced. If you have K3, and the flop is K83, you have two pair, kings and treys. If an 8 comes on the turn, you "improve" to kings and eights, but the trey in your hand no longer plays, and the relative strength of your hand has dropped.

**Crying call:** A call with a hand you think has a small chance of winning.

**Cut the pot:** To take a percentage from each pot as the profits for the person or the casino running the game.

**Dead hand:** A hand a player may not continue to play because of an irregularity.

**Dead money:** Money put in the pot by players who have already folded their hands.

**Domination:** When two players hold a card of the same rank, but one holds a smaller side card, the player with the smaller side card is dominated. Someone with ace-king dominates another with ace-jack.

**Drawing dead:** Drawing to try to make a hand that cannot possibly win because an opponent already holds a bigger hand. A player drawing to make a flush when an opponent already has a full house is drawing dead.

**Draw out:** To improve your hand so that it beats an opponent who had a better hand than yours prior to your draw.

**Double belly buster:** *See* Open-ended straight.

**Early position:** A position on a round of betting in which you must act before most of the other players.

**Edge:** An advantage over an opponent.

**Effective odds:** The ratio of the total amount of money you expect to win if you make your hand to the total amount of bets you will have to call to continue from the present round of betting to the end of the hand.

**Equity:** The value of a particular hand or combination of cards.

**Expectation:** The average profit (or loss) of any bet over the long run.

**Favorite:** In poker, before all the cards are out, a hand that has the best chance of winning.

**Family pot:** A pot in which most of the players at the table are involved.

**Fifth street:** The fifth and final community card on board.

**Fill:** To draw a card that makes a hand. For example, to fill a flush is to draw a fifth card of that suit.

**Fill up:** To make a full house.

**Flat call:** To call a bet without raising.

**Flop:** The first three exposed community cards, which are dealt simultaneously. The word is also used as a verb. For example, to flop a set is to make three-of-a-kind on the flop.

**Flush:** Five cards of the same suit.

**Fold:** To drop out of a pot rather than call a bet or raise.

**Four-flush:** Four cards to a flush.

**Four-of-a-kind:** Four cards of the same rank. Four jacks is four-of-a-kind.

**Fourth street:** The fourth community card on board.

**Free card:** A card that a player gets without having to call a bet.

**Free roll:** A situation where two players have the same hand but one of them has a chance to make a better hand.

**Full house:** Three cards of one rank and two of another. A♣A♥A♦9♠9♥ is a full house.

**Giving a hand away:** Playing your hand in such a way that your opponents should know what you have.

**Good game:** A game in which there are enough players worse than you for you to be a substantial favorite.

**Gutshot:** A draw to an inside straight. Also called a belly buster.

**Heads-up:** Playing against a single opponent.

**Hidden out:** A card that does not directly improve your hand (i.e., by pairing one of your cards or by making a straight or flush) that still gives you the best hand. If you have AK, your opponent has K3, and the board is K853, the remaining eights and fives are hidden outs.

**Hourly rate:** The amount of money a player expects to win per hour on average.

**Implied odds:** The ratio of the total amount of money you expect to win if you make your hand to the bet you must now call to continue in the hand.

**Inside straight:** A straight which can be made only with a card of one rank, usually somewhere in the middle of the straight. When you hold ten-nine-seven-six, only an eight will give you a straight. Thus, you are drawing to an inside straight, or you have an inside-straight draw.

**Kicker:** A side card.

**Late position:** A position on a round of betting in which you act after most of the other players have acted.

**Legitimate hand:** A hand with value; a hand that is not a bluffing hand.

**Limit:** The amount a player may bet or raise on any round of betting.

**Limp in:** To call a bet rather than raise. (This usually applies only to the first round of betting.)

**Live one:** A loose, weak player with a lot of money to lose.

**Lock:** A cinch hand. A hand that cannot lose.

**Long shot:** A hand that has little chance of being made.

**Loose:** Playing more hands than the norm.

**Loose game:** A game with a lot of players in most pots.

**Mathematical expectation:** The mathematical calculation of what a bet can be expected to win or lose on average.

**Middle pair:** Pairing the second highest card on board.

**Middle position:** A position on a round of betting somewhere in the middle. In a ten-handed game middle position generally refers to those players four or five seats to the left of the big blind.

**Monster:** A very powerful hand that is the overwhelming favorite to win.

**Muck:** To discard a hand; the pile of discards in front of the dealer.

**Multiway pot:** A pot in which more than two players are involved.

**Negative expectation:** The amount a wager may be expected to lose on average. A play with negative expectation is a play that will lose money over the long run.

**Nuts:** The best possible hand at any given point in a pot.

**Odds:** The chance, expressed mathematically, that an event will occur. Also, in the term *pot odds,* the ratio of the size of the pot to the amount of the bet you must call to continue.

**Off-suit:** Not of the same suit.

**One card draw:** A draw to a hand that uses only one card from your hand and four from the board. If you hold one spade, and there are three spades on the flop, you have a one card flush draw.

**On the come:** Playing a hand that has not yet been made. For instance, if you bet with four cards to a flush, you are betting on the come.

**On tilt:** Playing much worse than usual because, for one reason or another, you have become emotionally upset.

**Open-ended straight:** Four cards to a straight, which can be made with cards of two different ranks. Thus, nine-eight-seven-six is an open-ended straight, which can be made with either a ten or a five. Theoretically, jack-nine-eight-seven-five is also open-ended in that either a ten or a six will make the hand. The latter hand is also called a double belly buster.

**Outkicked:** To have the same pair as someone else, but to lose to a larger kicker. If you have ace-queen, and an opponent has ace-king, you are outkicked if an ace flops.

**Outs:** Cards which will improve your hand. Also, ways of improving your hand. The term is used particularly in reference to a hand that needs to improve to become the best hand.

**Overcall:** A call of a bet after another player has already called.

**Overcard:** A card higher than any card on the flop, or any card higher than those in your hand.

**Overpair:** A wired pair that is higher than any card on board.

**Pair:** Two cards of the same rank. Two eights is a *pair.*

**Partial out:** A card that will give you the best hand a percentage of the time.

**Pass:** To check. Also, to fold.

**Pay off:** To call a bet or raise when you don't think you have the best hand.

**Pay station:** A player who calls bets and raises much more than is correct. He's also referred to as a *calling station.* This type is great when you have a legitimate hand, but he's just about impossible to bluff out of a pot.

**Position:** The spot in the sequence of betting in which a player is located. A player in first position would be the first person to act; a player in last position would be the last person to act.

**Positive expectation:** The amount a wager may be expected to win on average. A play with positive expectation is a play that will win money over the long run.

**Pot:** The total amount of money wagered at any point in a hand. A hand itself is also referred to as a pot. Thus, three people in the pot means there are three active players still playing the hand.

**Pot equity:** The percentage of time that you expect to win the pot, multiplied by the size of the pot. If you expect to win the pot twenty percent of the time, and the pot contains $100, your pot equity is $20.

**Pot equity edge:** You have a pot equity edge if you expect to win more often than an average opponent. If you have four opponents, the average player expects to win twenty percent of the time. If you expect to win thirty percent of the time, you have a pot equity edge.

**Pot odds:** The ratio of the amount of money in the pot to the bet you must call to continue in the hand.

**Protecting your hand:** Betting or raising while there are still cards to come for the purpose of forcing opponents with weaker hands to fold or pay to draw.

**Put someone on a hand:** To determine as best you can the hand (or hands) an opponent is most likely to have.

**Pure nuts:** The best possible hand. If the board is A♥7♦8♦K♣4♣ a player holding a 65 has the pure nuts.

**Rag:** *See* Blank.

**Raise:** To bet an additional amount after someone else has bet.

**Raiser:** A player who raises.

**Rake:** An amount retained by a casino from each pot, usually no more than $3 or $4.

**Represent:** To make your opponents believe you have a better hand than you really do.

**Reraise:** To raise after an opponent has raised.

**Reverse implied odds:** The ratio of the amount of money now in the pot to the amount of money you will have to call to continue from the present round to the end of the hand.

**River:** The fifth and last community card.

**Round of betting:** A sequence of betting after one or more cards have been dealt. A round of betting continues until each active player has either folded or called.

**Royal flush:** An ace-high straight flush. A♠K♠Q♠J♠T♠ is a royal flush.

**Running pair:** Fourth- and fifth-street of the same rank (but of a rank different from any of the other cards on board.)

**Rush:** Several winning hands in a short period of time.

**Sandbag:** To play weakly with a strong hand. To check-raise or slowplay with the probable best hand.

**Score:** A big win.

**Seat charge:** In public card rooms, an hourly fee for playing poker.

**Second pair (third pair):** Pairing the second (third) highest card on board.

**Semi-bluff:** To bet with a hand which you do not think is the best hand but which has a reasonable chance of improving to the best hand.

**Set:** Three-of-a-kind made using a pair in your hand and a matching third card on the board.

**Share:** Your share is the percentage of the time an average person expects to win the pot. If you have three opponents, your share is 25 percent. Usually used in a comparison, as in "winning more than your share."

**Short odds:** The odds for an event that has a good chance of occurring.

**Short-handed pot:** A pot contested by only a few players (i.e., four or fewer)

**Short-stacked:** Playing in a game with a relatively small number of chips remaining.

**Showdown:** The turning up of all active players' cards at the end of the final round of betting to see who has the best hand.

**Side pot:** A second pot for the other active players when one player is all-in.

**Slowplay:** To check or just call an opponent's bet with a big hand in order to win more money on later rounds of betting.

**Speculative hand:** A hand that will win only rarely, but that will make a big hand that can win a large pot when it does win.

**Starting requirement:** The minimum initial hand a player considers he needs to continue in a pot.

**Start the action:** To make the first bet in a particular hand.

**Steal:** To cause your opponents to fold when you probably do not have the best hand. The term is used especially in reference to stealing the antes — that is, raising on the first round of betting so that everyone remaining in the pot folds.

**Steam:** To play badly because you are emotionally upset — especially to play considerably more pots than you normally would when your hands do not justify it.

**Straight:** Five cards of mixed suits in sequence. T♦9♣8♥7♦6♥ is a straight.

**Straight flush:** Five cards of the same suit in sequence. T♥9♥8♥7♥6♥ is a straight flush.

**Strong draw:** A draw that has a good chance to be completed. Examples are an open-ended straight draw or a flush draw.

**Structure:** The limits set upon the ante, forced bets, and subsequent bets and raises in any given game.

**Stuck:** Losing money, especially a substantial amount of money, in a given session or over a period of time. We might say, "Sammy is stuck $1,500 in the game." That is, Sammy has lost $1,500.

**Sucker:** A player who can be expected to lose money, especially one who is not as good as he thinks.

**Suited:** Two or more cards of the same suit.

**Tell:** A mannerism a player exhibits that may give away his hand.

**Three-of-a-kind:** Three cards of the same rank. 7♣7♦7♥ is *three-of-a-kind*.

**Tight:** Playing fewer hands than the norm.

**Tight game:** A game with a small number of players in most pots.

**Top pair:** Pairing the highest card on board.

**Top pair hand:** A hand that wins often by making top pair, but that will rarely make a big hand.

**Trips:** Three-of-a-kind made using a pair on board and a matching third card in your hand.

**Turn:** The fourth community card. Some "old time" players also refer to the flop as the *turn*.

**Two flush:** Two cards of the same suit.

**Underdog:** A hand that does not have the best chance of winning.

**Under the gun:** The first person to act on the first round of betting is under the gun. On later betting rounds, the player to the immediate left of the bettor is said to be under the gun.

**Up:** Expressions like aces up, kings up, and sixes up mean two pair with two aces, two kings, or two sixes as the highest of the two pair. Unless an opponent has a top pair of the same rank, the rank of the second pair is of no importance.

**Value:** What a hand is worth in terms of its chance of being the best hand.

**Wager:** A bet.

**Weak draw:** A draw that has only a small chance to be completed. Examples are bottom pair or a gutshot straight draw.

**Wired pair:** A pair in the hole.

**World Series of Poker:** An annual series of poker tournaments with buy-ins ranging up to $10,000, which is held each spring at the Horseshoe Casino in Las Vegas. The competition is generally recognized as the premier competition among the best poker players in the world.

**Worst of it:** A situation in which a wager will be unprofitable in the long run.

# Index

# NOTES